Happy Birthday 1982.
from
David & Helen

Maritime England

Maritime England

Michael Shea

Country Life Books
in association with the

Frontispiece
H.M.S. *Victory* at the
Royal Navy Museum,
Portsmouth.

Published by Country Life Books
and distributed for them by
The Hamlyn Publishing Group Limited
London · New York · Sydney · Toronto
Astronaut House, Feltham, Middlesex, England

First published 1981
ISBN 0 600 36803 3

Composition in 10/12 Bembo by Filmtype Services
Limited, Scarborough, North Yorkshire

Printed and bound in England by
Balding + Mansell, Wisbech, Cambs.

Contents

Author's Acknowledgements

In writing this book I have been enormously assisted by many people, principally, Patricia Pierce of Country Life Books, whose contributions are acknowledged in the text. Patrick Roper, and Fiona Campbell of the English Tourist Board have provided me with much valuable comment and criticism. In addition, without singling them out. I would like to thank the representatives of the many organisations who sit on the Maritime England Advisory Committee, for providing me with a great deal of useful material, and, as important, much of their time. Additionally, I would like to express my appreciation to Admiral Leslie Townsend who read the majority of the chapters in draft and who gave me much guidance and suggestions for improvement, and to Dr Alan McGowan of the National Maritime Museum who gave me similar guidance on the historical chapters. I am grateful to the Society of Authors as the literary representative of the Estate of John Masefield, for permission to include excerpts from 'The Ship' and 'Cargoes'. As always, I would, finally, like to express the debt I owe to my wife, for all her help and encouragement during the writing of this book.

Introduction

The sea that surrounds this our island – our archipelago of islands – means something that is both special and different to each and every one of us. Recollections of a barefooted childhood on endless sands; of breaking waves and wild sea journeys; of school history books, each packed with maritime adventures and famous naval victories that seemed to stretch from the dimmest recesses of the past right up to the present – these are but a part of the many-faceted pattern of any child's growing consciousness and awareness of this nation and its inheritance. The experience and the memories of the sea and all things connected with it remain intense and lasting.

That we as a nation are surrounded by the sea means that this factor, more than any other, has dominated our past, our present, and our foreseeable future. Since no point on the English mainland is more than seventy miles from the sea, it has been an historical inevitability that this land should, quite apart from her geographical position, produce great seafaring men and women. Above all, her capital, London, is on the sea, unlike those of many other great seafaring nations such as France and Spain.

The sea has, consequently, served as the basis for this country's past prosperity – and frequently the lack of it – both in pure economic terms, and in the political, defence and social arenas. Our trade was and is with the world, and it is a trade that, even in this age of air-freight is still basically seaborne.

That we were, once, the richest nation on earth as well as the most powerful, was a direct result of our relatively advanced capability to conquer and utilise the oceans for transport, exploration, exploitation and defence. That we have a unique history as a nation never conquered, (in recent centuries at least), and a democratic political system which is enviably independent, is also largely the result of our invincibility, protected as we are by the seas, straits and channels that lie all around us. In social terms, the peculiarities of the English way of life are again as much attributable to our isolation on our islands, as to any innate and uneasily explained 'national characteristics'. As a nation we and our ways owe much to the sea.

It is perhaps appropriate here to mention something about national definitions. This book is concerned with maritime 'England', but even the most partisan Englishman will recognise that, in much of what is to follow, the geographic, political, social and economic entity is in fact 'Britain'. Our seaboard has no visible barriers at the Severn, Solway or the Tweed; for centuries, along with union of Crown and Parliament, much of the history and the heritage is indivisible, the Royal Navy being one pre-eminent example. Yet in this book it is with England and her particular maritime wealth and variety that we are concerned. It is not only on maps that England was and remains a distinct, proud and fundamental part of the greater commonwealth.

There are many facets to the maritime England story. The author's approach has been to divide the book into two parts: the first concerns itself with England's maritime heritage, its history and development both for good – the Royal Navy, shipbuilding, discovery, trade – and for bad – smugglers, pirates and their kind. The second part deals with the present and the strengths, both natural and man-made, that make their contribution to the theme – and the dangers that threaten if the inheritance is misused or abused. The method is to take up the story on a subject-by-subject basis rather than to set out on a expedition round the English coastline.

With a subject of this scope one can only paint with a broad brush, whetting the appetite, and pointing out what is on offer, in the context both of history and of the tremendous variety presented today by the nation's greatest natural asset. To assist those who wish to see as much as possible of the maritime attractions available on any given stretch of littoral, the English Tourist Board and the twelve English Regional Tourist Boards have extensive literature and advice to back up what is set out here.

Publication of this book coincides with a major promotion of the same title, 'Maritime England', co-ordinated by the English Tourist Board. Together with many other organisations and individuals interested in and involved in the development and protection of our rich maritime heritage,

the Board has brought together a huge package of events devoted to all aspects of the subject. Historical ships, maritime museums, the many-sided attractions of seaside resorts, water-sporting activities, and our heritage in the arts, theatre and music are all part of this enterprise. Nautical Institutions such as the National Maritime Museum, the RNLI, Trinity House, British Shipbuilders, the Council of British Shipping, Lloyd's, the Maritime Trust as well as the Royal Navy itself, have worked together to focus the attention of everyone on the disparate range of our natural and historical sea-related inheritance.

One of the delights of writing this book has been the enormous wealth of subject matter available. So much of our day-to-day life is, in one way or another, touched upon or affected by the sea and life along our coasts. Not a static phenomenon, it is constantly developing in a variety of exciting ways.

Equally stimulating has been the constant process of discovery and rediscovery of the coastline and the seashore with its myriad faces – faces that change enormously from season to season. For each person there is a favourite beach at a favourite time of the year. Brighton beach in a winter storm, is, to this writer at least, more appealing than the same beach on a crowded summer day. Likewise, the long deserted shores of Northumberland or the West Country have as great a fascination in bleak November or in January as they do in the high weeks of the tourist season. England's seashore is for all seasons.

By definition, the range of subjects touched upon in a book of finite length is vast. That the existing literature on the varied aspects of maritime England is also vast, underlines the quandary of what to include and how much. I therefore felt that a short select bibliography would be most helpful as a guide for those who wish to know more about some of the subjects discussed.

One of the greatest of all English historians, G.M. Trevelyan, wrote in his *History of England* that

> she has always owed her fortune to the sea, and to the havens and rivers that, from earliest times, opened her inland regions to what the sea might bring. Long before she aspired to rule the waves, she was herself their subject, for her destiny was continually being decided by the boatcrews which they floated to her shore.

It is therefore proper to begin by looking at England's maritime inheritance in its historical setting.

OPPOSITE *Salmon fishing at Berwick-upon-Tweed, Northumbria. A port and the northern-most town in England, Berwick is noted for its salmon fisheries and as a holiday resort.*

BELOW *Thousands throughout the country enjoy water-skiing. There are over 150 clubs with members participating in numerous events and competitions. The 1980 European Overall champion was, in fact, English.*

Part I
The Sea our Heritage

The Eye of the Wind *off the coast of Costa Rica. This magnificent brigantine was the base for 'Operation Drake' 1978–1980*

Richborough Castle, the Romans' main fort on the Channel crossing. One of the Saxon Shore forts, it was also designed to stop Saxon pirates from going around the blind side between Thanet (then an offshore island) and Kent. The site was the landing-place of Claudius' invasion of AD *43, then became a prosperous little port, later the site of a grand monument (the Channel was marked with a triumphal arch), then a fortified look-out, and finally, around* AD *250, an impregnable castle. The Saxon Shore Way, a recently opened path that traces these seaboard of 2,000 years ago, passes close by Richborough. The walk is 140 miles long: from Gravesend along the Kent Coast and across the Sussex border into Rye.*

1 Beginnings

The search for food, the urge of primitive man to maintain life at the most basic of levels, probably prompted the first migration to these northern isles tens of thousands of years ago. Dynamic patterns of migration continued through the following millennia. These early travellers doubtless dug themselves canoes out of logs with the help of fire and simple tools, just as men in remote, undeveloped parts of the world do to this day. If trees of sufficient dimensions were lacking, others may have constructed wicker frames and covered them with skins to form coracles, and these, we know from recent simulations, were capable of making long and dangerous journeys.

Nobody knows when, in geological terms, Britain first became an island, but it is thought to have been connected to the European Continent by a marshy belt across the southern part of the North Sea until a few thousand years BC. So migration would have been across channels of water, some narrow, some wide. Evidence of their food-gathering activities is to be found in the traces of primitive 'middens', comprised of foraged shells and small animal bones, located along the coastline.

Other motives for this migration were probably the urge to escape from dangers of involvement with the warring tribes on the European Continent, and the search for a better life. But there may have been more mystical reasons for some migration. Perhaps it was a search for the rich and legendary 'isles of the sunset', where the dead would live again. Later, there were more organised tribal motives: to conquer, to search for gold brought from Ireland, or to gain access to the much valued tin in Cornwall. The Beaker Folk arrived around 2,000 BC.

The greatest migration started in the Mediterranean area, coming over a period of time and from many directions. Some immigrants came from Portugal, via Brittany, a difficult journey by canoe or coracle. These early men took their skills and treasures with them when they travelled, leaving much archaeological proof of their wanderings. Styles of pottery, tools and arrowheads link distinct parts of Britain and Europe.

ABOVE *The Rillaton Gold Cup. Found in a Bronze Age barrow in Cornwall, the cup dates from* c. *1600–1400* BC. *According to one school of opinion, the bell shape and the handle indicate that it was most probably made by the Beaker Folk.*

When they reached England they tended to stay close to the shore for a very long period. In this way they kept their escape route open while they gained the experience, knowledge – and courage – to explore the dangerous hinterland.

Long before Christian missionaries used the same sea to travel on, these early voyagers came with their religions and beliefs, erecting great stones and burial cysts. We have their mysterious monoliths to remind us of their expert skills as hewers of stone, but no such artefacts to recall their undoubted skills as seafarers. For they must have been fine seamen and, interestingly, some of their journeys by sea were to

BELOW *The Battersea Shield was acquired by the British Museum in 1857. Dredged up from the Thames, this Celtic bronze shield is decorated, and enriched with studs set with red stones. It is 2 ft 6½ in. in height and dates from around the first century* BC.

transport the much treasured stones of their religion. For example, the huge blue stones from Pembrokeshire were brought by boat or by raft, by sea and by river, to the many sites where they can still be seen today.

Over the centuries individuals, family units and small tribes grouped together for defence and support. Early trading patterns, studied by archaeologists are the best indications we have of life and conditions in the first semi-organised communities along England's coastline.

In the early Bronze Age trade between Ireland and Cornwall is known to have been extensive and constant, bronze being the principal 'industrial' metal of the time. However, wares had long been imported from Ireland. At first the gold route was from Wicklow to north Cornwall, then from south Cornwall on to Brittany. Later this seems to have been superseded by easier and more direct routes from Wicklow to Wales and Scotland.

Cornish tin was a very important item in the extensive pattern of trade that existed in this period. Along with bronze and gold, tin has been found in definite geographical patterns through much of western Europe. There is some dispute amongst historians as to whether it was the finished article or the raw material that was traded, but whoever is correct, it is certain that the trade was widespread and well established.

To support this early economic activity there must have been boats and boat builders, sailors and navigators – and harbours or havens to receive them. England's maritime history had truly begun.

With the arrival of the Iron Age in Britain around 500 BC, axes and swords of flint and bronze became outdated. Though bronze and tin long continued to be used domestically, the Irish and Cornish dominance of the metal trade declined. Iron ore is commonly found in Britain, the Romans finding iron bars in use as currency when they arrived. One important consequence of the use of this new metal was that a man could cut down large trees much more easily and shape the wood, thus being able to build ever bigger and better boats.

The Veneti, Bretons who were some of the best builders and navigators in north-west Europe at the time of Caesar's invasion of Britain, seem to have specialised in this activity and we can assume that there were others as well. The Veneti used boats built of oak and because, as a tribe, they must have traded across the Channel, their skills as shipwrights and seamen would have been brought to the most accessible settlements along England's south-eastern coast.

These fortified groups of huts where cargo was off- and on-loaded were the forerunners of ports as we know them. London, with its excellent and navigable river was just such a settlement, even before the Romans made it their military supply base in the first century AD. The Romans were expert at choosing the best sites both for defence and for communications wherever they went and wherever they conquered. Having chosen London, they then developed it. Evidence for the growth of trade through ports such as London is shown by the minting of coins – one of the first indicators of organised economic life and one which helps historians plot the growth of trade to and from these growing centres of population.

While Roman nautical influence must have been considerable, we can only speculate on how the

Coracles

Coracles, bowl-shaped fishing boats without keels, have been known for centuries in Britain. They were the direct successors to the small skin-covered vessels that Caesar first saw in Kent, an idea he later adapted for his own use and then wrote about in *Civil War*, Bk.1:

> As things were reduced to such a strait and all the roads were blocked . . . Caesar orders his men to build ships of the kind that his experience in Britain in previous years had taught him to make. The keels and the first ribs were made of light timber, the rest of the hull was wattled and covered with hides.

There is a historical reference to a seven days' voyage made by missionaries in AD 878 from Ireland to Cornwall in a coracle made of two-and-a-half hides. The sea-going type of coracle was probably similar to the curragh still used by Irish fishermen off the coast of Connaught.

River coracles were built at Ironbridge on the Severn and are now displayed there at the Ironbridge Gorge Trust Museum. Coracles are still used today on several rivers in Wales. (In 1807 a contemporary observer wrote of Cenarth, Wales: 'There is scarcely a cottage in the neighbourhood without its coracle hanging by the door.') Both design and method of handling varied from river to river, depending on conditions. The weather, speed of flow and depth of the water and rapids all affected the design, in which there were also elements of tradition and individual preference.

In past centuries the frame of woven grasses, reeds and saplings was covered with horse or ox hide, the size of the coracle being directly related to the size of the hide. Later, tar-coated flannel replaced the hide and today pitch-coated canvas or calico has replaced the flannel. Coracles were, and still are, used primarily for netting salmon.

These marvellously innovative and functional little boats could easily be carried on a man's back or hung on his head like a hood, leaving his hands free to use his oar as a stick when walking or climbing. They weighed between 25 and 36 pounds and were from 50 to 60 inches in length. PP

Fisherman in a coracle, Cilgerran, Dyfed, Wales.

native tribes applied the newly available knowledge of maritime skills. Generally, England lacks the preservative climate, seabed muds and sands that have kept very early wooden boats intact in other parts of the world, so this source of information is usually unavailable. Also, in the barbarian ages following the collapse of the Roman Empire many traces of the previous way of life were erased.

For evidence of the design and rigs of Romano-British shipping we must look abroad, just as we must for pre-Roman vessels. But there are glimpses: parts of a Roman vessel were unearthed at Blackfriars on the Thames and we can see contemporary pictures of vessels painted on vases and represented in frescoes, mosaics, and even on memorial stones.

One of the Romans' lasting contributions was the building of our road network, which served the country for centuries until the great road-building programme of the past two hundred and fifty years. Their use of roads must have reduced somewhat the need to make some journeys by water. Successive races ensured, by their neglect of these magnificent Roman constructions, that travel by water was often more convenient, especially for goods traffic.

The Roman system of colonisation gave a tremendous impetus to foreign trade and commerce, this being another major influence of the

Empire. Obviously, these wares had to have considerable value to warrant being imported by sea. Such items would have been the amphorae containing wine or oil, pottery and metal goods, along with other items which we know were landed at and distributed from London and the smaller ports along the Kentish coast. English exports included cattle, hides, iron ore and slaves; even 'sporting dogs' were exported to Europe in the first century AD. The successive waves of destruction that eventually drove the Romans from Britain and the rest of northern Europe did not totally obliterate the awareness that goods could be bought and sold or bartered internationally to the advantage of all.

During the centuries of their rule the Romans must have been fundamentally dependent on the sea, particularly on the Channel, for their supplies, communication and trade. This Channel traffic was defended by their fleet, the *Classis Britannica*, which was based at Dover and Boulogne.

From about AD 275, when their Empire was gradually declining, the fleet came under increasing attack from Saxon and Frankish pirates. The Roman shore bases were equally vulnerable. Consequently, from Brancaster by the Wash round to Porchester fortifications were raised against seaborne attack.

The Roman Palace, Fishbourne, Sussex. Near Chichester, this major ruin is thought to have been the palace of Tiberius Claudius Cogidubnus, the local tribal king, who was also a puppet-king for the Romans. It is the largest Roman residence yet found in Britain, and was larger than Nero's palace in Rome. Particularly outstanding are the mosaic floors, of which the remains of twelve can be seen in situ *under a modern cover building.*

Lifting the Graveney Boat

The wooden timbers of this tenth-century Anglo-Saxon boat – a merchantman – were discovered in September 1970 when an improved drainage system for the Graveney Marshes in the Thames estuary was nearing completion under the supervision of the Kent River Authority. Due to the interest and persistence of Roy Botting, the driver of one of the mechanical excavators, the find was recognised and saved. A task force was assembled from several local museums and groups under the direction of the Canterbury Archaeological Society.

The British Museum and the National Maritime Museum became involved in this important find almost immediately, each contributing a variety of skills and services. Many others were involved and it was with considerable human effort that this important boat was lifted from the heavy mud of the marsh that cold, bleak autumn. The Kent River Authority gave their permission and, with the channel due to be flooded in two weeks' time, the owner of the land agreed that the vessel be recorded and lifted.

Seventy per cent of this clinker-built vessel, about forty-six feet long with a beam of over thirteen feet, had survived. The heavy marsh clay was excavated from the vessel with some difficulty, the slowly revealed ancient wood being kept as wet as possible. A polythene shelter and scaffolding were built over the vessel, a full photographic survey was made and soil samples taken. The massive ribs, nine in all, were removed by cutting through the wooden trenails (dowels) holding them to the hull. Then a plaster-of-Paris mould was made of the inside of the shell by the team from the British Museum, who had made the plaster cast for the Sutton Hoo ship.

The boat was dismantled and lifted piece by piece, each timber being sealed in heavy-duty polythene. Kneeling helpers dug under each timber with their hands, to prevent planks from being scratched and to search for objects in the mud. In this way the timbers were freed from the mud. Quickly, just before a timber came free, they slipped a piece of plywood underneath to bear the weight.

A special framework was built to fit the eighteen-foot-long keel as it sat on a ridge of mud with a trench to one side. The keel was lashed to the framework with plastic webbing that had been pushed through holes made by hand in the mud ridge. The keel was then rocked from side to side until it came away from the mud and was rolled over to rest on its framework. The keel of the 'Gravy boat', as it was affectionately dubbed by volunteers, was raised on the penultimate day before flooding.

The timbers were placed in a conservation tank at the National Maritime Museum where they will remain until full conservation can take place. A full-size cast in fibre glass of the boat is on display in the new archaeological gallery.

Radio-carbon and tree-ring dating have provisionally fixed the building of the Graveney boat at about AD 927 and it was probably abandoned about twenty years later.

Particularly interesting is the fact that the boat has modified previous generalisation about ships of this period. Instead of a sweeping double-ended shape with curving helm and stern, it has a definite heel at its stern. Illustrations of similar ships have been found in Scandinavia. PP

The Graveney boat embedded in the mud of the marsh. Finds in or near the boat included wood, pottery, tile, stone, bone and shell. Unfinished millstones found on board came from the middle Rhine and, with hop plants, were probably the cargo. Cooking pottery on board came from northern France.

Partial model of the Blackfriars ship, a Romano-British sailing barge dating from the second century AD. *The solid structure of the hull and the large iron nails can clearly be seen. The origin of this method of construction is found in north-west Europe, probably among the Celtic peoples of the Iron Age. A reconstruction of a cross-section of the ship with some of the original timbers in place, can be seen in the Roman Gallery, Museum of London. There is also a display of its cargo of Kentish building stone.*

Among the most important of these fortified sites was that of Richborough, known as *Rutupiae*. This, though now two-and-a-half miles from the sea, is believed to have been the major cross-Channel port through Roman times. It was first a base camp, and then, for a century and a half, a prosperous little port. Suddenly, around the year AD 250, it had to be fortified, perhaps after a pirate raid. Its fortifications were then strengthened continually.

The collapse of cross-Channel trade paralleled the collapse of Empire, and England gradually slipped back into a long period of primitive self-sufficiency. Internally she remained fairly peaceful until late in the fourth century. But along the coast pirates and sea-raiders ruled unchecked until their place was taken by the new marauders of the Viking Age. As with the Roman settlements, towns and villas, the ports of England slipped or were cast into ruin. If there was a maritime economy, except for some inshore fishing, we know nothing of it today.

2 Vikings, Priests and Merchants

The end of Roman Government broke the trading ties with the Empire. Though the evidence is scarce, it is clear that maritime trading did not cease entirely in the so-called Dark Ages. Settlers from across the North Sea, collectively known as Angles and Saxons, raided and then settled in England, in later centuries to be attacked by the fierce Viking raiders of Scandinavia. They were also subject to a sea-borne spiritual invasion whose influence was of lasting effect – the Christians from Europe and Ireland.

Vikings and missionaries had two things in common. They both used boats as a means of transportation in an age when it was exceptionally difficult and dangerous to travel by land. Also, to both the sea was a defence, as is betokened by traces of Viking and monastic settlements on nearly every island of note around the entire English coastline. Their aims and methods had few other similarities.

There were, of course, many other tribal and social processes going on in England over that long period, including the great Norman Conquest in the eleventh century and all that stemmed from it. In strictly maritime terms these events were much less significant, but there followed a rebirth of the trade that the Roman occupation had first established. This was eventually to usher in England's great mercantile age.

In the past few years there has been a trend towards rehabilitating the reputation of the Vikings. The popular notion that they were motivated by a basic bloodlust and desire to rape and pillage is now modified somewhat by the realisation that they were survivors in a perilous age. Now their considerable accomplishments as artists, heroic explorers and successful traders are emphasised.

There is no doubt that the Vikings and the Viking tradition had a fundamentally important effect on the development of the indigenous English into a maritime nation. Pillaged the villagers were, but in turn they learned much from these Scandinavian raiders. As has occurred several times in the course of English history, great developments were generated only as a reaction to a grave external threat.

The aims of the Vikings were first, simple looting, then territorial expansion, then trade. In the beginning they were entirely pagan, later becoming aggressive in the pursuit of their new-found Chris-

A large memorial stone from the Swedish island of Gotland. Such stones have given invaluable information about very early boats.

The Gokstad Ship, an amazingly complete Viking longship of about AD *900.*

tian faith. With their impressive navigational skills, they met little or no seaborne resistance, giving them free access, not only to the coastline settlements, but also deep into England's interior. With their highly manoeuvrable, shallow-draught boats, they were able to make these inroads via the Humber estuary and its river system, through the whole drainage area of the Wash and along the Thames – just as earlier invaders had penetrated into the very heart of the English countryside.

Viking power came, above all, from well-designed ships and superlative seamanship. We have learned about longboats from old carvings which show the great skill that went into their marine architecture and from actual vessels that have been preserved in the muds of Scandinavia. Among the most famous of these relics is the Gokstad Ship, an amazingly complete Viking longship, now preserved in Oslo's Viking Ships Museum.

From contemporary reports we know of the English wonderment at the appearance of the Viking ships, due to the speed and manoeuvrability of these vessels. The longboats needed little depth of water and could easily be beached on sand or shingle enabling the Norsemen to jump out and do battle immediately. It also meant that they had no need for sheltered harbours. Except for the North Sea crossing, they did prefer to stick to the coasts and the crews probably encamped ashore at night when they could. In addition, by using both sail and oar, they had less dependence on the winds; however, lacking a deep keel, the longboats must have rolled fiercely in high seas.

Viking ships varied in size from the 'skuta' of thirty oars to the 'skeid' with up to sixty-four oars and a crew of around 250 or more. In construction, the ships were open and clinker-built, that is, made from planks each overlapping the one below. Usually built of oak, the decking, masts and booms were of pine, which was more easily dressed with the primitive tools available. They were slender in the beam and the simpler ones were bound with stout roots – this, according to some sources, allowed the vessels to 'give' with the waves. In the earlier centuries of Viking supremacy the vessels tended to have symmetrical bow and stern and were easily adaptable for sail and oar; steering was with a large starboard-mounted oar. They might also carry small oak-built rowing boats as dinghies. As recently constructed life-sized replicas have demonstrated the

Viking longboats were fine and seaworthy ships.

Some were very large: the Gokstad Ship, built with wrought-iron nails, is nearly 77 feet long, with a seventeen-and-a-half foot beam. Remains have been found of even greater longboats, some being almost 100 feet in length. The largest one on record is a massive 120 feet from bow to stern. Despite their size they could have a draught of as little as three feet, clearly demonstrating how close inshore and how far up rivers the Norsemen could navigate.

The masts were stepped on a great block of wood fixed to the keel; the simple rigging, probably consisting of a forestay and shrouds, would have allowed the mast to be raised and lowered easily. The square sail was hoisted on a beam or yard which might, as on the Gokstad Ship, be up to forty feet in length. These longboats could have up to sixty-four oars, although half that number was more common. The oar holes or rowlocks were closeable when not in use, and the topsides could be hung with multi-coloured shields as added protection for the oarsmen. On later ships especially, there were elaborately carved and decorated figureheads at the prow in the shape of weird sea monsters. From archaeological discoveries we also know something of the equipment carried on these vessels, such as spare rigging, metal anchors and skins and casks for fresh water.

What real legacy did the Vikings leave? Most important, the Vikings had the gradual effect of forcing the development of an organised naval defence by the 'English tribes'. As Alfred the Great, the first to have been inspired to deal with the Vikings in their own fashion, later demonstrated, the challenge offered by Norse ships and military seamanship was one that had to be met and mastered by increasing the size and speed of England's own ships of war.

As well as negotiating politically with them the king knew that he had to have the power, the military backup, to make the treaties he signed with them stick. Around the last decade of the ninth century he therefore ordered the building of an English

Alfred the Great

Alfred (AD 849–899) was King of Wessex, a Saxon kingdom in south-west England, from 871–899. He is remembered for many things including his fine character, a great interest in learning, his administrative ability, his code of laws – and the development of a navy. In 886 he captured London bringing all of the English under his rule.

He first saw active service when he went with his brother, King Ethelred, to help Burgred of Mercia when a large Danish army took possession of Northumbria. The Danes invaded Wessex itself in 871, the very year in which Alfred succeeded his brother as king. The Danes were strongly repelled by Alfred, and there was some respite from attack for a few years. But the invasions started again and in a surprise attack in 878 the west Saxons submitted, all except King Alfred. Alfred harassed the invaders from a fort in Somerset, while he secretly assembled an army, with which he defeated them. The king of the Danes was baptised and all finally settled in East Anglia. The great overall danger subsided, although there were further attacks and battles.

Alfred took defensive measures to maintain a stable rule. Old forts were strengthened, new ones built and all were manned. The army was re-organised and he used ships as part of his defence as early as 875 – adopting the tactics of the Danes themselves.

About 897 he designed his own 'long ships' which he then had built to use against the coastal raiders. From the 'Saxon Chronicles':

> They were full-nigh twice as long as the others; some had sixty oars, and some had more; they were both swifter and steadier, and also higher than the others. They were shapen neither like the Frisian nor the Danish; but so as it seemed to him that they would be most efficient.

When Wulfstan, an Englishman, made a northern voyage, Alfred was interested in hearing details of the countries he had seen. There is no evidence that Alfred sent men on exploratory voyages, although many fabulous stories exist about his achievements. PP

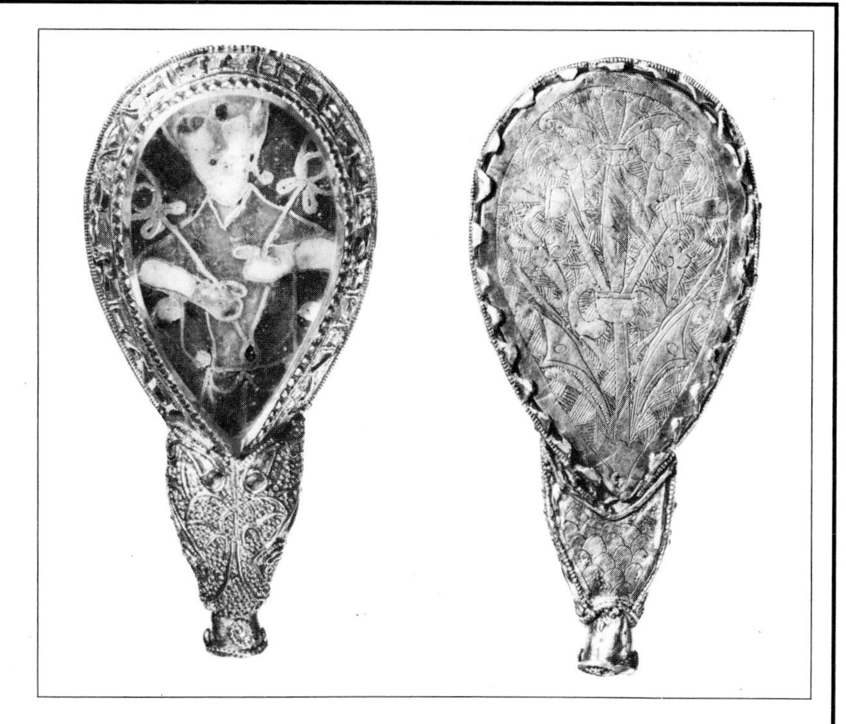

A portrait, believed to be of King Alfred, in cloisonné enamel on the Alfred Jewel. It bears the inscription 'Aelred het me gewyrcan' *(Alfred caused me to be made). This ninth-to-tenth-century Jewel is at the Ashmolean Museum, Oxford.*

RIGHT *A page from the magnificent Lindisfarne Gospels, now in the British Museum. Bishop Eadfrith compiled the Gospels, about* AD *700. With the Viking attacks, the surviving monks fled from Lindisfarne, taking the Gospels and other treasures with them.*

OPPOSITE, TOP *Menacing figurehead from the Oseberg ship burial. University Museum, Oslo.*

OPPOSITE, BOTTOM *St Guthlac being conveyed to Crowland in the Lincolnshire Fens in a fishing boat; from the vellum Guthlac Roll, a scroll illustrating his life of religious seclusion in a series of drawings. The isolation of the Fens attracted monks and hermits.*

fleet, the ships of which, according to the contemporary 'Saxon Chronicles', had sixty oars or more and were twice as long as the Viking vessels. The Chronicles subsequently tell of numerous battles in which the enemy boats were captured or destroyed. The foundation of an English naval power and the resolve to master the sea and those who used it, was thus the principal legacy of the Vikings.

A parallel effect was that these Danish, Swedish and Norwegian adventurers dominated much of the 'foreign relations' of England, particularly eastern England, from around AD 790 to the end of the eleventh century. The first recorded raid on southern England was in the year 789; four years later they were consistently sacking coastal villages up and down the country, including the well-documented raid on Lindisfarne Abbey in AD 793, when almost all the monks were massacred.

But the Viking bequest was not only in the realms of warfare and defence. The infusion of tough, seagoing blood into these land-loving tribes must have had no less an important effect. Equally, their navigational skills, their boatbuilding expertise, their opening up of Europe in terms of establishing sea routes, were all essential to the creation of a maritime, trade-oriented England.

England was pillaged, but was also converted to Christianity, as she had been to the earlier ancient and mysterious religions from across the seas.

When the great missionaries and saints reached England, they tended to keep their bases and retreats by the coast or on the islands that lay offshore. They then moved onwards by sea in their eventually successful bid to convert all of England. There is no doubt that the outstanding names of early Christianity must have been not only strong in their faith, but also good seamen. Christianity, a seaborne faith, was carried forward in very humble vessels indeed, probably no more than coracles or the most rudimentary trading and fishing hulks.

Christianity spread inland from Northumberland, from Cornwall and the Kentish ports. It had come a long way: Augustine, who landed at Thanet, had come all the way from Rome, while Theodore had come from Tarsus. Each carried with him his special skills. It is possible that some Mediterranean fishing and navigation techniques reached England in this way, brought here by people whose calling was basically as fishers of men.

Cross-Channel trade now came to the fore to stimulate the maritime interests of England, the forces of war and religion having opened up routes and a range of contacts with the European mainland to a degree unknown since Roman times. By the tenth and eleventh centuries, with the Vikings defeated and gone, there is increasing evidence of a substantial pattern of such overseas trade developing outwards from the south-east of England in particular. Small communities of foreigners engaged in this cross-Channel trade settled in several parts of the growing town of London. The Cinque Ports were also developing as active trading ports, their townspeople and merchants building and owning their own shipping fleets.

Documents from the period, set out rules and regulations governing, for example, the import of certain commodities such as wine and fish from Rouen and Normandy. In the Domesday Book it is further recorded that, to prevent fraud and treachery, laws had been established to ensure that 'far-coming men', or foreign traders, identify themselves by their ensigns, by 'horn-blowing' or by singing known 'sea-shanties' before being allowed up the Thames to unload their Rhenish wines. Otherwise, strange ships might too easily be mistaken for the pirates and sea-raiders that troubled the English coasts.

The commodities first imported were simple and confined mainly to a few staples. Soon significant imports of wine, spices and other luxuries, such as silks and other fine cloth, gems and gold, dyes, oil, glass, ivory and brass were also included. More com-

St Augustine

Christianity, very much a seaborne faith, was brought to these shores from faraway places by missionaries like St Augustine. St Augustine (d.*c.* 604), the 'apostle of England', became the first Archbishop of Canterbury and is considered to be the founder of the Christian church in southern England.

He was prior of St Andrew, Pope Gregory's monastery in Rome, when Gregory chose him to lead forty other monks on a mission to England, which was mostly pagan in the south. It was an unusual expedition and the monks were fearful of what lay ahead, even though something was known of the country, including the fact that there was some Christianity. The monks left Rome in June 596, but before going very far, Augustine, reluctant to proceed, as were the others, returned to the Pope questioning the necessity of such a dangerous journey. He was reassured by Gregory, who gave him letters of safe conduct and a letter of encouragement to the monks. As recorded by Bede:

> Since it is better not to begin good works than to have second thoughts and withdraw from those that are begun, you must, my dearest sons, zealously complete the good work you have begun . . .

He rejoined the monks and they proceeded, landing on the Isle of Thanet in the Spring of 597. Ethelbert, King of Kent, after due consideration, for he feared the magical arts, crossed to Thanet to meet them. A tolerant and sensible man, whose wife already was a Christian, he assured Augustine that his monks would not be molested. Noting the king's growing interest and eventual conversion others followed in great numbers. In 597 Augustine was consecrated Bishop of the English at Arles.

Augustine probably would have been content with the conversion of Kent, but Gregory had formulated a much greater plan. In 601 he sent Augustine the pallium, symbol of metropolitan authority, along with a supply of sacred vessels, vestments, books and more missionaries. Gregory revealed his plan for the ecclesiastical organisation of England and Augustine was directed to

St Augustine as depicted in a fifteenth-century French volume.

consecrate twelve suffragan bishops, he himself now the archbishop. During the following years all the Saxon kingdoms of England gradually accepted the faith.

Augustine founded the monastery of Christchurch, Canterbury, which established Canterbury as the primatial see. He tried to unify the British (Celtic) churches of North Wales, but the Welsh remained unconvinced, even when Augustine performed a miracle.

Augustine had a grave and accomplished mind, but was seemingly bogged down by organisational difficulties and frequently wrote for instruction to the Pope, whose replies were full of advice and sympathy for the difficulties the missionaries were experiencing.

Augustine's impact on southern England included a new style of architecture as well as written laws and learning.

In a most moving part of the Enthronement ceremony held at Canterbury Cathedral the Archbishop of Canterbury takes his corporeal oath on the illuminated Canterbury Gospels believed to have been sent by Gregory to Augustine. PP

mon imports included dried fish, timber and salt.

As far as English exports were concerned, from the tenth to the thirteenth centuries, these were entirely of raw materials and foodstuffs. Quantities, like the ships that carried them, were undoubtedly small; nonetheless, it was profitable to send corn and other meal to Scandinavia, while lead, tin, cheeses, skins and hides went to other parts of Europe. Royal 'levies', the taxes of the time, were charged on many types of ship cargo out of English ports.

Wool was the main English export and the wool trade, above all, was to be of prime importance to

LEFT *Illustration of English merchants watching cargoes arrive, about 1350. Bodleian Library, Oxford.*

BELOW *Ruins of Tynemouth Priory dating from the eleventh and fourteenth centuries. The priory was founded in the eleventh and twelfth centuries by the Benedictines on the site of an earlier seventh-century monastery.*

England's economy and to her merchant marine for many centuries. The growth and prosperity of many an English port depended on this trade and it was the major source of foreign exchange for merchant and monarch alike.

From the twelfth and thirteenth centuries on there were, particularly in the larger ports, merchants with considerable overseas trading interests. Certain London merchants, chartering or owning their own ships, were engaged in trade both to Ireland and to Europe. Much of this trade was financed by Jewish businessmen, but, equally importantly, by Italians. There were comparatively large firms operating in thirteenth-century England that dealt mainly in wool, whose bases were in Florence and elsewhere in Italy. These Italians acted as early bankers, issuing letters of credit which sea captains, pilgrims and merchants could cash abroad. They grew to dominate much of England's trade until Edward III suddenly repudiated his debts with them and their heyday was over at a blow. From then on it was the turn of rich English merchant shipowners to watch nervously when successive monarchs – who were inclined to 'borrow' with little option to the lender – ran out of money to finance their foreign wars.

Over this period, there was a fairly permanent excise tax on exports which was administered through semi-official bodies called the 'Merchants of the Staple', who dealt in one or other of the major commodities, particularly wool. Calais, being an English possession, was for almost a century and a half, from 1363, the centre of the Wool Staple – the market and organisation of this principal commodity. His-

St George's Guildhall, King's Lynn, Norfolk, for centuries a port and market town on the River Ouse. The Guildhall, with its striking chequered flintwork, dates from the fifteenth century.

torians argue that this first permanent settlement of English merchants overseas, marks the beginning of the centuries of prosperity for English merchant shipping.

We are fairly knowledgeable about the growing success of this merchant shipping because we have access to an increasing wealth of statistics in customs accounts and port records. Economic historians can, for example, give figures for the number of bales of wool shipped overseas in the year 1290, and also the names of the ports from which they were consigned.

Wine easily came at the top of the list of imports. It is interesting to note that it was probably easier to get French wine in any English village inn on the south coast in the thirteenth century than in the early years of the twentieth. The greatest wine fleets sailed out of the Thames, and later from Bristol, during the three centuries when the English ruled Gascony and Bordeaux. In addition, nearly every other coastal town, from Chester round to Ipswich, had some stake in the Bordeaux wine trade. On the west coast of England much of it was shipped via Ireland, as evidenced by the fact that Edward I, in the year 1282, in the middle of his wars with the Welsh, could order up six hundred tuns from there.

After the loss of Bordeaux in 1453, the trade decreased rapidly and from then on, imports had to come from further afield: 'malmsey' was brought from the Mediterranean and 'sack' from Spain and the Canaries. The longer distances involved was one of many reasons why larger ocean-going vessels were built.

During the fifteenth century, exports of wool also fell away, hitting the ports of Southampton, Hull and Boston, with great severity. What trade survived, was largely carried on through London's Merchants of the Staple.

3 The Age of Sail: Ships and Shipbuilding

The foundations of the age of sail were really laid in previous centuries when simple and inefficient vessels were replaced by galleys. The galley, used right up to the fourteenth century, could be quite sophisticated; with possibly two or three banks of 'sweeps' or oars and up to seven men on an oar, it was obviously labour intensive. Inefficient and ponderous for long and rough sea journeys and with regard to provisioning for the crew, it was inevitable that a replacement would be found.

The sailing ship, by comparison, needed only a tiny crew and by the tenth and eleventh centuries sail had begun to supersede the oar as a method of propulsion. In its earliest version it would have been a simple square sail used only for going before the wind, as an auxiliary to oars.

The cargo ship of the age was the 'cog', a relatively clumsy, blunt-nosed and broad-beamed tub. It had one square sail on a single mast and was therefore rather slow, sailing best before the wind. Its size was measured in terms of its cargo-carrying capacity. Given the importance of the wine trade to England, this was done very generally by 'tuns', a tun being a cask containing some 250 gallons. Until around 1300, cogs of about thirty 'tuns' were the average, indicated by the fact that the twelfth-century Crown was apt to levy a tax or 'prise' of one tun before the mast and one after (something like six-and-a-half per cent import tax).

In the fourteenth century, larger ships came under construction and some of over 200 'tuns' are recorded. Such vessels began to need two masts and to have stern rudders in place of the earlier steering oar, a development that is noted from the twelfth century.

The proliferation of the use of gunpowder had the most telling effect on ship design. Earlier, guns had been fired from the bows. Now tactical benefits and the need for stability led to guns being carried along the sides, firing through portholes. As the national fleets of the French and Spanish developed in the latter decades of the fourteenth century, an increasing number of specialised warships were built, though converted merchant ships continued to be pressed for naval duty. The guns and the need to manoeuvre rapidly also led to the development of new hull designs and rigging to give maximum seaworthiness and speed.

A cog depicted on the seal (1359) of Stralsund, a member of the Hanseatic League. Cogs were merchant vessels, clinker-built, i.e. with overlapping boards.

Richard, Coeur de Lion, is specifically credited with improving the English naval fleet in the course of fighting the Crusades. At his peak, in the last decade of the twelfth century, the king is reputed to have had, sailing with him out of Dartmouth, a fleet of no less than 110 vessels, with twice that number under his command by the time he and his navy reached the Mediterranean. Most of these ships would have been armed merchant ships.

From about the fourteenth century they were built with an increasingly high freeboard, with fore, top and stern castles–literally 'castles' of wood–and with centre-line rudders. Though evidence is scant, other improvements included carvel construction for bigger ships and the three-masted ship rig – a standard sail and mast lay-out for the rest of the age of sail.

King Henry V, another important figure in the history of the English fleet, is credited with building huge vessels of up to 1,000 tons. The largest of these was called *Jesus of the Tower* at 1,000 tons, with a sister ship *Holigost of the Tower* at 760 tons, though most of his fleet would have been about half that size.

Shipbuilding techniques and experience in this period were often drawn from the Continent, where the Spanish, Venetians and Portuguese were generally considered to be ahead in many aspects of ship and rigging design.

This was the age of the great discoveries of Columbus (1492), and Cabot (1497). These men sailed in vessels of quite limited size and with tiny crews; for example, John Cabot took only fourteen men on his voyage of discovery to Newfoundland.

Merchant ships of the day were, however, gradually increasing in size: at the beginning of the fifteenth century, the wine ships sailing into Bristol were around eighty to ninety tons; a century later, twice that size was not uncommon. The standard form of these vessels was also improved. Finer lines and more intricate sails and rigging were adopted, though, of course, local trade as well as fishing would continue to be by small single-masted vessels.

Tudor England saw further developments in ship design, generally of the 'bigger and stronger' variety, to cope with longer sea voyages and the growth in strength of the other great maritime nations, Spain and France. On warships, several tiers of guns were not uncommon, and experiments were widespread in terms of varied numbers of masts and of rigging design. Two, three, even four masts appeared and a mixture of square, and fore and aft sailing rigs are described in contemporary accounts.

Shipbuilding always was an important industry – one that is vital to an island race. In the centuries up to 1500, it had become a major employer, particularly in the Thames area, where shipwrights, Freemen of London, were settled at Wapping, and, even more importantly, at Rotherhithe.

Apprenticeship to this most exacting profession was strictly regulated; in a late-fifteenth-century wage statute, we find the 'Maister Ship Carpynter', in charge of the work, with, under him 'the Hewer', the 'Able Clyncher', the 'Mere Holder', 'Maister Calker' and 'Meane Calker'. The Master Carpenter probably took on contracts from prospective shipowners, who produced the necessary supplies of the increasingly scarce timber. He then assembled his team to complete the task. Unfortunately, on both the technical and the economic side, we know less that we would like about the industry at this time.

Shelter, a good depth of water and a skilled work force were the essential requirements for a shipbuilding location. Many such sites for boat and shipbuilding by the sixteenth century were largely those that, to some extent, still have a toehold in the industry today; in the seventeenth century, East Anglia, mainly Suffolk, was an important area as well.

A considerable impetus to the industry was given by Henry VIII, who took especial interest in shipbuilding, particularly for his fleet. He founded

A woodcut of the first Ark Royal. *Originally the* Ark Ralegh, *she was re-named when bought by Queen Elizabeth. This vessel was the flagship of the Lord High Admiral of England and took part in the attack on the Spanish Armada.*

Royal Dockyards at Woolwich and Deptford and during his reign much attention was given to improved designs of hulls, sails and rigging. Other civilian shipyards were at Southampton, Dover, Hull, Boston and Bristol, though, because few boroughs had shipwrights' guilds, little is known about them, their size or their output.

There would also have been many small enterprises in coastal and riverside villages, building small craft for the coastal trade and fishing. For it must be remembered that, until the later seventeenth century, while 'great ships' are all that feature in contemporary texts, the majority were still very small.

Our knowledge will soon be enhanced by one of the most important discoveries of recent times – the wreck of the ship the *Mary Rose*, which was built in the sixteenth century on the orders of Henry VIII. It has recently been found on the bed of the Solent, and plans are well under way to raise it. The *Mary Rose* is an example of a so-called 'carrack' – a large square-rigged vessel – whose popularity spanned four centuries eventually being replaced during the sixteenth and seventeenth centuries by the more navigable and efficient galleon.

The English galleons of the late sixteenth century were much improved versions of the Portuguese and Spanish vessels of the time and set the standard for warships over the next 100 years. They were also the forerunners of the great 'Ships of the Line' of the eighteenth century.

An excellent impression of England's maritime strength is shown by the fact that, in the year 1588, facing the 132 ships of the Spanish Armada (the largest at 1,300 tons) was the English fleet of 197 vessels, of which only around thirty belonged to the Royal Navy. The largest of these was the 1,000-ton *Triumph* with the flagship, the *Ark Royal*, at 800 tons, carrying fifty-five guns. The majority of the rest were armed merchantmen.

A principal result of the defeat of the Armada was a very large increase in mercantile activity, an analysis of which will be discussed later on in this book. Suffice it to say that from then on, English merchants largely abandoned their previous practice of chartering foreign ships, preferring in future to build and own vessels that were entirely English. This gave an enormous incentive to the growth of English overseas trade and a further impetus to English shipbuilding and ship design.

Over this period shipbuilders and owners started to organise themselves more effectively. In 1605, James I granted Corporation status to the Shipwrights' Company of England, though the Company (which today has 500 members and is the largest Livery Company in the City of London), claims that its history goes back several centuries before that date, with its earliest ordinances dating from 1456. In the reign of Charles I, the 'calkers' and other artisans made demands to have their own corporation, but eventually had to make do with getting representation on the Board of the Shipwrights' Company. There was, over the next century or so, a growing amount of rivalry between the builders and the shipowners who tended to dominate this sector of the economy.

Samuel Pepys (1633–1703), is remembered for his unique diary, although his influence on the Navy was substantial. He was twice Navy Secretary, and author of Memoirs of the Royal Navy *(1690).*

When James II came to the throne, and with Samuel Pepys as Navy Secretary, Sir Anthony Deane, the best naval architect of the age, introduced many changes in ship construction. He borrowed largely from the superior skills of the French, since the study of naval architecture had reached a much higher level there. Naval historians agree that, even up to the beginning of the nineteenth century, some of the most successful English ships were either of French design or had been captured from them. But the advantages of English oak for shipbuilding remained considerable and domestic marine architecture was also improved by a new wave of skilled naval ship designers, who contributed to England's pre-eminence at sea.

At that period, the mercantile marine was, in terms of ship size, still maintaining the tradition of using much smaller vessels. For example, the East

The Mary Rose

The wreck of the *Mary Rose* is surely one of the most exciting archaelogical finds ever made – a unique time capsule of Tudor life on a warship in active service.

The wreck lies one mile offshore from Southsea Castle in the lee of the Isle of Wight and the busy waterway of the Solent. Henry VIII's *Mary Rose* was a 700-ton carrack which sank in July 1545 at the height of an attack on Portsmouth by a French invasion force – an attack that itself made little impact on history, but left to us this fascinating wreck of major historical importance.

Built in Portsmouth from 1509 to 1511, from the beginning the *Mary Rose* was a success. In 1513 Sir Edward Howard reported on her performance to the King, 'your good ship, the flower I trow of all ships that ever sailed.' But with her refit in 1536, also in Portsmouth, she became a revolutionary new type of ship. Her tonnage was increased from 600 to 700 tons and her armament increased to a total of 91 muzzle-loading and breech-loading guns. Major alterations were probably made to her structure as well, so that she emerged as a carvel-planked vessel (the planks flush with the seams) mounting a broadside battery of guns between decks with lidded gun ports. Thus, she was the first warship purpose-built as an independent fighting machine, capable of carrying guns between decks and firing broadsides. She carried a crew of 200 mariners, 185 soldiers (archers and pikemen) and 30 gunners.

The circumstances of her sinking remain something of a mystery. As Henry VIII watched from Southsea Common, four French galleys, mobile oared vessels, moved forward to exchange shots with one of the English ships; at this moment the *Mary Rose* heeled and rapidly sank beneath the surface of the calm sea. Her loss appears to have resulted from a combination of poor handling, some lack of discipline, overcrowding – she may have been carrying over 700 men (of whom less than three dozen survived), and gun ports open ready for action (through which the water poured as she began to heel). The King heard the screams of the drowning men as the pride of his navy went down. This question of why the *Mary Rose* sank may be resolved when she is lifted in 1982.

Several Tudor attempts to salvage the vessel failed, but the site was remembered for many many years, memories that eventually dimmed, leaving the ship forgotten, but safe, in the preservative soft seabed silts of the Solent.

In 1836, John and Charles Deane, pioneer helmet divers, were working on the wreck of the *Royal George*, also in the Solent, when local fishermen asked them to investigate an area where their lines frequently snagged an underwater obstruction. On diving, the Deanes discovered the fishermen's lines caught on an old piece of timber, and then noticed more timbers and a large bronze gun, which they recovered. A number of remarkable guns, loaded and primed, were brought up. The elaborate inscriptions established that this was the lost ship *Mary Rose*.

In time, the location of the ship was again forgotten until 1965, when Alexander McKee initiated 'Project Solent Ships' and the present-day search for the *Mary Rose* began, enthusiastically supported by members of the Southsea Branch of the British Sub-Aqua Club. Most opportunely, in 1966 a chart compiled in 1841 was found in the Hydrographic Department of the Royal Navy; the spot where the Deanes had found the *Mary Rose* was marked with a red cross. The site was inspected and a shallow depression suggesting a totally buried wreck was found. Outside help was sought with the result that the site was searched using side scan sonar and a sub-mud profiler – both of which use acoustic sounds to reflect changes in density. The results were excellent, showing a buried anomaly the right size and shape.

Deciding on the best way to conduct a methodical investigation of what is probably one of the most important wrecks in Northern Europe presented many problems. In 1967 the Mary Rose Committee was formed, including representatives of the Royal Navy and the Society for Nautical Research, with commitment 'to find, excavate, raise and preserve for all time such remains of the ship *Mary Rose* as may be of historical and archaeological interest.' The Committee obtained a lease to the seabed from the Crown Estate Commissioners and began to organise the excavation and survey of the site. The *Mary Rose* was one of the first ships to be protected under the 1973 *Protection of Wrecks Act*, and the Committee was licensed to work on the site by the Department of Trade, making all other diving there illegal.

Various artefacts were recovered, but it was not until 1971 that the first timbers of the ship were found – 426 years after she sank. In 1978 a major trench was dug across the ship at the bow which revealed that the orlop and the main decks were intact and that personal possessions were strewn across the deck exactly as they had fallen.

The wreck of the Mary Rose. *A diver hand-feeds silt into an airlift, which sucks it up and discharges it downstream. In this way no artefacts will be lost during excavation.*

The magnitude and complexity of excavating and raising a ship that pre-dates known ship plans and drawings became apparent and at this point several important decisions were made. It was agreed that the *Mary Rose* should be completely excavated and recorded *in situ*, and, after all the objects have been removed from inside the ship, that she should be recovered to be the centrepiece of a Tudor Ship Museum. In January 1979 the Mary Rose Trust was formed with the Prince of Wales as its first president. Within weeks the Trust's newly acquired base diving vessel, *Sleipner,* was moored over the site and a £3 million scheme to complete the archaeological work, recover the ship, and build the first stages of the museum had begun.

The 1980 season involved a rota of 30 divers, drawn from an international register of more than 200 volunteers, working in shifts. In that season 7,025 dives were made. Thousands of objects have been recovered so far – many unique. The *Mary Rose* has yielded a whole range of archery equipment, scores of longbows and hundreds of arrows. (There is only one other Tudor arrow in the whole country.) A popular sixteenth-century musical instrument (forerunner of the oboe), a shawm, has been found – the only English example in existence and possibly the oldest in the world. There are gold coins, a pewter flagon and candlesticks, wooden bowls and plates, sword scabbards, a wooden comb inside a leather purse, shoes, two pocket sundials and the Barber Surgeon's silk velvet coif (in remarkably good condition). The Barber Surgeon's chest contains a fascinating array of objects: razors, syringes of pewter and brass, turned-wood containers, flasks and ceramic pots – still containing ointments and bearing the fingerprints of the last people to use them. Archaeological director of the project, Margaret Rule, explains: 'The *Mary Rose* is important because of the opportunity she affords to study archaeological evidence in its totality.' Advanced techniques are being used to conserve the artefacts; wooden and leather objects have been freeze-dried, for example.

Among the numerous avenues to explore when the ship is fully excavated and all the information assembled will be the evolution of shipborne gunnery; how Tudor ships were manned – for remains are being found in their 'correct' positions – and operated; and, physiological data on the large group of men who died by accident rather than disease.

Portsmouth, where the ship was built, refitted, and near where she sank, will become the location of a major new museum. The Executive director of the Mary Rose Trust, Richard Harrison, maintains that the project has 'enormous implications both in terms of its importance to the Portsmouth area and in wider terms of human knowledge.' PP

Elevation of a Merchant-Ship with all her Masts, Yards, Sails & Rigging.
more particularly designed for that which is the Subject of the Poem.
Bowsprit and Rigging.
1 Bowsprit.
2 Jibb boom & Horses.
3 Bobb stays.
4 Gammoning.
5 Spritsail & Yard.
6 Spritsail Topsail & Yard.
7 Spritsail lifts, see lifts.
8 Spritsail Braces.
9 Spritsail Clue lines.
10 Spritsail Sheets.
Spritsail Topsail
7 Lifts.
8 Braces.
9 Clue-lines.
10 Sheets.
11 Hallyards.
12 Jibb furl'd on the Boom
13 Jibbhallyards.
14 Jibb Stay.
15 Fore topgallant Stay.
16 Fore topmast Stay.
17 Fore topmast Stay Sail.
18 Netting for Ditto.
19 Forestays
Fore Topgallant
1 Mast.
5 Yard & Sail.
6 Shrouds.
7 Lifts. 11 Hallyards.
8 Braces.
9 Clue lines.
10 Sheets.
3 Cap.
Fore Mast
Main Mast
Mizen Mast
Mizen Topgallant
1 Mast.
5 Yard & Sail.
6 Shrouds.
7 Lifts.
8 Braces.
9 Clue-lines.
10 Sheets.
2 Cap.
25 Stay.
Mizen Topmast & Riggin
3 Cross Trees.
25 Stay and Staysail Hallyards
6 Shrouds.
4 Back Stays
5 Yard and Sail.
Mizen Topsail
7 Lifts.
8 Braces.
9 Clue-lines.
16 Bunt-lines.
10 Sheets.
17 Bow-lines.
11 Hallyards.
Mizen Mast & Rigging
5 Yard & Sail.
3 Top.
25 Stay.
26 Stay Sail.
6 Shrouds
27 Brails
10 Sheet & reef
5 Cross Jack Yard
21 Crowfoot.
19 Lannyards.
Foretop Mast and Rigging
3 Cross trees.
6 Shrouds. 11 Staysail Hallyards
4 Back Stays.
5 Yard & Sail Hoisted
Fore Topsail
7 Lifts.
8 Braces.
9 Clue-lines.
12 Reef Tackles.
13 Reefs.
14 Points.
15 Earings.
16 Bunt-lines.
11 Hallyards.
17 Bow-lines.
Fore Mast and Rigging.
Fore
5 Yard & Sail. 21 Crowfoot.
6 Shrouds.
18 Rattlings. 3 Top.
19 Lannyards. 20 Dead eyes.
Fore
11 Tye and Jears.
22 Tacks.
10 Sheets.
9 Clue-Garnetts.
16 Bunt-lines.
23 Leech-lines.
17 Bow-lines.
7 Lifts.
8 Braces.
24 Horses and Stirrups.
Maintop gallant
1 Mast.
5 Yard & Sail.
6 Shrouds.
7 Lifts.
8 Braces. 17 Bowlines.
9 Clue-lines.
10 Sheets.
2 Cap.
25 Stay. 11 Staysail Hallyards.
11 Hallyards.
Maintop Mast & Rigging.
3 Cross trees. 25 Middle staysail stay & Hallyards.
6 Shrouds. 4 Back stays.
25 Stay & Staysail Hallyards.
5 Yard & Sail
Maintopsail
7 Lifts.
8 Braces.
9 Clue-lines. 10 Sheets.
16 Bunt-lines.
11 Hallyards.
17 Bow lines. 12 Reef Tackles.
Main Mast & Rigging
Main
5 Yard & Sail.
6 Shrouds.
18 Rattlings. 21 Crowfoot.
25 Stay. 3 Top.
19 Lannyards. 20 Dead eyes.
11 Tye and Jears.
22 Tacks.
10 Sheets.
Main
9 Clue-Garnetts.
16 Bunt-lines.
23 Leech-lines.
17 Bow-lines.
7 Lifts.
8 Braces.
24 Horses and Stirrups.
Parts of the Hull
A. Head.
B. Rails.
C. Cutt Water
D. Bow. E. Chains.
E. Catt Heads. F Boat on the Booms.
G. Chess Tree.
H. Quarter.
I. Taffarel.
K. Poop. L Poop Lanthorn.
M. Ensign.
N. Companion.
O. Binnacle.
P. Wheel.
R. Hawse Hole.
J. Bayly

India Company's fleet of ships running on that longest of voyages, to China, were all between 200 and 300 tons. It was not until the eighteenth century that merchant navy vessels increased in size to any substantial degree. Even then, in the first half of that century, many of that company's East Indiamen were still only around 500 tons. The small size had, however, less to do with technology than with the owner's financial expediency. It was a high risk trade and smaller ships were often a better bet even with their more limited cargo-carrying abilities.

By contrast, at the beginning of the same century, a Royal Naval 'Ship of the Line' would average about 1,500 tons, and might carry up to 100 guns. But many other naval ships did not match up to these high standards and in the 1750s, attempts were being made to rectify the situation. One such was the building of the ill-fated *Royal George* in 1756. At 2,000 tons, it had 100 guns and a huge crew of 750 men, most of whom perished when it sank at Spithead in August 1782 – one of the Royal Navy's greatest tragedies. A few years later, Nelson's flagship, *Victory*, was launched with slightly larger dimensions. The frigates of the period, about half the size and carrying between thirty and forty guns, were highly developed and manoeuvrable, though often reputedly outclassed by French vessels of the same type.

Back with the merchant marine, we begin to have more reliable statistics from the year 1760, which give some indication of numbers and size of the fleet. Great Britain, in that year, was said to 'own' over 7,000 ships with a 'reputed tunnage' of just under 500,000 tons. Of these, about one in seven were Scottish. Because registration was not compulsory, it is estimated that the real figure was some fifty per cent higher than this. One fact drawn from this is that the average vessel size could still only be seventy-odd tons. Many of these were still foreign-built, bought or captured. Dutch vessels were particularly prized, especially the 'flyboat' or 'flute', a single decked 'shell' of 200 to 500 tons, useful for bulk cargo-carrying. They were comparatively slender, four to six times as long as they were wide.

OPPOSITE *Sail plan of a merchant vessel, 1762.*

BELOW *An early-nineteenth-century Suffolk boatyard, part of a tradition of building – sometimes fairly large vessels – simply and informally in the open air, close to wood and water. In the painting below by Constable, an inlet has been dug from the river. This would have been flooded to float out the completed barge. This method was also used to repair boats.*

Their major other advantage was that they were workable by a very small crew.

While the building of smaller vessels continued at many places along the English coast, the larger ships of the late seventeenth and eighteenth centuries were built mainly on or near the Thames. The techniques used remained surprisingly unchanged right up to the middle of the nineteenth century, when the last wooden warships were built. One widespread innovation was, however, the process of sheathing the hulls of vessels in protective copper sheet to protect the wood against ship-worm, barnacles, weed and rot. Daniel Defoe criticised the concentration of shipbuilding in the London area, a cry oft repeated since. He argued that this had seriously injured shipbuilding in towns such as Ipswich, Southampton and Dartmouth. In the Thames itself there were a number of increasingly prosperous yards, which certainly lends support to Defoe's complaint. For example, Blackwall Yard, also known as Johnson's Yard at Blackwall, which operated from the seventeenth century or earlier, and Wells and Company in business somewhat later, were by repute much larger than the neighbouring Royal Yards; and there were a number of other substantially similar yards all along the Thames.

As native woods and Baltic sources were rapidly becoming worked out, one new development for English shipbuilders, was that both the Navy and the merchant marine could now procure the needed wood for their great sailing ships, particularly for masts and spars, from the Americas. The New World, especially New England, started up in competition, being so well-placed with regard to raw materials; they concentrated on building ships to ferry troops, emigrants and the famous 'tea' across the Atlantic. At its peak, just before the Declaration of Independance, the American colonies were building over 100 square-rigged sea-going ships a year, and in the early nineteenth century Canadian yards exported many ships to English shipowners.

The beginning of the nineteenth century brought with it a growing demand for fast ships to speed cargoes home from the farthest parts of the globe. It was, after the end of the Napoleonic Wars, also a time of relative peace. The wooden warships of the day, which were around the 3,000-ton mark and carried over 100 guns apiece, became outmoded by mid-century.

The same decades saw enterprising merchants expanding their trade to all parts of the globe. Australia and South America were of growing importance, and the end of the East India Company's monopoly of the Far East trades was another stimulus.

In the Atlantic meanwhile, this was the age of the packet ship, running between English and North American ports. The latter's cargo included mail and, increasingly, the emigrants who were seeking a better life for themselves in the New World. American yards were concentrating on building for speed, and England quickly followed suit, developing the clipper ships, the great square riggers with three tall masts and yacht-like lines.

The English clipper owners were also developing their tea trade with China and for the very high paying trades like the Australian Gold Rush traffic of the early 1850s. The clippers themselves were driven very hard and, as a result, had relatively short lives. With the introduction of wooden planking on an iron framework, such as was the style of the *Cutty Sark*, the working years of a ship were, however, considerably prolonged.

The age of steam and iron came in gradually.

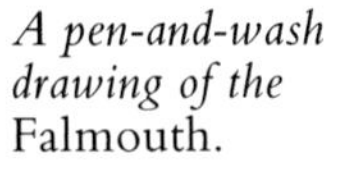
A pen-and-wash drawing of the Falmouth.

Blackwall Yard

Blackwall Yard, also known in the past as Johnson's Yard and East India Yard, is probably the oldest private business in England, or was until recently when Blackwall Engineering Limited formally became part of British Shipbuilders.

The yard was probably laid out in 1597 and over the centuries has had a bewildering number of owners. The ship-list, now at Greenwich, contains the names of all the ships known to have been built at the yard, with only a few gaps; the yard numbers run consecutively from number one, the East Indiaman *Globe* (1612), to number 260, the *Queen* (1842).

In 1639 Henry Johnson was apprenticed to Phineas Pett, his cousin and the Royal shipwright. In 1653 he built the *Dreadnought* at Blackwall. At the same time the Commonwealth was building a great fleet with the yard contributing at least two battleships. There is a short gap in its history, but in 1661 Pepys went to the yard to see the East Indiaman *Royal Oak* being built. Henry Johnson died in 1683, having built ships for both Commonwealth and King.

Between the years 1756–67 thirty-one large ships were built, of which twenty-seven were East Indiamen. In 1789 Joshua Boydell wrote:

> The Dockyard . . . is at this time more capacious than any other private yard in the Kingdom, or probably in the world . . .

Handsome passenger ships and Blackwall frigates are strongly associated with the yard, but many other types were built as well. In 1821 the firm (now Wigram & Green) launched their first steamer, the *City of Edinburgh*. There were tea clippers, a packet ship, paddle-steamers, and around 1850 the yard built its first opium clipper, one of five. One of their failures was the *Beaver*, built for the Hudson's Bay Company. Steam was not yet able to provide compact auxiliary power, so the *Beaver* voyaged to Vancouver Island under sail with the engine in her hold; later the engine was successfully used by the ship on coastal voyages.

Ships were built for both the Napoleonic Wars and the Crimean War. After the turn of the century, the size of ships increased and shipbuilding on the Thames declined; the last work completed in the slipways was steel barges for use on the Thames. During the First World War the firm (R. & H. Green and Silley Weir & Co.) took advantage of the large amount of skilled labour, probably immigrants, in London to convert merchant ships into troopships. In the Second World War many destroyers were repaired and refitted, and in the latter stages of the war the yard assembled and launched landing craft.

Mooring buoy built at Blackwall's for BNOC's Thistle Field in the North Sea.

Right up until recent years the two dry docks have been used for ship repair with some very historic ships being dry-docked, notably the *Cutty Sark*, before going to Greenwich and, more recently, the *Pekin*, an iron-hull sailing boat, which was surveyed and repaired prior to being towed to America for preservation. The larger of the dry docks is still in use to maintain Port of London Authority floating cranes.

Blackwall Engineering Limited is a self-contained yard which provides extensive general engineering facilities to a wide variety of industries throughout the world.

Steel-fabrication work, oriented to North Sea oil, has been brought in. Blackwall's have completed several major projects, among which are: a Thistle 'A' platform tower control module which houses the controls for the up-ending of the rig after it has been towed to site (for the North Cormorant Oil Field); a 200-ton sub-sea template which rests on the sea floor (Occidental Petroleum [Caledonia] Limited); a wave force measuring tower for the National Maritime Institute; the firm was also responsible for the steel work on the national data buoy (*see* p. 131). PP

Lithograph of the Sussex, *a graceful clipper ship.*

There were experiments with auxiliary sail, not always very successful, and for a long time sailing vessels held their own in the commercial world because of the cost and bulk of coal as fuel. Iron and, later, steel hulls could be made ever larger and where speed was unimportant, as with cargoes of coal and wheat, the sailing ship had an even longer life. At this time many types of rig, too numerous to mention, were tried out, as they had been throughout previous centuries.

In the 1860s steam-driven ships became more economical through improved engines and boilers. Coal bunkering ports were better organised, and, above all, the opening of the Suez Canal in 1869 added a major incentive to the long-distance steamer trade. This put hard pressure on the sailing ship owners to continue to run at any profit. As late as the 1890s, there was a brief revival of sail with the building of iron and then of steel-hulled ships, constructed to carry as much as possible with a very small crew.

Since those days, however, very few other sailing ships have been built in England. The glorious days of sail sadly drew to a close, though even today there are some twenty great sailing ships still operational around the world, all used for training purposes.

4 The Lawless Seas

The history and legends of the sea are brimfull, not only of great feats of seamanship, exploration and naval battles won or lost, but also of tales, sometimes true, of a less salubrious maritime past. In fact, lawlessness on land was well matched by lawlessness on water.

Setting the subject in the context of its varied times, past centuries were wilder; human life was cheaper; the possibility of reaping untold wealth from crime was greater; above all, the forces of law and order were much less capable and organised than they are today. The heyday of smuggling and disparate sorts of piracy tended to occur in times of war, against Frenchmen, Spaniards, Americans, Dutch. Many was the pirate who gave his all and his loyalty to the Crown when he was needed; then, when peace came it was difficult to break the habit of plundering, booty-seeking and capturing ships as prizes – even with the threat of the gibbet in the background. Equally, with life on board Royal Naval and merchant vessels often indescribably harsh, the mutiny, justified or not, was all too common and understandable.

Piracy, armed robbery on the high seas, has long been considered a crime, not only against an individual state or nation, but also against all law-abiding maritime countries. There were, of course, pirates and pirates, the distinction between them and privateers always being a slim one. Pirates were subject to no laws – and in case one is inclined to believe that they belong entirely to past centuries, there are many cases of piracy in this century as well. Ships of opposing countries are, for example, often accused of 'piracy' in times of near war: the US courts held that the sinking of the *Lusitania*, by a German submarine in 1915, was such an act. Piracy in Chinese waters is still a problem today, but in the main, it died out several centuries ago in English waters.

Up until Tudor times, English ships had, by and large, always more to fear from foreign than from indigenous priates. For example, the famous Barbary Pirates, sea-robbers operating out of Algiers and other North African ports, were, for centuries, hated and feared by all who sailed the Mediterranean.

The Tudor reigns in England were particularly notorious for piracy in almost all domestic waters. Especially favoured were the areas south of Ireland, particularly round the Isles of Scilly; isolated islands such as Lundy were also feared as pirate bases. Such islands offered safe haven away from the power of the Navy and the excisemen, and made excellent staging posts for the later disposal of captured booty. There were many other pirate lairs round the English coastline, and nowadays a number of little museums exist where relics and mementos of this nefarious trade can be seen.

As late as the seventeenth century, piracy was still common and there continued to be many instances of semi-'legal' piracy in English domestic waters. For example, ships from the 'civilised' Cinque Ports, set out from time to time to plunder, or at the very least to extract heavy 'dues' from passing coastal traffic, in order to fund their civic debts.

Throughout, there seems to have been a fairly common use by pirates of the evil 'Jolly Roger' or 'Black Jack', the skull-and-crossbones flag. Sometimes a whole skeleton was represented, though each pirate chief tended to have his own insignia. The apparent object of flying this flag was to strike such fear in the prey that the pirates would gain their objectives with less trouble and fighting.

Gradually, by dint of much more forceful measures and law enforcement directed against piracy in home waters, the pirates, many of them from famous English families, set off to loot in new and less well-patrolled areas of the globe. Favourite haunts of English-crewed or captained pirate ships were the West Indies, the coasts of New England, and along the increasingly busy trading routes of West and East Africa. The West Indies were particularly favoured, since, with their myriad islands, they offered the safest of all possible refuges. Pirate gangs even made these island bases into tiny 'kingdoms', one being the famous island of 'Tortuga', or Turtle Island, that lies close to the island of Hispaniola, now Santa Domingo. From such hideaways

Captain Teach, alias 'Blackbeard' the pirate, from a History of Pirates, *1725.*

the booty could then be trans-shipped, as legitimate freight, to markets in England, Europe, the New World and the Colonies.

One reason piracy flourished was because successive British governments, as with those of Spain and France, tried to insist, with their Navigation Acts, that their colonists traded only with their own country. It was inevitable, therefore, that the colonists would try to defeat these regulations by buying cheaply what they could, without questioning the origins of the goods in question. Another reason was that, particularly in the aftermath of war, there were more ships and seamen around than legal trade and shipping could accommodate. Every crew member had a share in the booty of every prize, so it was a fair temptation to the unemployed mariner thrown out of a peacetime navy to re-enlist with these irregulars.

One strangely generous reaction to piracy was the English custom, from the reign of William III up to that of George I, of granting the 'King's Pardon' to those pirates who surrendered by a given date. It was a measure introduced mainly out of weakness: there was no chance of most of them being caught, but it gave many notorious men a new break – and an opportunity to spend their ill-gotten gains with impunity. In the Bahamas in 1718, for example nearly 2,000 pirates surrendered and were granted such a pardon.

Harsh penalties were more common and, at Execution Dock near Wapping on the Thames, those found guilty of piracy on the high seas were, by tradition, executed. The early method was to tie the accused to piles driven into the mud so that, when the tide rose, the man was drowned. In later times, culprits were hanged in chains until their bodies rotted, as a warning to all who passed up or down river.

Famous pirate names abound, though most reputations were a mix of fact and fancy. One of the most notorious of them all, Captain Kidd, or Kydd, was probably not a pirate at all, though he was condemned as such in the end. Other household names were Captain John Avery or Every, known as 'Long Ben', who operated in the last quarter of the seventeenth century. His stamping ground was East and West Africa. and his most famous 'booty' was captured from the so-called 'Great Mogul', whose fortune and beautiful daughter both fell into Long Ben's clutches; Avery later died in poverty in Devon. Another notorious figure was the Welshman, Bartholomew Roberts, who reputedly captured and looted many hundreds of ships during his turbulent career. 'Blackbeard', whose real name was Edward Teach, was eventually trapped and killed by the Royal Navy in November 1718. The lawless Barbary Pirates operating out of Algiers, Tunis and elsewhere had their English recruits as well; the much-feared Captain Fleming, with the Arabic alias 'Murad Reis', raided many a ship and seaside settlement as far afield as Britain and Ireland, to seize people for the profitable slave markets of North Africa.

There is much confusion about who was a true pirate or buccaneer and the privateer. The buccaneers, first of all, were a group of piratical Englishmen, often working with Dutch, Portuguese and French crews, who operated in the West Indies during the seventeenth century. They took their name from meat cured by 'boucanning' – a mixture of smoking and sun-drying – and they were united only by their opposition to Spain. A mix of sailors and colonists, they were at times little better than pirates; for most of the seventeenth century they earned much unofficial English blessing as the scourge of Spanish-American trade in all its forms. They operated eventually not only in the Caribbean, but also along the whole coast of the western seaboard of North and South America.

The most famous of the buccaneers was undoubtedly Henry Morgan, a Welshman, who ruled from Jamaica during the latter part of the seventeenth century. Much of his success was due to the fact that those nations, including England, who were opposed to Spanish interests and monopoly in the area, largely turned a blind eye to his activities and adventures. After a brief spell of imprisonment in the Tower of London from 1672 to 1674, he was released and returned to the West Indies, as Lieutenant Governor of Jamaica, a fair testament to his eventual loyalties and abilities. In the long run, the fact that the buccaneers were of so many different nationalities, eventually led to indiscipline and lack of cohesion and their inevitable collapse as a unitary force. They did, however, succeed in breaking Spain's monopoly and opening the door to Britain's future colonial interests in the area.

By contrast, privateers were a sort of 'civilian navy' though, in essence, they ran armed merchant ships belonging to private individuals. In the Mediterranean Sea they were also often described as corsairs. Among their ship's papers they had legal

Captain William Kidd

William Kidd (*c.* 1645–1701) was a British privateer who has become a semi-legendary figure. Treasure-seekers continue to search for his plunder, some of which undoubtedly still lies buried in secret places, 280 years after his death.

He probably went to sea as a youth becoming, by 1689, a legitimate privateer against the French in the West Indies and off the coast of North America. Such legitimate privateers were commissioned by letters of marque, which licensed them to take prizes in times of war – unofficial action which suited the ruler of the day very well. By 1690 he was an established sea captain and ship-owner in New York City. At various times he was employed by both New York and Massachusetts to rid the coast of enemy privateers.

In 1695 he received a Royal Commission to apprehend pirates who molested the ships of the East India Company. Accepting this commission led to his downfall, for, some time after reaching the Coromo Islands off East Africa in 1697, it seems that he turned to piracy. He had not taken a prize ship and, therefore, according to the usual privateer's agreement, there was no pay for the captain or the crew. He then captured several small ships, but his refusal to attack a Dutch ship nearly led to mutiny; in a fight Kidd killed his gunner, possibly accidentally. This murder was later one of the charges brought against him. In 1698 he captured his most valuable prize, the *Quedagh Merchant,* owned by the Great Mogul, and scuttled his own, by now unseaworthy, vessel.

On reaching Anguilla in 1699, Kidd learned he had been denounced as a pirate. He got rid of the booty and the ship and bought a new one, in which he sailed to New York. He unsuccessfully pleaded his innocence with the colonial governor, who sent him to England. Here he was found guilty of murder and five indictments of piracy. He was hanged at Execution Dock, Wapping, amid charges that vital evidence in his favour had been suppressed. The proceeds from the sale of his effects and his ship were given to the Greenwich Hospital by Queen Anne. Part of this money was used to purchase the property which is now the National Maritime Museum. Guilty or innocent, the romanticised concept of the daredevil pirate adventurer is linked forever to the name of Captain Kidd. PP

Illustration by Howard Pyle for Harper's Monthly, *1902.*

OPPOSITE, TOP *Custom House, King's Lynn. The square Custom House was built in 1683 by Henry Bell for a local wine merchant, Sir John Turner.*

OPPOSITE, BOTTOM *Caricature of delegates in Council during the mutiny at the Nore; an engraving after Cruikshank.*

authority both to trade and to engage the enemy. These authorities or commissions, given to them by the Crown, were known as 'letters of marque'. In practice this frequently led to a sort of legalised piracy, since, when they failed to get their prize-money from one of the enemy's vessels, it was easy enough to turn their attention to peaceful trading ships. Sir Francis Drake was one of the best known of all privateers, but England's maritime history is full of other famous names, to whom it was a perfectly respectable calling.

By the time of Nelson however, they were universally considered no better than pirates, though only finally made illegal in international terms by the Declaration of Paris in the year 1856. This ruled that an armed merchantmen must be under the full control of the state whose flag it flew. The United States was one of the last countries to use privateers which were, for example, commissioned by the President during the American Civil War.

With shipboard life in both Royal Naval and merchant vessels extremely hard, discipline often had to be very strict and punishments severe: flogging, keel-hauling or even execution were the order of the day. In consequence, throughout English maritime history, mutinies – the refusal by a group of sailors to obey a lawful order and the consequent resort to force by the mutineers – were not uncommon. The penalty was death by hanging from the yardarm. The most notorious British naval mutinies were at Spithead and the Nore in the year 1797, when sailors of the Fleet mutinied against low pay and conditions on board. A less serious modern mutiny was with the Fleet at Invergordon in 1931, the result of a maladministered reduction in naval pay.

The most famous and much recorded mutiny of all was on the *Bounty* in 1789, when an officer, Fletcher Christian, led a revolt against the harsh discipline of his Captain, William Bligh. Christian and some of his followers in the end found refuge on Pitcairn Island in the Pacific; Bligh and eighteen loyal men, cast adrift in a small boat, eventually reached Timor after a heroic journey of some 3,500 miles.

The illegal importation of prohibited goods or of goods which are subject to customs duties, has a long history. The peak periods for smuggling in England have been ones when protectionism has been at its height, despite the fact that heavy penalties for being caught have been in force in one form or another since the fourteenth century. The major problem for the exciseman has been constant, right up to the present day: smuggling has always had considerable public popularity and support. One reason for this in early centuries was that customs officials tended to be private individuals operating under contract, often to their own benefit.

BELOW *Watercolour by Thomas Rowlandson (1756–1827) entitled 'Lord Howes victory or French prizes brought into Portsmouth harbour'.*

In the early Middle Ages, one of the most prolific aspects of smuggling was that of illegally minted coinage; this was doing such damage to the economy in the reign of King Edward III that it became a treasonable offence. But throughout the high days of smuggling which lasted until the repeal and virtual abandonment of many excise duties in the nineteenth century (they came again after the reintroduction of heavy duties on imports after 1918), the goods smuggled were always the traditional luxuries – wines, spirits and tobacco. At various other times, heavily taxed items, such as silk, or prohibited items (certain drugs and guns in our own times) have been popular smugglers' items.

During the Napoleonic Wars, smuggling flourished, backed by the French and infiltrated by Napoleon's highly effective spy system. A century earlier it had obviously been just as bad, with Daniel Defoe writing that 'Smuggling and Roguing. . . was the reigning Commerce. . . of the English coast from the mouth of the Thames to Land's End.' While inward smuggling in his day was of silks and brandy, there was also 'outward' smuggling of English wool, particularly from the grazing areas of the Romney Marsh. This was in contravention of regulations which were directed at keeping all domestic wool for English manufacturers.

Those caught smuggling have always been penalised by forfeiting their cargo in addition to any fines or prison sentences which may be imposed. To

RIGHT *Clovelly, Devon. An exceptionally pretty village, its famous cobbled main street drops 400 ft to the harbour in a series of steps. A fishing village, it was once also famous for its smuggling. Cars are banned from the cobbled streets.*

BELOW *The revenue cutter* Greyhound *– used between 1780 and 1808 for the suppression of smugglers in the English Channel.*

administer this, the government of the day has long employed officers of the Crown – excisemen, customs officials, coastguards – to thwart this illegal practice.

During the reign of William III, when high customs charges were levied, the manning of a fleet of customs vessels was required for the first time. But the increase in the scale of foreign wars meant that there were not always men available to serve in this less immediate line of duty. After the Napoleonic Wars, patrolling tended to be undertaken by the Navy, with ratings manning shore stations and Martello Towers. It was only later in the century that the modern coastguard service was finally established.

The areas of the English coastline traditionally favoured by the smugglers have always been the remoter ones. Devon and Cornwall loom high both in schoolboy mythology and in reality. Equally, the great ports – London, Liverpool, Bristol – have long histories of coping with this, to some, almost glamorous trade. Caves and islands and ghostly Fen Country are all very well, but a busy seaport with overworked customs officials is just as attractive an entry point. As it was in the past, so it is today.

5 New Worlds

The discovery of so much of the world out of English ports was a complex process. Knowledge of the nature of the world's geography was not only acquired by those voyages that were spectacular in historical terms, but also by a gradual process of discovery by many whose names are now forgotten. It is, however, helpful to look at the process of exploration through the exploits of those great Englishmen who opened up the world for trade, colonialism and the Empire and Commonwealth that were to follow.

As far as can be ascertained, up until the late fifteenth century, with the notable exception of the Vikings, no European sailors had ventured far beyond the safety of their own or North-African coastal waters. Quite apart from the widespread belief that the world was flat and that one was in danger of falling off the edge somewhere to the west of the Scillies, navigational skills were largely undeveloped, and the ships of the day were ill-equipped for long sea voyages.

However, by the late fifteenth century both navigational skills and shipbuilding techniques were fast developing. In addition, the incentive that drove men to travel further afield was produced by the lure and fascination of trade with the Orient, with its offerings of silks, spices and other precious goods. The old overland routes which had run across the Mediterranean and through Asia were closed after the fall of Constantinople in the mid-fifteenth century and the general hostility of the Ottoman Turks in the aftermath of the Crusades. The only alternative was to try to find a sea route, either to the south round Africa, or – because of a gathering awareness that the world was round – by sailing west.

The Portuguese, among them Vasco da Gama and Bartholomew Dias, were the pioneers in exploring the route round the Cape to East Africa and on to India. Then came Columbus and his New-World discoveries. Following close on his heels were the Spanish, bent on exploring the coasts of Central and Southern America. The remarkable fact is that all this happened in the course of thirty short years, so that by around 1680, all the continents, with the exception of Antarctica, were known about.

In the next stage the Spanish and Portuguese began to found settlements along the newly discovered Central and Southern American coasts, ensuring that these areas were closed to English ships. This, along with the realisation that they were losing out on rich trading benefits, gradually spurred the English into the game.

There were roughly three main areas of fascination to English explorers after the discovery of the Americas. The first goal was pursued by those who decided to seek a 'North-West Passage'; this was the presumed sea route round the top of Canada from the Atlantic to the Pacific, sought by those wishing to find the treasures of 'Cathay' or China. The second goal was the 'North-East Passage' round the north of Europe and Asia, while the third and most adventurous, was the aim, by increasingly varied expeditions, of circumnavigating the globe. It was however the first of these three that always had most attraction to English explorers because of the political and trading benefits such a discovery would bring to England by a northerly outflanking of the Spanish and Portuguese who had never tried for this route at all.

If one is looking for a milestone by which to mark the beginning of the English contribution to the process of discovery, it comes in 1497, when, fascinated by stories of Spanish achievements, the Venetian-born John Cabot (1450–98), set sail from Bristol towards the New World. He was backed in his venture by a group of Bristol merchants, and he set out accompanied by his son Sebastian and a crew of fourteen. He eventually made landfall on Cape Breton Island to the north of Nova Scotia and then sailed on to Newfoundland before returning to England. Convinced that he had reached the shores of Asia, he announced that he had discovered the land of the 'Great Khan'.

With Henry VII's backing he set off again with five ships and 300 men, and, according to many accounts, was held to have reached Greenland,

John Tradescant

From the beginning, explorers, plant hunters, naturalists and adventurers brought back a great variety of plants to enrich English life. While Darwin is perhaps the most famous, there were many others who made a contribution – men like the Tradescants, for instance.

John Tradescant (1570–1638) was gardener to the Cecils at Salisbury House in the Strand and at Hatfield House, where he laid out formal gardens. He was sent on several journeys to Europe to find and bring back new varieties of fruit and vegetables. From France he brought mulberries (to promote silk-weaving), vines and roses, and reputedly brought the Cos lettuce from Greece. Tradescant eventually became naturalist and gardener to Charles I and Henrietta Maria and continued to build a collection of natural history objects, some of which he acquired on additional journeys abroad. He was the first botanist to visit Russia – he joined a diplomatic mission to carry out his plant-hunting – bringing back larch, bird-cherry, and Muscovy rose. During the trip, on 20 July 1618, he had

> One of the Emperor's boats to cari me from iland to iland, to see what things grewe upon them, whear I found single roses, wondros sweet, with many other things whiche I meane to bring with me.

In 1620, as a gentleman volunteer, he joined an expedition to fight the Barbary pirates; he visited Alicante in Spain and Algiers in North Africa, bringing back 'Argier Apricocke' and the Persian lilac.

With his son, also John Tradescant (1608–1667), who followed in his footsteps as naturalist and gardener to Charles I, he helped finance the colony of Virginia. The elder John obtained a number of American plants; forty are named in his garden-list of 1634.

Young John visited America in 1637, 1642 and 1654. It seems that he brought back the Virginia creeper, phlox, a form of michaelmas daisy, the red maple, the tulip tree, the swamp cyprus and the common spiderwort, now a popular garden plant. Linnaeus gave the last mentioned the generic name, *Tradescantia*, in memory of these two men.

The Tradescant Collection became famous, for it was the first collection in England of natural history objects of such quantity and quality. A number of sea captains brought back material for the collection. Their museum and physic garden in Lambeth was popularly known as 'Tradescants' Ark', for they collected an immense variety of curiosities. After the death of the second John, Elias Ashmole acquired the collection and gave it to Oxford University in 1683, thus founding the Ashmolean Museum. Some of the original items from their collection may still be seen there, along with portraits of both Tradescants; the museum opened a Tradescant Room in which the Founder's collection is housed.

On a memorial to both men in the churchyard of St Mary at Lambeth they are described as:

> Those famous Antiquarians that had been
> Both gardeners to the rose and lily Queen.

This church, now redundant, has been leased by the Tradescant Trust and will become a Museum of Garden History. Elias Ashmole is buried in the church and Captain William Bligh of the *Bounty* is buried in the churchyard.

Explorers and adventurers brought back an enormous assortment of plants of all types, including potatoes, tomatoes and tobacco, many of which became totally assimilated into English life. PP

The Tradescant monument in the churchyard of St Mary at Lambeth and the portraits of both men; from a publication of 1793.

Labrador and Nova Scotia before sailing down the New England coast as far as Delaware and then returning home. More reliable historically is the sadder and simpler story that, after setting sail in May 1498, nothing more was heard of him or his ships. His son, Sebastian (1476–1557), backed by the experience of having sailed with his father, spent most of his life away from England, and there is dispute over whether he reached the mouth of Hudson's Bay in the years 1508 and 1509. In later years however he returned to Bristol, helped found a company of Merchant Venturers there, and sponsored various attempts to discover the North-East Passage in the years 1554 and 1555.

The next to venture on the North-West Passage route was Sir Martin Frobisher (*c.*1535–94), who was also bent on finding a route to Cathay, though he realised that Asia must lie much further to the west. A considerable seaman and a hero of the wars with the Spanish, his driving force was the pursuit of the gold which he believed would be found there. His expeditions were well equipped for the age: one such, in the year 1578 had fifteen ships under his command, though in terms of size, his own vessel was a mere twenty-five tons. He discovered no gold, but did give his name to the strait and bay which he discovered to the north of Labrador.

A contemporary of Frobisher was the navigator and explorer John Davis (d.1605), who was haunted by the same dream of finding a way round the north of the American continent. He, like Frobisher, made three separate attempts, the last in 1587. He is credited with discovering the Falkland Islands, having failed to make it round the southern tip of South America. Later in life, as well as writing two successful books on navigation, he went on various other voyages of discovery to the Far East in the employ of the East India Company.

The next famous name is that of Henry Hudson (d.1611), who, in his early days, had experience of trying to find the North-East Passage. He made two voyages – in 1609 and again in 1610. On the first (having failed to find a polar route to the East), he went west, to Virginia, and then 150 miles up New York's river that now carries his name. His second trip, to Hudson's Bay, ended in tragedy. His mutinous crew cast him and his son adrift in a small boat, and left them to an unknown fate.

In the final years of this first phase of exploration, William Baffin (1584–1622), an experienced navigator, was pilot of the ship *Discovery* which was charting the Hudson and Davis straits. In 1616, he discovered the great north Canadian bay which now bears his name. He was also involved in early surveys of the Red Sea and the Persian Gulf, when at a later stage, he, like Davis, served with the East India

Portrait of Sir Martin Frobisher by Cornelius Kekel, 1577.

ABOVE *On his expedition to the Arctic in 1819 in search of the North-West passage, Parry took the ships through a channel to the north of Banks Island. Parry was in H.M.S.* Hecla*, while Matthew Liddon captained H.M.S.* Griper. *Here the ships are in winter harbour – a charming engraving after a sketch made on the spot by Lt Beechey.*

OPPOSITE *Replica of Drake's* Golden Hind *at Tower Pier in London. This replica was commissioned by the Golden Hind Company Limited and built by J. Hinks & Son of Appledore, Devon, specialists in building wooden vessels. The ship took eighteen months to build and was launched in 1973.*

Company. Baffin was followed by two minor explorers, Luke Fox and Thomas James, whose voyage in 1631 determined that there was no through-route to the west from Hudson's Bay itself.

From that date there was very little in the way of seaborne exploration of the North-West Passage until, 200 years later, the formation and development of the Hudson's Bay Company led to a gradual mapping of the land area of northern Canada. In 1819 Sir Edward Parry (1790–1855), took H.M.S. *Hecla* and H.M.S. *Griper* through a channel to the north of Banks Island. Following him, Sir John Franklin (1786–1847), using steamships for the first time, also tried and, in one of the greatest tragedies in the history of exploration, perished in the winter cold along with 134 of his men in the year 1847. The search for Franklin by a variety of English relief expeditions led, gradually, to an understanding that while some such passage might one day be discovered (it eventually was, by a Swede in 1878), it would remain an impossible route for all practical purposes. Even with present-day ships, equipment and knowledge, it is a difficult, arduous and highly seasonal journey.

While parts of the North-East Passage across the north of Europe and Asia were doubtless known to the Vikings and the Russians themselves, the first Englishmen to explore the possibilities were Richard Chancellor (d.1556) and Hugh Willoughby (d.1554), followed later by the ill-fated Henry Hudson with his two expeditions in 1607 and 1608. Chancellor, who was one of those captains backed by Sebastian Cabot, sought out the passage via the White Sea in the year 1553. While he failed in his main objective, he did make contact with Czar Ivan the Terrible and his Court. Though Chancellor was to share the same fate as Willoughby (who is noted for discovering the Lofoten Islands to the north of Norway) and perish in a later voyage, the attempts by these men led to the development of English trade with Russia and the eventual formation of the Muscovy Company. Hudson, when he came to follow Chancellor's route, was in fact employed by that company to find the passage, but was defeated by the ice each time he tried.

Having followed the course of these early expeditions, let us turn to look in more detail at the achievements of two of England's greatest explorers: Sir Francis Drake (1543–96) and Captain James Cook (1728–79). Drake's claims to a major place in maritime history are many and varied. He was, in turn, naval captain, trader, piratical adventurer and explorer, and his exploits are referred to in many sections of this book. Born around the year 1543, on a farm near Tavistock in Devon, he grew to maturity serving in coastal ships and later in West-African waters where his experience of Spanish behaviour led to his life-long feud with them.

Following years of privateering and slave-

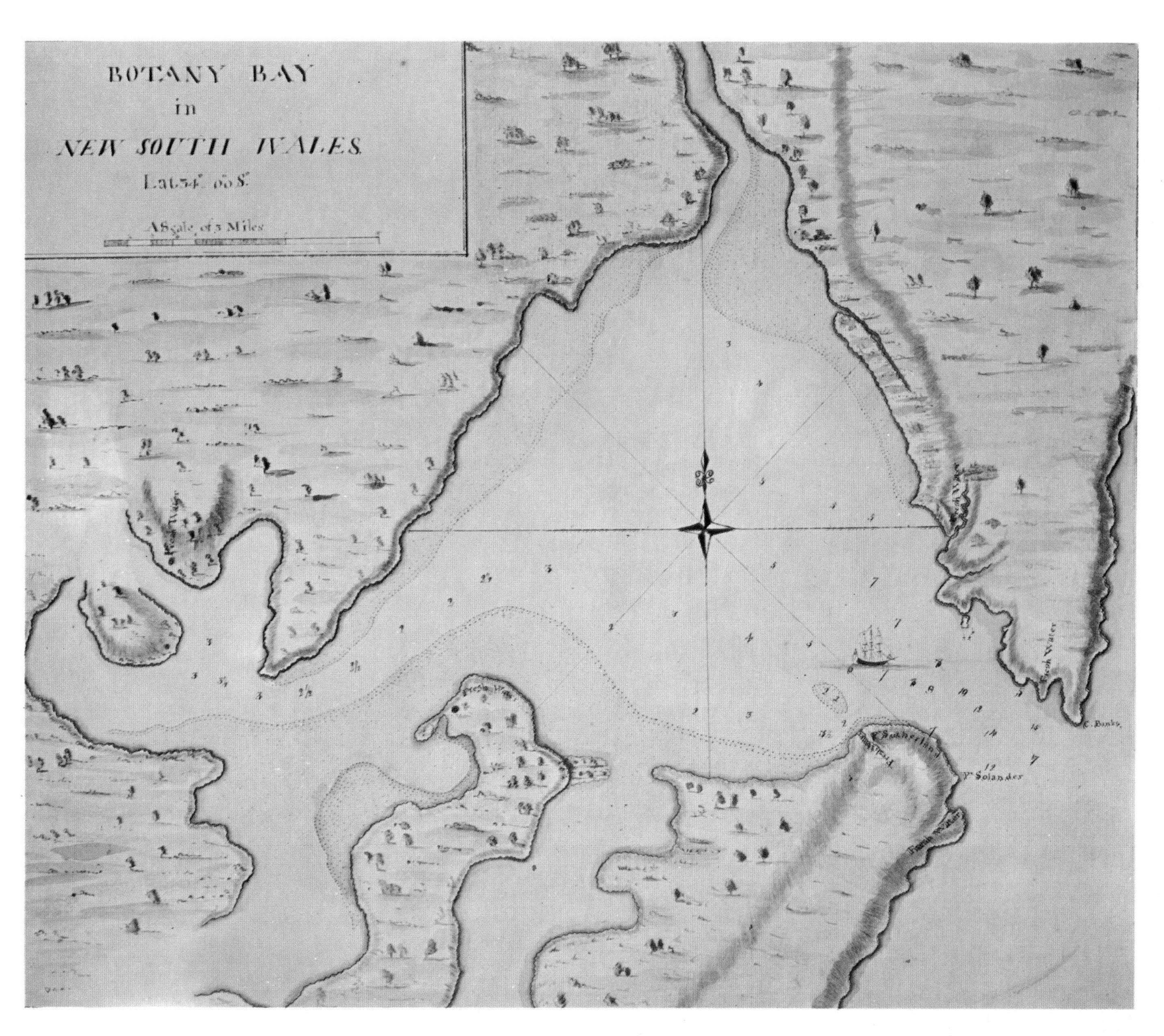

trading, he was given command of *Pelican* (renamed *Golden Hind* in the Pacific). With four other ships, he set off on his voyage of circumnavigation. He followed the route discovered by Magellan, round the tip of South America, progressing north again through Spanish waters, booty-seeking as he went. He eventually returned, across the Pacific and round the Cape, to a hero's welcome at home in the year 1580. His voyage of exploration, was also an expression of determination to show the English flag and to make it clear to the Spanish that they did not rule the oceans of the New World. Drake was well due his reward – to be knighted by his Queen on board his ship at Deptford. His house, Buckland Abbey near Plymouth, was bought with his plunder. It is now a museum, in memory of his life and exploits.

A century and a half later, Captain James Cook of the Royal Navy, made three major and highly significant journeys of exploration: the first from 1768 to 1771, the second from 1772 to 1775, and the third from 1776 to 1780. He was perhaps the greatest of all of England's navigators and explorers, by virtue of the fact that geographical discovery was his aim rather than territorial expansion, military conquest or the search for the riches of the Orient. His mission was to discover what land masses might or might not exist in the southern Pacific. The discovery of New Zealand in 1769 was his first triumph. He charted these islands with considerable accuracy before he went on, in April 1770, to find the eastern seaboard of Australia.

His second voyage was a complex tour of the Pacific, approaching from the west and giving the lie to stories of some mythical continent – which eventually turned out to be the scattered Polynesian Islands. In all he sailed some sixty thousand miles and in the process he and his colleagues made very considerable advances in navigational techniques.

His third voyage, which included trying to find

OPPOSITE Resolution *and* Adventure *at Tahiti, visited by Captain Cook in July 1773; painting by William Hodges, who accompanied Cook on the second voyage.*

ABOVE *Cook's chart of Botany Bay, Australia, made on his second voyage. Cook made accurate charts of the areas he visited.*

Captain Scott took dogs and ponies with him on the Terra Nova *for the British Antarctic Expedition, 1910–1913, to search for the South Pole. The latter were, of course, totally unsuited to the conditions.*

the North-West Passage (he, like so many before him, was defeated by ice), ended tragically with his murder by the natives of Hawaii in February 1779. Cook, unlike most of those who had gone before him, was a true explorer and navigator for the sake of knowledge itself. It was for those that followed him to open up, populate and exploit the Australasia that he had discovered.

* * *

To the south of Australia all was still unknown, though Captain Cook was probably the first to cross the Antarctic Circle. Whatever was beyond, he declared, the 'World would derive no benefit from it.' English sealers were the first to find land in the Southern Polar Regions, and later, America sent in various expeditions to survey and chart the area. The first British expedition with similar purposes did not take place until 1841. It was under command of Captain James Clark Ross (1800–62), who had experience of that other supreme testing ground, having also tried to find the North-West Passage. His triumph to the south was to claim a large area of Antarctica for Britain.

The next substantial follower to Ross was Captain Robert Falcon Scott (1868–1912), a naval officer who commanded the survey ship *Discovery*. Accompanying him on his 1901 voyage, during which he charted a route to the pole, was Ernest Shackleton (1874–1922). Shackleton, in turn, tried to reach the pole over the years 1907–08, but failed by a mere hundred odd miles. Then followed Scott's over-hasty, heroic yet tragic, second expedition, which culminated in his being beaten to the pole by Roald Amundsen of Norway. On the return journey of over 800 miles, Scott and his party, beset by misfortune and tragedy, perished in a blizzard only a few miles from the safety of their base camp.

Shackleton returned again to Antarctica in 1914 with the intention of crossing from one side to the other. But his ship the *Endurance* was caught and crushed in the pack ice and the team were rescued only after Shackleton himself sailed one of the small open ship's boats the bitter 300 miles to South Georgia for help. And so it was not until as late as 1957–58 that Sir Vivian Fuchs made what has been called 'the greatest journey in the world', by successfully completing the trans-Antarctic crossing.

There is another more human, and in many ways much more fundamental, aspect of the 'opening up' of the world out of English ports. This was the vast tide of human emigration that moved out to the new worlds, the United States, Canada, Australia, New Zealand, East and Southern Africa – indeed to

Mayflower Monument, Southampton. On their way to Plymouth from Boston in Lincolnshire the Pilgrim Fathers stopped here. Southampton became a port of great importance in the heyday of the passenger liner.

almost every part of the globe. Such emigration by ordinary people – men, women and children – mapped and populated the world in a different, but just as significant, a way. From the days of the *Mayflower* and the Pilgrim Fathers in 1620, on to our own century, this tide has been a huge and far-reaching one. It was partly a colonising process for trade, political and defence reasons. Usually voluntary, it could be highly involuntary as in the case of convict shipments to Australia. It began with a tiny trickle, mainly those fleeing political or religious persecution as the Pilgrim Fathers had done; it became a vast flood during the European pogroms and the rural poverty of the nineteenth century, as new cheap land became available.

Convicts were first shipped to Australia in 1788, the last recorded sailing being in 1868. Conditions on these prison ships were bad, but probably no worse than on the emigrant ships which, before regulations were introduced in the 1850s, were uncontrolled in terms of overcrowding and provisioning. Indeed, for the poorer emigrants, the holds of cargo vessels were all that was available. Liverpool was the main English port of embarkation, not only for the English themselves, but also for many destitute Irish emigrants escaping the starvation brought about by the failure of successive potato crops. The gradual introduction of steamships, from the 1860s, led to slightly better conditions; while fewer of the emigrants from then on were of English origin, many of the vessels carrying them across the Atlantic and to the far side of the world remained English-owned.

The rich, the famous, refugees, convicts and the poor – these are some of the well-known and the forgotten of English navigation, exploration and discovery. But among the great there were many others who could well justify pages of their own: people like Thomas Cavendish (1555–92), who successfully circumnavigated the globe in the years 1586–88; or William Dampier (1652–1715), who began life as a buccaneer and then undertook several

The landing of the Pilgrim Fathers at Plymouth, 22 December 1620.

Matthew Flinders

Flinders (1774–1814), a hydrographer who charted the coastline of most of Australia, and circumnavigated Tasmania and Australia, entered the Royal Navy in 1789 when he was only twenty. He was still a midshipman when he arrived at Botany Bay on the R.N.'s *Reliance* in 1795, fascinated with the idea of the hundreds of miles of uncharted and unexplored coast on either side of the Bay. Cook had made a general chart of the east coast, but the west coast had previously only been sighted in a few places. With no official encouragement, Flinders and his friend, George Bass, the ship's surgeon, with a boy as crew went exploring in a small boat. They accomplished so much that they were then given a whaler with convicts as crew. In this they discovered that Tasmania was an island. In 1878 they took a sloop, *Norfolk*, with eight naval volunteers and surveyed all of Tasmania and the strait. These amateurs took great delight in exploring this beautiful untouched territory.

The charts were very professionally done and, when the men returned home, came to the notice of the President of the Royal Society, patron of explorers. He in turn persuaded the Admiralty that the work should continue. Although there was war with France, Flinders was put in charge of a ship, the *Investigator*, an old North Sea collier.

In it he returned to Australia, intending to sail right around the continent surveying every small harbour as he went. He sounded every harbour he came to in a rowing boat, named it, took bearings from hill tops, and had his staff study the flora and fauna, while he tried to converse with the natives.

As well as being a hydrographer of the highest order, Flinders made scientific studies, particularly in correcting the deviation of the compass caused by the iron components in a ship. The compensating bars around a magnetic compass are named after him.

Hundreds of miles from help the *Investigator* began to leak and when closely inspected was found to be so rotten that the survey was abandoned. On the return to Port Jackson (now Sydney) the crew suffered from scurvy and there were some deaths. Flinders' health was permanently damaged.

Intent on returning home he took passage on a ship, one in a convoy of three. His ship and another ran onto a reef at night. The third abandoned them, leaving the crews marooned on a sand bank. Flinders rowed and sailed in a small

boat 600 miles back to Port Jackson for help – an amazing example of initiative and endurance. He then led a relief expedition to the sand bank, borrowed a twenty-six ton schooner and set off for England again. This boat eventually sprung a leak and had to put in at what is now Mauritius. The French governor, disbelieving his story, detained him as a prisoner-of-war for six and half years.

On release he returned to England, but never sailed again. He lived long enough to write his journal, *Voyage to Terra Australia* (1814) – published the day he died.

In 1795 the Admiralty had appointed its first hydrographer, the beginning of a department which, in the 1800s, charted all the coasts and oceans of the world. PP

valuable journeys of exploration round Australia and across the Pacific, journeys which were, unfortunately, beset by mutinies, due to Dampier's over-harsh behaviour to his crews. Matthew Flinders (1774–1814) was yet another considerable navigator who undertook valuable charting work and made many advances in navigating techniques in the course of circumnavigating Australia. The list is almost endless and the achievements of these English maritime adventurers very great indeed. Many of their names have been perpetuated in the Royal Naval Hydrographic ships of today.

Emigrants at dinner on board a ship en route *to the United States, 1850.*

6 Ruling the Waves: The Royal Navy and English Sea Power

The long and distinguished history of the Royal Navy has been recorded in volumes about every aspect of its foundation, development, ships, skills and victories. We can nonetheless sketch out the main strands of that history in the context of the growth of English seapower across the centuries, first around her own coastline and then on to cover the farthest oceans of the globe.

Whichever king one credits with having founded the Navy, there is no doubt that it was, from the first, a truly 'Royal' force. As we have seen, the Saxon King Alfred ordered the building of a navy of sorts in response to the Viking maritime presence. But the Saxons and other English tribes had forgotten their seamanship to such an extent that he had to call for a great deal of help from Frisian mercenaries. Nonetheless the present-day Royal Navy credits Alfred the Great (849–*c.*899) with its foundation.

Following Alfred, King Canute, born a Dane, but King of England from 1016 to 1035, is renowned for having kept a semi-permanent navy of over forty ships, though most of them doubtless doubled as merchant vessels as well.

William the Conquerer reputedly first granted rights and privileges to the Cinque Ports (Hastings, Romney, Hythe, Dover and Sandwich, with the towns of Rye and Winchelsea as later additions) over self-government and tax exemptions, on condition that they should stand prepared to supply fighting ships and men to their King, when required. This obligation, scant though it was, represented virtually all of England's medieval navy for the three centuries that followed. The Cinque Ports' importance only waned with the establishment of a per-

Mighty Dover Castle – a defence against invaders for more than 2,000 years.

OPEN
Lyons Maid

manent navy during Henry VIII's reign and declined further as the new Atlantic ports, such as Bristol and Portsmouth, developed to meet the requirements of the New World.

While the navy that existed in the reign of Edward III, was largely a merchant force, the King was sufficiently sure of its comparative strength to claim, to be 'Lord of the English Seas' after his victory over the French at the battle of Sluys. The English ships had briefly united under the King for this battle, but they were still mainly traders or pirates with little other uniting discipline. In order to demonstrate and improve his authority, the King, for the first time, appointed a 'High Admiral', John de Beauchamp, to oversee the running of the fleet. Henry V, in turn, did something to build up the fleet under royal command, but made few significant advances. Right through to Henry VII's reign there was some encouragement of the Merchant Navy, and few ships designed for fighting purposes only were built.

Henry VII gave a determined and powerful new direction to the overseas interests of the English people, and it was during his reign that the Royal Navy is often said to have been constituted as a significant, organised and semi-permanent service. As with the response to the Viking menace in former centuries, its creation was brought about largely as a result of external threat. The new worlds were, with the help of the Pope, neatly and firmly divided be-

OPPOSITE *Rye, one of the Cinque Ports, was also famous for its smugglers. Now, this beautiful little town is sought out by tourists.*

LEFT *Twelfth-century seal of Hythe, confirming it as one of the original Cinque Ports. Note the rudiments of fore and after castles on the boat. In vessels such as this the men of the Cinque Ports defended king and country.*

BELOW *The* Henry Grâce à Dieu *or 'Great Harry', 1546; from the Anthony Roll, Pepysian Library, Magdelene College, Cambridge. On state occasions her sails were of gold damask.*

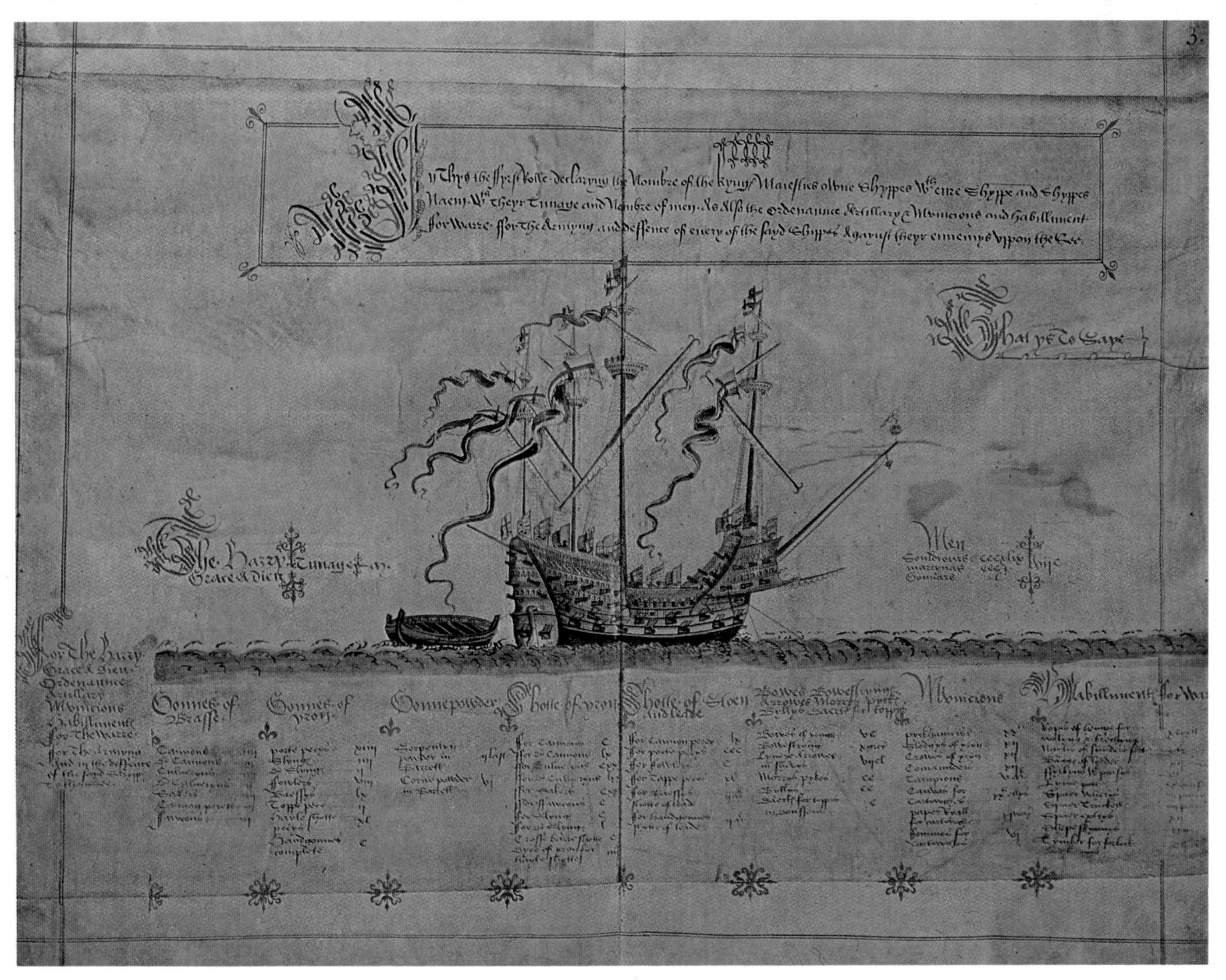

RIGHT *Detail of a painting of Sir John Hawkins.*

BELOW *Defeat of the Spanish Armada, July 1588; oil painting by an unknown artist from a design for a tapestry.*

tween the Spanish and the Portuguese. As a consequence, and coupled with the ever-present threat from France, the infant Royal Navy was additionally strengthened to help establish England's right to the freedom of the oceans in the New World. The continual opening up of these new worlds to the west and to the east, meant that access had to be safeguarded for purposes of exploration, plundering or trading, and that the ships themselves had to be better equipped, both in size and design, for longer and longer hauls. A new breed of seaman was another result.

Henry VIII, 'the father' of the Navy, was equal to these challenges. He not only built an effective Royal fleet, but also created Royal Dockyards at Woolwich, Portsmouth and Deptford. He additionally founded the five-man Navy Board to control civil and military aspects of the Navy, and also Trinity House, whose role will be described fully later. Above all, his ships were built and crewed for war: to fight for King and State alone. The vessels themselves were now ocean-going rather than coastal craft, and they were increasingly designed and rigged to give maximum manoeuvrability in

Peter Pett with Sovereign of the Seas. *He built this ship with his famous son, Phineas Pett, who also designed it.*

battle. Gone were the squat semi-trading tubs that preceded them.

These new ships of war were at least three times longer than their beam – a new breed altogether – like Henry's 1,000-ton *Great Harry* with her twenty-one huge bronze guns, 231 lighter weapons, and a crew of 700. Gone were ancient methods of war dating back to Greek and Roman days, such as prow-ramming followed by boarding. This was the new age of gunpowder: cannon set in rows, ready for that most famous English naval technique – the broadside, first developed by Hawkins in 1569. The King himself was personally much involved with all these developments. From then on, England was to be all powerful in naval matters. As a first test of might, she defeated the French fleet which attempted to invade England in the year 1545 – the year in which Sir Francis Drake was born.

England was very well positioned to dominate and control the new sea routes, first for trade and then for the colonisation which followed so rapidly. Throughout the late Tudor reigns the English people became more aware of the advantages of their geographical position. Along with the development of naval power came an exciting period of world exploration, with, as we have seen, many of the outstanding figures of the time acting both as warriors and discoverers. In the latter part of the fifteenth century the Cape route to India was discovered. The treasures of the east no longer had to be brought home by land caravan and then across the Mediterranean (which, as its name implies, had until then been the maritime centre of the known world). With this discovery and the realisation that there was an American continent, came the clear message to the English nation: they were in danger of losing the

The Dutch in the Medway, 1667; painting by Soest.

ownership of these new lands to their traditional enemies. The Spanish and the Portuguese were well ahead and had staked out the best colonies for themselves; France would have followed suit, had she not been too much involved with her European and internal political and territorial problems.

With the dawn of the Elizabethan age came the great names of England under sail. This was the era of Sir Francis Drake, the first of the great privateers and later (ranked with Nelson) to be the greatest of all England's Admirals. He, unlike the Spaniards, knew that in ocean warfare, maritime skills of negotiating and manoeuvring came before the skills of soldiers. The Spanish, by comparison stressed the latter, which, as much as anything else, contributed to their eventual defeat. Drake was very particular to ensure that his fighting men and his sailors worked well together; the feudality of Spain made the sailor a mere serf to the aristocratic soldiers who were always taken on board in large numbers.

Warfare, commerce and exploration went hand in hand throughout the age, with at times little to differentiate between those involved in these disparate aims. In the decades leading up to the Spanish Armada of 1588, Queen Elizabeth I, still nominally at peace with Philip of Spain, aided and abetted English privateer attacks – by captains such as Frobisher, Howard and Drake – on Spanish ships and colonies, particularly in Spanish America. With hindsight, it proved good training for the English naval forces and crews for the years to come, quite apart from the contribution that the plunder provided to the sometimes rather empty Privy Purse.

One particularly useful appointment at this time was of Sir John Hawkins, as Treasurer and Controller of the Navy. He it was who was largely responsible for the new design of warships that were to defeat the Spanish Armada. The high poops and forecastles which had made for bad sailing and poor stability were gradually eliminated, thus allowing for greater manoeuvrability particularly in sailing closer to the wind.

Despite the internal turmoils that preceded the Spanish Armada, the English – Catholic and Protestant alike – were united in opposition to the designs of Philip of Spain. The Spanish fleet was crewed by men from many Mediterranean countries, there 'to sail the Spanish Army' to conquer England. By contrast, the English fleet, under an experienced Lord High Admiral and with men like Drake, Hawkins and Frobisher in command of its ships, was very able and experienced. This mixture of Royal Navy and merchant marine was well equipped, not only with guns, but also with greater expertise and seamanship, particularly in coping with wild northern seas. The Spanish soldiers waited, lined up on deck, ready to fight an enemy that never came near enough to fight.

One hundred and thirty ships, the largest of them at 1,300 tons, faced a British fleet of 197 vessels, only thirty of which were strictly Royal Navy. The largest of the English ships, at 1,000 tons, was the *Triumph*, while the flagship *Ark Royal* was a mere 800 tons, and carried fifty-five guns.

The varied natural misfortunes to which the Spanish fleet was subjected, helped by the punishment that Drake and the others afforded them, led to total rout. Battered by storms and without stores or water, they fled round the north and west of Scotland and Ireland, leaving many wrecks on their way. Less than half of their 130 ships ever reached Spain again. The defeat of the Armada and the attack on Cadiz broke the power of Spain and emphasised that England's Navy had begun to rule the waves and that her merchants, colonialists and indeed pirates, could roam the New World with a new, if not yet absolute, freedom.

The war with Spain dragged on till the death of Elizabeth in 1603. Over that period, the Royal Navy reigned supreme, though, despite many famous naval victories like the last fight of the *Revenge* off the Azores or the sacking of Cadiz, it was not powerful enough to bring about the final dismemberment of Spain's American empire. One reason for this was that England had yet to evolve an army adequate enough to back up her new-found naval might. From the Elizabethan age on, the Royal Navy was to become the real bulwark of the State in every foreign war right up until the Great War of 1914–18.

In Stuart times, James VI of Scotland and I of England, always short of money, was less than resolute in his support for the Navy, though during much of his reign, 'private' war continued to be waged against the Spanish without the backing of the State. This helped usher in the age of the buccaneer and gave a new lease of life to the privateers discussed earlier. By the end of the Stuart period, the lack of control over these freebooters led to widespread piratical robbery and abuse of every kind on the high seas. The prey were no longer just Spanish ships; even England's own East India Company had to defend its ships against English-born adventurers. One result was that English power at sea was almost totally extinguished over the next thirty years and the Channel itself became a hunting ground for Barbary Pirates. Where naval heroes remained, they were powerless; even Raleigh himself was eventually arrested and executed to appease the Spanish.

This series of events gave rise to a deep resentment against the House of Stuart by the English maritime community, despite Charles I's later attempt to remedy matters and rebuild a Navy that had largely been abandoned by his father. It contributed to Charles's own downfall and, during the Civil War that followed, the majority of the Navy consequently sided with the King's enemies. Even the major seaports, with their dependence on a free-trading mercantile marine, came out in support of the Parliamentary Roundheads. Nonetheless, it was during Charles I's reign that the largest warship in the world at that time was built, the *Sovereign of the Seas* – designed by the famous naval architect Phineas Pett and built by him and his father. Although estimates

The Siege of Gibraltar, 1779.

Press gang at Tower Hill. Pressed men were paid at a lower rate than those who volunteered.

Press Gangs

'Press gang' was the popular name for a group of seamen, commanded by an officer, who brought in men more or less by force to serve in the Navy. Impressment was a royal prerogative in times of war and was used to recruit men for both the Army and the Navy; it was more closely associated with the latter because of the unpopularity of the Navy, where the pay was less than that of the Merchant Navy but the discipline greater, and the large numbers of men needed. The legality of impressment was laid down for the first time in an *Act of Mary Tudor* (1556) in which a request by the Thames watermen to be exempt was refused. There were further Acts in the following reigns, outlining groups that were to be released from this duty. In the reign of George II, for example, a proportion of the men from each colliery were exempt. Vagrants and minor criminals were often sent to the ships to make up the numbers. Later, there was a series of Quota Acts to ensure that each town and county contributed their share of men.

In times of war during the eighteenth and early nineteenth centuries recruiting centres were frequently set up in taverns, an essential feature being a strong lock-up room.

Regulating captains hired and paid the press gangs and saw that the men collected were taken in a press tender to the receiving ship in one of the home ports.

Impressment was widespread, the gangs usually operating in seaports, but occasionally going inland to a town or village where they believed seamen resided. A cruel and arbitrary system, men didn't have a chance to say goodbye to their families. Impressment was employed at sea as well, part of the crew sometimes heartbreakingly being taken off a homeward-bound ship after voyages lasting years. Later, one had to accept the 'King's shilling' to be made to serve, but this was circumvented by slipping a shilling into a man's beer.

Press gangs were last used in Britain during the Napoleonic Wars, 1799–1815. By 1853, when a pensionable career in the Navy became possible, the need for impressment faded.

During the two World Wars of this century Acts of compulsory national service were passed by the government of the day to recruit the large numbers of men required for the defence of the country. The *Military Service Act of 1916* was abolished in 1919. The *Compulsory Training Act of 1939* was abolished in 1963, as was the *National Service Act of 1947* in 1960. PP

of her length vary, it seemed she was about 167 feet long, displaced 1,600 tons and carried 102 guns.

When their turn came, the Roundheads took it upon themselves to revive naval strength and, with it, England's seapower. This revival occurred despite the fact that something like a third of that Navy had stayed loyal to the Monarchy, and, under the command of Prince Rupert, was operating out of European ports. This renegade 'Royal' Navy constantly threatened English commercial shipping both in the Channel and the Thames itself.

Consequently, the Cromwellian Navy, the 'Fleet of the Commonwealth', was urgently transformed under its brilliant commander, Admiral Robert Blake. His expertise and successes, first against Rupert, then against the Dutch, French and Spanish, place him with Drake and Nelson among the greatest of English Admirals. He was by training a soldier rather than a sailor, but his tactical skills and administrative abilities were outstanding; as measure of this, his new style for the Navy was retained, even after the Restoration. It was, for example, under him that annual estimates for the Fleet were obtained by Parliamentary approval.

Blake, as well as beating Rupert and introducing the Navy into the Mediterranean, was also successful in the war which the Commonwealth fought with Holland over the years 1652 to 1654 – the two greatest fleets of the age battling with one another – and later against the Spanish at Tenerife on which occasion he destroyed their fleet. At the end, Cromwell's Fleet, consisting of 154 vessels, one third of which were two deckers, was exceptionally well-equipped, well-manned and well-practised in every new naval technique.

With the Restoration, Charles II and his Parliament, learning from the mistakes of the past, took a well-informed interest in the Navy and in ensuring that the Admiralty was well staffed. Samuel Pepys, the diarist, was the Naval Secretary most credited with the reforms ushered in from that time on.

Yet neglect of the Navy continued, through Parliament refusing to vote money to pay its crews. This led to at least one disgraceful episode when the Dutch fleet, piloted by English seamen, sailed up the Thames and Medway and destroyed or captured the finest ships of the Fleet as they lay at anchor at Chatham. Such incidents and the later wars with Holland were largely for control of Channel trade and North Sea fisheries. By 1690, with the power of the Dutch broken, the English Fleet, with 180 odd ships and an estimated manpower of forty-two thousand, was well equipped for the struggle to dominate trade and exploration.

The wars with the European powers during the following reigns and particularly in William III's time (1689–1713), are usually discussed in terms of land campaigns. But it is important to bear in mind

*Aquatints by Rowlandson of (*LEFT*) a Midshipman in uniform and (*RIGHT*) an Admiral, from a series illustrating a Ship's Company, 1799.*

The Battle of the Nile, 1798: the French Fleet was devastated, due to the initiative of the young Nelson.

that the land campaigns would never have been crowned with the successes that followed without the English Navy as back-up. There were famous sea engagements as well, including at La Hogue, when the French fleet were roundly defeated in the year 1692. But the main achievements were the consolidation of English seapower in the western Mediterranean, particularly after the capture of Gibraltar, in addition to the supremacy they gained during this period on the other side of the Atlantic. Britain really did rule the waves almost unchallenged. To ensure that this position would not be eroded, an additional Naval Dockyard at Devonport was first established during William III's reign. The other yards were increased in size and scope so that, at the peak, the Fleet numbered 270 ships with a total dead weight of 160,000 tons.

The Royal Navy further consolidated its international position during the Hanoverian reigns, helped by the destruction of a reborn Spanish fleet off Sicily in 1718. In the decades that followed, especially under Pitt's leadership, the Navy continued to be strengthened and the best available men were generally placed in command. As Prime Minister, Pitt's great strategic achievement lay in ensuring that Army and Navy worked well together as they did in the successful capture of Quebec in 1795 under Wolfe.

This too was the period in which naval uniform first came into use for officers (1747). Naval Regulations were more strictly defined and administered, and the overall manpower of the Fleet increased substantially owing to the continuing French threat from across the Channel. In social terms, however, it was also a time of the press gangs. They were considered necessary evils in a constant struggle to find crews to help defeat the French in the struggle for Canada and North America.

The final years of the eighteenth century were less happy. Despite Sir Samuel Hood's victories at Toulon and Corsica, the combination of the French and Spanish forces and lack of political determination by the British Government left the Navy without a base in the Mediterranean. Penny-pinching and maladministration resulted in the mutinies at Spithead and the Nore with sailors protesting at harsh treatment, poor food and corruption over their pay.

Admiral Jervis, who was then blockading Cadiz, took the decision in 1798 to send Nelson through the Straits into the Mediterranean, culminating in his victory at the Battle of the Nile. This was the turning

The Royal Marines

The Marines, 'Per Mare Per Terram' (By Sea by Land), were formed in 1664 and were known as the Duke of York and Albany's Maritime Regiment of Foot or the Admiral's Regiment. The Duke's favourite colour was yellow, hence the first uniform: yellow coats, red breeches with stockings and gold braided hats.

Basically, they were soldiers trained for service at sea. For many years raised in war-time and disbanded in peace, the Corps was permanently established in 1755 under the Board of Admiralty. Since then it has provided a military force within the Royal Navy.

Known as 'soldiers of the sea' during the French Wars, the Marine Corps was present at every naval engagement, including the Battle of Trafalgar, in which 3,000 men took part.

In 1802 they were granted the prefix 'Royal' and in 1804 Artillery Companies were added to the Corps. Later all Marines took on a gunnery role, remaining the nucleus of armed landing.

During the Second World War the majority of Marines trained as commandos. They provided, for example, complete formations for the defence of naval bases, overseas crews for landing craft, and armoured units for close support on the beaches. They have furnished detachments for H.M. ships, and R.M. pilots with the Fleet Air Arm. In the post-war years commando operations, including arctic warfare training, has been their main role. The green berets of the commandos are a familiar sight on NATO locations. PP

Two Royal Marines on reconnaisance in Arctic Norway.

Nelson mortally wounded at the Battle of Trafalgar, 1805; painting by Denis Dighton.

point in restoring British prestige and morale and the beginning of a century and a half of British Naval supremacy in the Mediterranean, a supremacy further determined by its powerful and well-equipped base at Malta.

By 1805 the Fleet consisted of around 150 'Ships of the Line' and over 400 other vessels, crewed by 120,000 men and marines. This was the age of England's greatest sailing ships, their sides studded with guns, ready to conquer at Trafalgar and a hundred other battles and encounters. It was this strength which won that greatest sea victory of all time. The place and time was off Cape Trafalgar on the twenty-first of October, 1805. Nelson's ships had chased the French fleet to and fro across the Atlantic. Eventually, after taking refuge in various French and Spanish ports, they came out to meet the British Fleet and were destroyed. From then on English naval power seemed invincible, and Nelson was classed for all time among the noblest of English heroes – not least because of his death in his hour of victory. It was the Royal Navy's greatest hour.

After 1815 and the peace that followed the defeat of the French, the number of ships decreased substantially though their individual fighting power and efficiency increased. Generally, the nineteenth-century Royal Navy, like other of the world's navies, was alert to the introduction of steam in place of sail and iron hulls in place of wooden ones. But by the end of the century the change was complete, and the age of the battleship had arrived.

Throughout the nineteenth and twentieth centuries, the Royal Navy remained the mainstay of Britain's imperial might, supporting colonial expansion, opening up and developing trade routes, exploring, charting, surveying. To Britain, as Trevelyan said, the sea and seapower continued to be at the heart of her very existence. It was central to her military, political, diplomatic and commercial relations both in the later nineteenth and in the early twentieth centuries. It was to be central also to Britain's very survival in the two World Wars.

7 Trade and the Flag

The enormous growth and expansion, both in range of goods and in value, of England's seaborne commerce occurred from the fifteenth century onwards. This international trade gave considerable impetus to the development of both England's Merchant Navy and of a Royal Navy – to protect her freedom to trade across the high seas. From the latter part of that century, the drive to find and import new and ever more exotic wares and the pursuit of fresh overseas markets also led to the great voyages of exploration, to the colonisation of the new worlds, and to the eventual development of the British Empire and Commonwealth.

The handling of the bulk of English trade was, by the end of the same century, being carried out by native Englishmen. The earlier practice of foreign merchants setting up and buying and selling out of London and the other major ports was in rapid decline. One reason for this, particularly in Tudor England, was a nationalistic reaction to the years when the Hanseatic Merchants – men from the Hanse towns of north Germany – had bought themselves enormous privileges from the English kings, keeping large fleets, fighting battles on a mercenary basis (for example, for Edward IV in the late fifteenth century) and, in return, paying smaller customs duties both on exports and imports than native-born merchants.

This new breed of English merchant started travelling abroad to sell, becoming known, in their organised groups, as Merchant Adventurers or Venturers. They replaced the less outward-looking Merchants of the Staple, who had been largely engaged in a single commodity trade – that of wool. The larger the groups or organisations of Adventurers were, the wider their interests and geographical patterns of trade. They organised themselves into civic-based societies: Hull had the Guild of St George; York had both Mercers and Merchant Adventurers, as had Newcastle upon Tyne. Above all, London had its Merchant Adventurers of England. Increasingly, as the centuries ad-

BELOW *East Indiamen off Deptford, 1721; painting by Isaac Sailmaker.*

vance, records and customs receipts reveal more and more about the Venturers themselves and the range and quantities of England's maritime trade. Gradually this trade became more and more varied and exotic, as English tastes for foreign produce developed, and as domestic producers matched their output and wares to European demand.

In addition, there was an increase in English coastal trade in the two centuries from 1500 on. One of the reasons for this was a growth in the demand for coal which had to be brought from the northern coalfields, due to a drying up in the supply of fuel wood in the south of the country. In the year 1630, for example, there were up to 400 vessels of various sizes working the coasts of eastern England involved in this trade alone. Much of the coal was destined for London but there was also a great deal of up-river trade, and cargoes were off-loaded at every port round the coast from Whitby to Portsmouth, especially at Lynn which, by the year 1725, was supplying coal to 'six counties in whole and three in part', to quote from contemporary reports by Daniel Defoe.

The next phase of development in English maritime trade occurred when those entrepreneurs who followed the Merchants of the Staple and their successors, the Merchant Venturers, began organising themselves in terms of market areas. Their aim was to keep a monopoly of all English trade with a given part of the world, using force if necessary. The greatest of these new Companies were the Muscovy Company, the Levant Company, the East India Company and the Hudson's Bay Company, but there were many others, including those trading to East and West Africa, and the Eastland Company which briefly operated in the Baltic.

The Muscovy Company, founded by charter in 1553, was the first English company trading on a joint stock basis. This meant that both costs and risks were shared by a group of merchants who sponsored trade missions sent on the dangerous route via the White Sea to treat with Russia. The first such expedition, under the leadership of Richard Chancellor, was undertaken in 1553. The Muscovy Company's trade with the Czar and then with the Shah of Persia was successful for a comparatively short period, the arduousness of the sea routes proving too expensive and taxing in the longer run. In the following century, England's merchants gradually abandoned this trade to the Dutch, who used overland routes to reach their markets. At a slightly later date, the so-called Company of Royal Adventurers began a similar venture in trading in Africa. It became the Royal Africa Company in 1672.

The last years of the sixteenth century saw the formation of a third aggressively monopolistic organisation, the Levant Company. It was also a joint stock organisation, composed of a group of so-called 'Turkey Merchants' who, from 1561, had dom-

The Merchant Adventurers of York

For seven centuries York was one of the great staple towns of England, dominated by the Ouse with its great river system, the wool trade and the Merchant Adventurers of York. This guild, under the powers of various charters, controlled the entire regulation of the foreign export trade of the city. No person could exercise his trade without becoming a freeman of the company – by servitude, patrimony, purchase, or obtaining its licence – and then carrying on his trade in strict accordance with its laws and ordinances.

The wool trade for the entire area was strongly focused on York when, in 1357, Edward III granted a licence to Johannes Frebois and thirteen York citizens to unite themselves into a charitable guild. From its initiation, the interdependence of this guild, the cloth trade and the municipal government is clear, for all were actively engaged in buying and selling cloth, and the majority were mercers involved in city government. Within ten years the guild had become so popular that it had members from Newcastle, Hull, Scarborough and Whitby. As a charity the guild had gathered land together, and completed a hospital by 1371. In the long and complex history of the guild, it was not until the royal charter of 1430 that the power was totally and irrefutably in the hands of the merchants, who retained full control until 1837.

The company today possesses a magnificent series of account rolls and leases, which cover the greater part of the fifteenth and the whole of the sixteenth centuries. They give a minute and consecutive history of the expenditure of both the Merchant Adventurers and the Mystery of Merchants.

The merchants met in Trinity Hall, over the Hospital, to discuss means by which the hated Hanse merchants, and the rival London merchants, could be prevented from interfering in the northern trade. They also, of course, drew up their laws, censured or punished riotous apprentices and recalcitrant members. Some samples of orders recorded in the minute book:

1557 Richard Murton fined 10s. for opening his shop and occupying as a Brother of this fellowship without license.
1559 John Middleton and Oswin Edwin each fined 5s. for that they did break the order of shipping in keels at Hull.
1680 Leave given to W. Raper to sell a parcel of iron.

The prosperity of the York merchants reached its high point early in the sixteenth century. Much of the trade in lead, and a number of other materials, had become focused on York over the centuries. The guild's resident agents in Emden and Hamburg had the sole control of the sale of goods from York, part of the extremely complex trading patterns that existed throughout Europe at that time. The merchants ruled York and, in fact, did good work for the whole of England. They assisted the Merchant Adventurers of England in the struggle against the Hanse merchants, while at the same time enthusiastically championing the rights of northern England against the aggressive policy of London. The York merchants, basically Royalists, successfully changed sides during the Commonwealth and as a result prospered.

With the Industrial Revolution came the rapid growth of Manchester, Birmingham, Leeds and many other places that the old order could no longer dominate. York, conscious of its magnificent traditions, of centuries of organised supremacy, did not give in easily. For one thing, it had a system whereby, after their eight years of apprenticeship, a man received money from funds built up over many years to help set up in business. In 1779 the guild solidly opposed the bill for the abolition of apprenticeship and wasted much time and money in fighting a lost cause.

The *Municipal Corporation Act of 1835* made it lawful for any person in any borough to keep a shop for the sale of lawful wares and merchandise. With this, the primary objects for which the medieval mercers formed their guild ceased to exist.

Today the Merchant Adventurers of York apply their resources to charitable purposes and in restoring their buildings, particularly Trinity Hall, now called Merchants' Hall, the Undercroft or Trinity Hospital dating from 1357 and Trinity Chapel – among York's finest treasures. PP

The Great Hall, Merchant Adventurers' Hall, Fossgate, York. Timber-framed and 89 by 40 ft, it is divided by central pillars, and has oak roof trusses of fifteenth-century type. The traditional Court meetings and feasts are still held here. In the fifteenth century Fossgate was a rich parish in York; many wealthy merchants had their houses near the Hall.

inated English trade in the Mediterranean. They were now looking for new markets further to the East, and were particularly interested in trading with the East Indies, using routes that had been opened up for them by the Spanish and Portuguese.

Following enthusiastic reports from English travellers to India, yet another group of a-hundred-and-one 'Adventurers' sought a charter to trade in that part of the world. This was granted to them in 1600, and the 'Honorable' East India Company was born. It was granted the right to organise four voyages to the East on which it would pay no duties

Thames Sailing Barges

Found on the Thames and elsewhere on the rivers and coasts of southern England, this type of vessel was used for the coastal transport of freight and carried every conceivable type of cargo – with a crew of only two men. They also regularly traded up to the Humber and the Trent, across the Channel to Normandy and as far west as Devon and Cornwall. The average barge was 80 feet by 20 feet and flat-bottomed with a big spritsail and jib-headed topsail, a foresail staysail and a small mizzen. Bowsprits were also carried and a jib set.

A Thames sailing barge had leeboards instead of a keel, so it could operate without difficulty in shallow water and remain upright when grounded or when the tide went out. The flat bottom also helped, of course. It could carry an average load of 150 tons with minimum draught of water. This enabled the barges to go quite far inland on small rivers and creeks to places like the East Mills above Colchester or Bradwell Quay on the River Blackwater. As one old barge skipper claimed, 'They will go anywhere after a heavy dew.'

The sailing gear on these barges was made to lower, so they could go under bridges, another feature that enabled them to go quite far inland on rivers. The Medway barges, were constantly 'shooting' Rochester Bridge fifty years ago. The gear worked so easily that the crew could sail on cargoes and also be permitted to export bullion to buy the promised spices and silks. The East India Company continued to hold a monopoly of this trade even after the Civil War, with Cromwell declaring that they 'stood for England in the East' in a way that no casual, free-trading group of merchants could. At the same time, there were Dutch, French and other European East India companies operating in the same area, and inevitable and constant conflicts arose between them.

The ships that the East India Company used for their trade were, by Royal Navy standards, of

right up to the bridge, lower the sailing gear smartly, 'shoot' through, and heave the gear up again on the other side, scarcely losing any time.

These small sea-going craft must have been a remarkable sight loaded high with hay. Called 'stackies', they put out to sea with up to twelve feet of hay on their decks and the mate on top of the haystack to keep a lookout and to give steering directions to the skipper at the wheel. The hold was probably filled with root crops. They carried the hay from farms on the Essex and Suffolk coast, then up the Thames to feed the large number of horses in London. They returned with cargoes of horse manure. Restored and preserved barges can be seen regularly at Pin Mill, near Ipswich, Maldon, Essex, St Katharine's Dock, London and at Faversham, although these craft are now used only for pleasure races.

Today the traditions of the Thames sailing barge are preserved at the Dolphin Yard Sailing Barge Museum at Sittingbourne in Kent, which has a number of barges, including *Revival* and *Oak*. The museum is most appropriately situated on an old barge building yard on the Bourne Stream off Milton Creek. Milton Creek was well-known for its production of bricks, cement and paper. One firm alone had a fleet of ninety craft in which it shipped away a million bricks a week. Fleets of this size were not uncommon. There were twelve yards on the creek in its heyday, all occupied in building and maintaining sailing barges. This one creek is known to have produced over 500 barges.

Throughout a long period of decline and the virtual disappearance of waterside industry on the creek, the yard of Charles Burley remained, continuing to repair the barges which were once used to transport Burley's 'Dolphin Brand Cement'. The last barge was sold in 1965, but the yard, the last complete example of its type, now has a new and unexpected life as a folk museum. There is a carpenter's shop and a sail loft in one building, while another houses the forge, which contains leather bellows and has supporting timbers made of sawn-up barge tillers (they went out of use when barges changed to wheel-steering in the 1880s). Alongside the sail loft, Thames sailing barges are once again undergoing re-rigging, repair and maintenance.

Several sailing barge clubs are active, including the Thames Barge Sailing Club, the Society for Spritsail Research and the Sailing Barge Association. This indicates the growing interest in these beautiful working vessels of which over fifty are now back under sail. There are often eight sailing barge matches every year – on the Swale, Orwell, Medway, Colne, Blackwater and the Thames at Southend and Greenwich, as well as a Passage Match from Gravesend to Pin Mill. PP

OPPOSITE *The barge* Redoubtable *taking part in the Swale Sailing Barge Match.*

BELOW *Sailing barges moored at Maldon, Essex.*

The Hudson's Bay Company

The demand in England and Europe for beaver pelts to make fashionable fur-felt hats was almost insatiable when two explorers and fur traders, Médard Chouart and Pierre Esprit Radisson, arrived at the Court of Charles II. Enthusiastic, and with the blessing of Prince Rupert, nephew of Charles I and a dynamic figure of the age, they persuaded the King of the advantages of opening trading posts around Hudson's Bay – the best beaver country – to which the Indians could take pelts.

In 1668 fourteen Englishmen set out on this preliminary expedition. The *Nonsuch* sailed into Hudson's Bay in September. The adventurers dug in for the winter. They returned to England in October 1669, keen to carry on. They soon transmitted their excitement and enthusiasm to the King.

A charter was granted by the King on 2 May 1670, incorporating 'The Governor and Company of Adventurers of England trading into Hudson's Bay', with Prince Rupert as the first Governor. The King also encouraged them to seek a north-west passage. This extraordinary document was the most comprehensive charter ever granted to a company. They had the right to trade in all parts of North America drained by rivers flowing into Hudson's Bay. Both law-makers and judges, they were authorised to, among other things, erect forts, and to commission and employ warships. The Governor and the Company of Adventurers thus became the absolute lords over these territories – territories so vast that they took in virtually all of what is now Canada and some of the United States.

After some initial difficulties the Company prospered. The capital of £10,500 trebled in 1690 and again in 1720, all from earnings. Trade routes had had to be established and there was strong competition. Almost from the beginning armed conflict with the French broke out, a struggle that eventually moved to the interior and became even fiercer. There was also very strong rivalry with the North West Company until it was amalgamated with the Hudson's Bay Company in 1821. In spite of these troublesome problems, the result, especially between 1821 and 1879, was outstanding commercial success.

The territories, known as Prince Rupert's Land, became part of the Dominion of Canada with the *Rupert's Land Act of 1868*. As part of a complete exchange the Company was given £300,000, chunks of territory around the trading posts, title to one-twentieth of the lands in the 'fertile belt' in western Canada and mineral rights to the land as well. The company remained in existence, although in a different form – happily transformed into the modern corporation it is today. One retail shop in Winnipeg has now grown into a nation-wide chain. In 1971 a Canadian charter supplanted the original royal one, finally making the company an entirely Canadian enterprise. PP

First page of the charter incorporating 'The Governor and Company of Adventurers of England trading into Hudson's Bay'.

medium size. Even by the year 1682, they were sending ships of only 200 tons all the way to China to trade, while as late as the 1740s, the standard size of East India Company vessels on the China run had reached only 500 tons. The most famous of the Company's ships, the aristocratic 'East Indiamen', were built at their own Company dockyard at Deptford, and while not a match for the Navy, were, nonetheless, the largest merchant vessels of the age. Internally and externally these ships were magnificently decorated and maintained with elaborately carved and gilded woodwork. The East Indiamen were fully armed both as a defence against pirates and also to protect themselves against their long-

LEFT *View of Broad Quay, Bristol, eighteenth century. The society of Merchant Venturers was founded here in 1552. Trade with new colonies stimulated the growth of industry around Bristol, a commercial port since the tenth century.*

BELOW *Bristol today.*

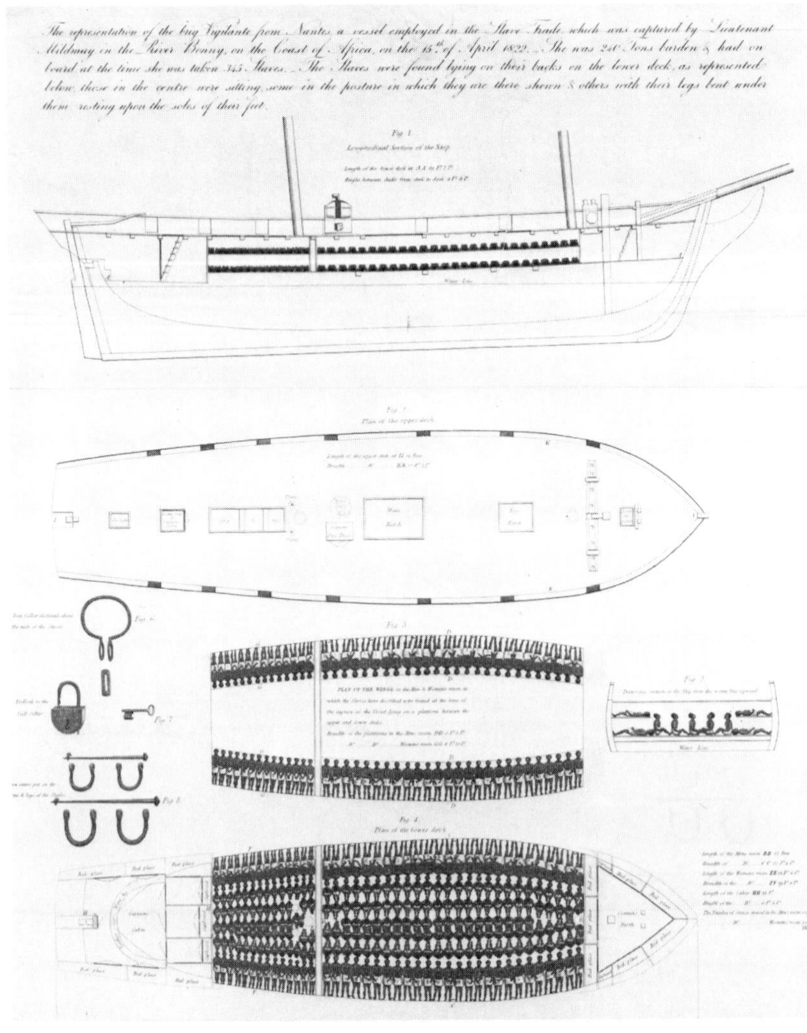

standing rivals, the French and Dutch Companies.

The success of the Company, which gradually acquired its own considerable legislative and judicial powers in the areas in which it traded, particularly in India, led eventually to conflict with the British Government. The latter subsequently had to take over responsibility for many of its operations, including the appointing of the top officers of the Company. In India itself, this change from commercial to governmental authority, in the latter half of the eighteenth century, was the most striking historical example of the 'flag following trade'. The monopoly of the Company in the India trade was eventually broken in 1813, but it continued to exist up until 1858 when it stopped trading.

One further organisation, the Hudson's Bay Company, has the considerable distinction in that it is the only one still to exist today. It was first chartered in 1670, and its 'territory' was all Canada. In the early days its trade was mainly with the Indians who exchanged beaver skins for guns and tools. Later it came to have great influence on the history and the geographical opening up of the Canadian provinces.

Economic nationalism was the driving force not only of these monopolistic companies but also of the foreign policies of all the European nations over these centuries. Trade discrimination measures were commonplace. While there had been many earlier attempts to protect English maritime trade, the so-called *Navigation Acts of 1651* and *1660* were the most far-reaching. They were directed mainly against the Dutch, and gave the English (and, after 1707, British) ships a complete monopoly in carrying all foreign produce out of and into English ports. This was to be applied particularly with regard to trade with the English plantations in the New World. Additionally, as well as stipulating that the ships themselves had to be English, and their crews at least three-quarters English, the Acts ruled that goods bound for the Colonies from Europe also had to pass through English ports. The passage of the Acts was intended to give an impetus to the English merchant marine and undoubtedly did just this, as well as stimulating activity at English ports, such as Liverpool and Bristol.

But these Acts were only part of a larger protectionist policy, developed and maintained by successive Westminster governments, which lasted until well into the nineteenth century. They were backed up by an increasingly complex system of customs dues and taxes that needed a large corps of excisemen to administer it. They also led, inevitably to a massive increase in smuggling, and, more importantly in the long run, to widespread feelings of grievance in the American colonies over the consequent inequities and restrictions to which they became subjected.

It should not be forgotten, sadly, that Britain, as

the pre-eminent maritime nation from the seventeenth to the nineteenth centuries, was not only involved with the great trades in wool, cloth, cotton, tobacco, wines and spices, but also in that most notorious of traffics – slaves. During this period there was a 'triangular' trade flow assisted by the 'trade', or prevailing Atlantic, winds. Ships out from Europe blown by these winds, carried manufactured goods to Africa, where the goods were bartered for slaves. These unfortunate negroes were shipped across the Atlantic to the West Indies or North America for sale. Returning, the ships brought back to England tropical produce such as cotton, tobacco and sugar. Ports like Liverpool and Bristol were particularly infamous for their part in this traffic in human misery. After the Treaty of Utrecht in 1713, England was world leader in the trade, having reached agreement with Spain to supply 5,000 slaves a year for thirty years to the New World. But by the 1750s, English ships were carrying nearly 40,000 'black cargo' a year. Some of the great names of maritime history, such as Hawkins and, less so, Drake, traded in slaves who had been rounded up in Africa. It was not until 1806, after William Wilberforce's anti-slavery campaign was launched in the House of Commons, that this type of 'cargo' was eventually banned.

With world trade growing enormously in the years after the Industrial Revolution, free trade and the repeal of the *Navigation Acts* followed in the second half of the nineteenth century. England, as the only fully developed industrial state up to the 1880s, found herself well able to hold her own without them. She managed until, in the face of German and other European and North American competition, new restrictive regulations and rules came to be necessary in the decades leading to the First World War.

Modernisation of ships, systems of marine transport and cargo handling were both inspired by, and gave their impetus to, this remarkable trade explosion. This was not just confined to the type and quality of the shipping used by the Merchant Navy (which by the 1820s probably amounted to two and a half million tons), but it also extended to the infrastructure with which it was intermeshed. Canals were built and rivers widened to bring goods from the industrialised interior of England.

Later, the growth of railways was to play a fundamental part in the whole pattern of supply, with the result that, between the 1850s and the 1870s England's overseas trade expanded fourfold.

OPPOSITE, TOP *Detail from a painting of William Wilberforce, who agitated in the House of Commons against the slave trade, and was a founder of the Anti-slavery Society. The bill abolishing slavery became law a month after his death.*

OPPOSITE, BOTTOM *The slave ship* Vigilante, *a brigantine of 240 tons captured by a Lt Mildmay off the coast of Africa, 1822. On board were 225 men and 120 women.*

BELOW *The Shropshire Union Canal at Chester.*

A24
SH214

Part II
The Life-Enhancing Sea

The splendour of Scarborough

Folkestone, a cross-Channel port, is also a working harbour for fishing boats such as these. In the old quarter of the town narrow streets wind down to the fishermen's quarter and the sea front. Folkestone is also a popular seaside resort, and has been since the mid-1800s. There is a fine promenade called the Leas, which follows the cliff-top for over a mile; terraced gardens connect the Leas and the beach. Rare plants and a variety of trees and shrubs grow in the Warren, a rugged land-slip basin nearby. There are many good picnic areas and pleasant walks on and around the town.

8 Gateways to the Sea: The Great Seaports

England has inherited one great maritime legacy, which, above all else, is important to a country and people who live by trade – her ports. Developed and expanded throughout the centuries, they are among the most modern and highly utilised in the world. Even in an age when an increasing amount of cargo is transshipped by aircraft, our ports are the gateways through which ninety-five per cent of our major exports and imports (by volume) are delivered. The network of rivers and canals – the arteries of England – help feed and supply both these ports and the country itself.

These English ports grew and prospered as a reaction to the economic forces and incentives of the time. Some based, and still do base, their prosperity on one staple commodity, coal; others have long been the points of exit and entry to a wide range of merchandise. Some are great and grow greater daily; others, sadly, are on the decline as the demands of modern life pass them by, or as geographical and other factors decrease their value.

In the second half of the sixteenth century coastal cities and towns started thinking about the general harbouring facilities they provided for vessels. The safety of the sea approaches to their harbours was a most important consideration for those civic authorities who wished to attract trade. Navigational aids, better charting, buoying and marking, lighthouses and so on were part and parcel of any port's attempts to improve the welcome to visiting ships. In place of moorings or simple quays, a more functional construction was needed to avoid the inconvenience of ships having to anchor in sufficiently deep water so that they did not dry out and damage themselves at low tides.

This led to the building of docks or basins with lock gates so the water level could be kept constant, thereby preventing ships from resting on the bottom. These docks were built with single or double lock gates, which were opened at high tide and then closed to retain the water as the outside level dropped. As skills developed, leakage from these docks would be made good by means of water pumps to keep constant levels. The earliest loading/unloading dock was built at Liverpool in 1715. This commercial dock was three and a half acres in extent and could accommodate 100 ships.

In the succeeding two centuries, ever larger and more efficient dock schemes were frequently combined with works to make rivers more navigable and the building of interlinking canals to feed them. Much of the impetus and need for such docks depended of course on the geographical location of the port. In Bristol and the Severn Estuary generally, there is a very large variation between high and low water; even in less extreme situations, tidal ranges generally required such dock gates. One exception is Southampton where prepared berths can remain tidal due to a local phenomenon known as 'double tide', which gives a prolonged period of high water.

English ports are still the gateways through which ninety-five per cent of the country's exports and imports pass.

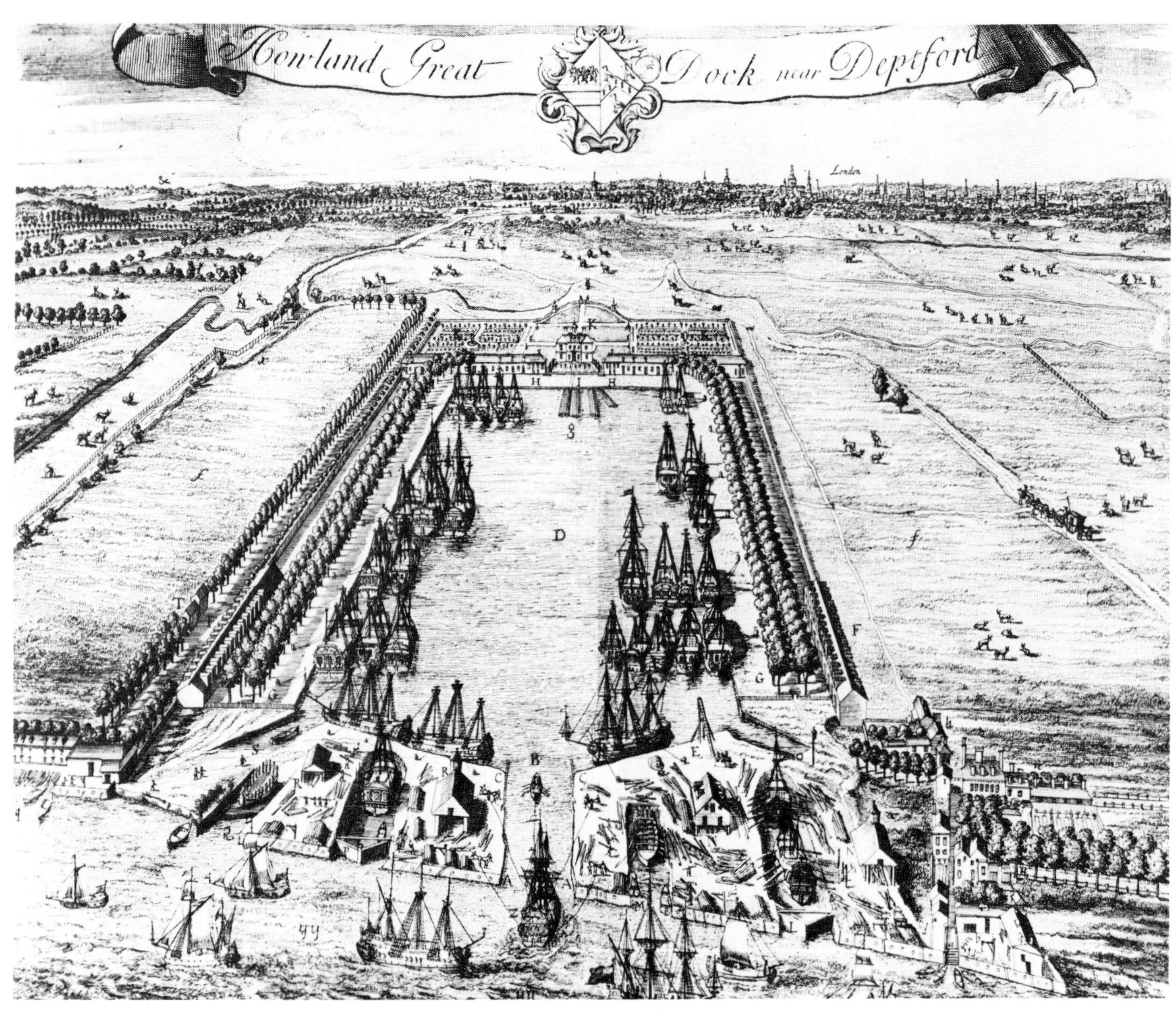

ABOVE *The seventeenth-century Howland Great Dock near Deptford. This dock was a winter laying-up berth for ships of the East India Company.*

Folkestone. On the hill can be seen one of the original seventy-four small forts called Martello Towers. They were built as a defence against an expected invasion by Napoleon.

Moving into the twentieth century, a major problem arose with the ever-increasing size of ships that had to be accommodated. Generally, with large, multiple-berth docks, the main consideration is to make the entry locks, the gates of which can weigh up to 300 tons or more, sufficiently large. Today, the largest lock in England is at Tilbury, 1,000 feet (304.8m) long and 110 feet (33.5m) wide. Yet even this means that it can only just accommodate some of the larger container-ships now in use. Dry or graving docks, where ships too large for a slipway can be brought in for maintenance and repair, blocked up by supports and then drained, are also part and parcel of any contemporary port.

The efficient administration of ports and harbours is a complex and expensive operation. In Britain today, there are some 250 port or wharf authorities, along with a further 800-odd organisations engaged in stevedoring, warehousing and lighterage.

The ports themselves are generally classified into four main types: nationalised undertakings; those run by public trusts; those administered by local authorities; and finally, a number that are run as statutory companies. Of the total, the nationalised ports account for over a fifth of the overall British capacity.

The British Transport Docks Board, founded in 1963, own a number of the largest ports including Southampton, Hull and Grimsby. Others, such as Folkestone, are run by British Rail, or, like Sharpness in Gloucestershire, are owned by the British Waterways Board. Ports controlled by public trusts include, pre-eminently, the Port of London and Liverpool, but also Medway, Tees and Hartlepool. Local authorities account for nearly a third of the overall total, this group including the major port of Bristol. Most of these different types of authority, through their membership of the British Ports Association, co-ordinate their policies and project their interests in a united and comprehensive manner.

By far the best known, the Port of London, which is run by an Authority, was set up as a public trust in the year 1908. Peculiarly, the responsibility for pilotage, lighting and buoying the River Thames is, however, in the domain of the Corporation of Trin-

Tilbury – the largest lock in England and the principal container port. The first docks were constructed here in 1884–86.

ABOVE *Jet foil at Liverpool, in service since 1980. Between May and October this jet foil carries passengers to Dublin and back, up to 250 on each trip.*

BELOW *Overview of St Katharine's Dock, London.*

ity House – the major English organisation connected with maritime safety. The Port of London is England's leading centre for non-fuel traffic and is also one of the largest in Europe. With the growing use of containers and bulk cargo handling, coupled with the ever-increasing size of ships using the port's facilities, there has been a tendency over the years to move its major port activities and developments further and further down river away from the centre of London. Such a trend is inevitable, given both the increasing need to be nearer deep water and also to be where land is less expensive.

Upstream, by comparison, the old docks, after a period of neglect and decay, are now being sold off for redevelopment or, like St Katharine's Dock, have been given an exciting new lease of life as yachting centre, recreation area, as well as, in this instance, being the location of a major maritime museum where ships can be seen in an attractive dockland setting. London's dockland, both old and new, today offers the visitor a fascinating glimpse of the past and of the future.

In terms of traffic-handling capacity, something like 350 million tonnes of cargo pass through Britain's ports each year. Of this, around a seventh goes through the Port of London alone. A third of the overall total is estimated to be coastal traffic, mainly in petroleum and coals.

Looking to the future, the development of North Sea oil has had a beneficial effect on some ports, particularly on the east coast, such as Tees and Hartlepool. But reduced petroleum imports, from the Middle East and elsewhere, have led to a falling level of activity at some of the traditional oil-importing terminals.

Perhaps the most significant and revolutionary development in port usage in recent years has been the increase in containerisation and the roll-on/roll-off traffic: wheeled containers that use stern-,

ABOVE *At Dover eleven million people use Sealink, Townsend Thoresen, Seaspeed Hovercraft and P & O Ferries to cross the Channel each year.*

LEFT *View of Dover in 1820; aquatint.*

side- or front-loading ships. Containerised traffic has increased threefold in the last ten years, and, with the delivery of oil to refineries, has contributed to the substantial move away from the larger more traditional ports, such as London and Liverpool, towards the Continental 'ferry' ports of Dover, Felixstowe and Harwich. The containers have been standardised to internationally agreed dimensions.

Because of this swing towards new methods of cargo carrying, English ports have, in recent years, been forced to spend large sums of money in order to meet these new demands. Container ships require handling facilities, such as heavy-duty cranes, that are substantially different from those needed by traditional cargo vessels. Available money has been spent on this and on tanker requirements at the expense of general port facilities.

Some of the most exciting new developments in recent years have been at Tilbury where the world's largest container terminal for refrigerated ships was completed in 1978; there have been other improvements at Bristol, Liverpool and Southampton as well. Equally, at roll-on/roll-off terminals, new ramps and shore bridges have had to be constructed to deal, not only with long-distance cargo traffic, but also with cross-Channel commercial and private ferry operations. Other developments in keeping with Britain's new marine technology, included the opening, in mid-1978, of a twelve-million-pound terminal at Dover, which marked an important stage in cross-Channel hovercraft operations. On the Tees a purpose-built oil terminal has further reflected the importance of North Sea oil development, while, at Great Yarmouth, the construction of a supply base for offshore oil and gas rigs has emerged as a result of similar demands.

Rivers, canals, the Broads, inland lakes and reservoirs, the waterways of the Fens, are, by extension, part and parcel of the seaborne life of England. Rivers from earliest times were the way to the heartland of the country, helping, as we have seen, Romans, Vikings, Saxons, merchants and many others to reach their diverse goals. Equally, they were gateways, for those living in the interior, to reach the sea. Today these great rivers, pre-eminently the Thames, are feeders or arteries for those ports and harbours on the coasts. Before the age of good roads and mechanised transport this was the cheapest and easiest, perhaps the only, way to carry heavy cargoes, such as coal, over long distances with relative ease. In many parts of England the bulk trade in coal would have been much less developed had it not been for the Severn and the Trent which could carry the 'stones that burned' from the collieries along their banks.

From the seventeenth and eighteenth centuries, men started to try to improve on nature and they began with what existed – the rivers – dredging them to make them more navigable. Rivers such as the Calder were opened up and the Mersey and Irwell were made navigable as far as Manchester.

Then came the great era of canal building, which began with the Sankey Brook Canal which was opened in the year 1757. Its principal function was to carry coal from the St Helen's coalfields. Four years later the Bridgewater Canal, built by James Brindley and named after and financed by the Duke of Bridgewater, was partly opened, again to transport coal. It ran from Worsley and later was extended to Manchester and Runcorn. With its aqueduct and

The Broads and the Norfolk Sailing Wherry

The Norfolk Broads, a haven for birdlife, angling and boating, lies within a wedge-shape formed by Beccles, Lowestoft, Great Yarmouth, Horsey Mere, Wroxham and Norwich. The term 'broad', meaning an open expanse of water with navigable approach channels, has been in use since the 1500s. Research has shown that these shallow lakes result in part from extensive peat or turf cutting over many many years in the Middle Ages. This explains why there is no concrete evidence of the existence of the Broads before the fourteenth century and why the Broads have comparatively recent names, usually being named after the parish in which they lie.

The Norfolk sailing wherry, unique in both shape and rig, was peculiar to the Broads. It had evolved over the centuries from a type of keel (a square-rigged, single-masted open boat) to become perfectly adapted to the conditions of this area. Clinker-built of oak with a double-ended tarred hull, there was one long hold for the cargo – of every type – which was protected from the elements by hatch covers. Trading wherries ranged from fifteen to fifty tons. A number of special features made them perfect for the Broads. Many had a false keel which could be detached in shallow water; detached, the draught was usually three to three-and-a-half feet when

OPPOSITE *The* Albion, *the last of her kind.*

LEFT *The Broads, serene and inviting.*

BELOW *Windmill on the quay at Cley next the Sea, Norfolk. Much of the marshland nearby is a bird sanctuary.*

fully loaded. The massive mast was perfectly counter-balanced by one and a half tons of lead at its keel enabling it to be lowered to go under bridges. The loose-footed sail was cleverly arranged, and controlled by a single halyard, so the peaks could be lowered easily in turbulent weather. This large black sail, positioned well forward and spread by a heavy gaff, was marvellously suitable for negotiating the winding rivers; when space allowed the boat could beat against a head wind, perhaps with some assistance from the quant (a long pole with a shoulder-piece); there were narrow plankways on either side of the boat for quanting when there was no wind.

The wherries were painted bright and distinctive colours. Each owner had his own selection of coloured bands, which were painted on the mast-head; the cabin in the stern, big enough for two, usually had a red roof, blue doors and yellow panels. A streamer of red bunting attached to a vane indicated the wind direction.

Among the thirty Broads, the five largest are Wroxham, Barton, Hickling, Ormesby and Filby. One can best appreciate the Norfolk Broads from a boat, a variety of which can be rented, to explore the 200 miles of Broads, rivers, streams and man-made channels. The Norfolk sailing wherry *Albion*, the last one in existence, can be chartered from the Norfolk Wherry Trust in Norwich. PP

lock system, it was rightly considered one of the engineering wonders of the age. Not content with this, Brindley also built the Grand Trunk (or Trent and Mersey) Canal which led from the Bridgewater Canal to the Trent. A further venture was the Staffordshire and Worcester Canal, which connected the Staffordshire Potteries with the Severn. Brindley's feats of bridge and aqueduct building and of lock construction, makes him a major figure of the industrial and economic revolution in England. His work eventually led to the linking of the rivers Mersey, Trent, Severn and Thames – a magnificent

Rennie's London Bridge, partially constructed. A Lord Mayor's Show parade is passing under the bridge, about 1829. The present London Bridge replaced this structure in 1973.

Sir John Rennie

Rennie (1761–1821) was a Scottish civil engineer of great resource, originality and energy, who built many important canals, docks, harbours and bridges in England.

At an early age he was allowed to spend time in the workshops of Andrew Meikle, the inventor of the threshing machine. Later, during school vacations, he worked as a millwright. After attending Edinburgh University, he visited Staffordshire to see James Watt, the inventor of the modern steam condensing engine. Watt employed him and this soon led to a position at the Albion Flour Mills in Blackfriars where Rennie designed all the machinery. This was notable because he was one of the first to use iron instead of wood for the gears, shafting and framing.

He started his own business in about 1791 in Holland Street, Blackfriars; from this location he, and eventually his sons, undertook vast engineering works, frequently of a maritime nature. At the beginning of a project he fully acquainted himself with local conditions before preparing his reports and estimates, which he did in great detail. His work was solid and has stood the test of time.

His achievements included the building of piers (Margate), canals (such as the Kennet and Avon, Rochdale, and Lancaster) and extensive drainage operations in the Lincolnshire Fens. He constructed important docks and harbours, among which were London Docks, East and West India Docks, Holyhead Harbour, Hull Docks, Ramsgate Harbour and dockyards at Sheerness and Chatham.

Rennie is also famous for his bridges: among others, Waterloo Bridge, Southwark Bridge and London Bridge. The latter, along with several other important projects, including the massive Breakwater at Plymouth – a wall a mile in length through deep water, were finished by his sons, Sir John and George. George also built the *Dwarf*, the first screw-propelled vessel to serve in the Royal Navy. PP

achievement and one which made a considerable contribution to the prosperity of the age. Equally foresighted were some of the great landowners and industrialists of the time, people who realised that a major canal and river system represented the cheapest possible means of transporting heavy and bulky materials over great distances.

After 1790 there was an even greater mania for canal building, with the result that by the end of the second decade of the nineteenth century, the system, for the most part unco-ordinated, was as complete as it ever would be, providing an intricate and interlinking network from coast to coast. At their peak, and with constant development and improvements, some 4,200 miles of canals, built by men like Brindley, Telford and Rennie, carried an estimated thirty million tons of raw materials and manufactured goods a year, bringing commodities to and from the harbours and sea ports as well as coping with much internal traffic.

The canal boats were drawn by horses walking the tow-paths; there were also passenger boats on many routes until the gradual development of the railways threatened and then took over not only the people but much of the merchandise as well. Even the advent of steam-driven canal boats could not halt the decline, and the gradual breaking-up of the canals as a comprehensive inter-locking system, a system that today's generations are again beginning to recognise for its real worth.

In present terms, inland waterways, both canals and rivers, are now in most commercial respects past their heyday. But this Victorian and pre-Victorian legacy is still of importance: nearly 1,000 miles of canals are still maintained by the British Waterways Board and other bodies, for the use of freight-carrying barges and other vessels. Most of the commercial boats and barges that use these inland waterways are privately owned, though the British Waterways Board itself operates two barge fleets as well as inland docks, warehouses and freight-terminals.

Canals and waterways are most excitingly coming into their own again today in the field of sport and recreation, assisted by post-war legislation and co-ordinated planning. Sailing, fishing, canoeing and many other sports are becoming increasingly popular and the British Waterways Board maintains around 2,000 miles of navigable canals suitable for cruising (this includes the figure mentioned above), quite apart from their 960 miles of other waterways. A further 1,600 miles of navigable waters are controlled by other bodies.

Canal-barge and river pleasure-cruiser holidays have a growing appeal to people who, with little day-to-day access to open waters and the sea, prefer to explore the English countryside with little to worry about in terms of navigational skills, boat-handling ability or stormy weather. The charm of canalside pubs, of travelling considerable distances away from the noise of cars and motorways is considerable. Inland waterways are also there to be enjoyed by canoeists, ramblers, anglers and nature study enthusiasts; the cruisers that can be hired have, themselves, a flavour of a different age. Many are not at all dissimilar from those one can, for example, see today at the Waterways Museum at Stoke Bruerne on the Grand Union Canal.

The importance of canals and river systems in historical terms, was to bind inland development with the ports and, through them, with coastal and foreign trade. It is, for example, notable that many of the magnificent churches and cathedrals of eastern England were constructed on their sites due to the presence of water nearby and built in their present form because it was possible to carry the necessary stone to the site by water. Even today, sea and water transport is still among the cheapest ways of moving raw materials.

Some canal boats are still drawn by horses – now for the pleasure of tourists. This picturesque scene is on the Shropshire Union Canal at Chester.

Campden Lock on the Grand Union Canal.

The Grand Union Canal

The Grand Union Canal connects London with Nottingham and the River Trent via Northampton and Leicester; for, with the completion of the Midlands' canals, it had become necessary to cut a waterway to London to link these two trade centres.

The Grand Junction Canal, now the longest section on the Grand Union system, was begun in 1793. From then until its completion in 1805 the Grand Junction offered almost insuperable difficulties to William Jessop, the engineer, and his assistant, James Barnes. Two long tunnels had to be cut through the intractable ironstone outcrops at Braunston and Blisworth, which consumed much time and money. The Blisworth tunnel alone held up completion of the canal for several years. During this period a tramway was used to carry goods over the hill to connect the two parts of the uncompleted cut.

The canal system revolutionised the transport of people and goods, in a way hard to imagine now. According to *The Times* of 19 December, 1806, troops were sent from Paddington to Liverpool by canal, the journey taking 'only' seven days, with the added advantage that the troops were not fatigued.

The last of the eight branches to be cut on the Grand Junction Canal was the Slough arm, completed in 1883. Regent's Canal is part of the system and, with the Thames, encircles the heart of the capital. In a spectacular accident a boat loaded with gunpowder blew up under the iron bridge at Regent's Park in 1874. Rebuilt, it is still called 'Blow Up Bridge' by present-day boatmen. A steam tug for towing barges through the Islington Tunnel was put into service by the Regent's Canal Company as early as 1826, and was used for many years.

In 1929 the Grand Union Canal system was formed by the amalgamation of several canal companies. By 1932 some 272 miles of canal had been absorbed.

On 1 January 1948 the waterways were nationalised and in the following year the *Transport Act* brought most of them into one unified system under the British Transport Commission. With the *Transport Act of 1962* the Commission was abolished and the British Waterways Board took over responsibility for Inland Waterways.

The Grand Union Canal ceased to be used for commercial cargo only around 1970, although there are still occasional coal boats selling domestic coal over the side of the boat. From the 1950s holiday cruising has become increasingly popular, the vast majority of canal traffic being private boats or hired pleasure boats; many old carrying boats have been fitted out as floating homes.

The Waterways Museum is located on the Grand Union Canal in the village of Stoke Bruerne, Northamptonshire. An old grain warehouse is used to display exhibits giving insight into the way of life of two centuries of working boatmen and their families. Among the displays is a full-size replica of a 'butty' boat cabin and outside, by the lock, a boat-weighing machine once used to ascertain the correct toll charges. The entrance to Blisworth Tunnel, the longest tunnel still in use on the waterways system, is only a short walk along the towpath. PP

9 Gateways to the Sea: Fishing Ports and Yacht Havens

The medium-sized and small harbours of England also have a fundamental role to play in the economy and life-style of her people. The survival of these smaller havens frequently depends on two staples: the fishing industry and water sports, especially yachting.

Many of these harbours have long and fascinating histories, some being much older than the enormous ports that have now superseded or bypassed them. They grew and developed to serve local needs and interests, each often with its own fleets of fishing smacks and trading boats involved in coastal traffic. Many are only a shadow of what they once were because of the decline in many local industries, particularly fishing, and the improvements in land transportation by road and rail. But many other famous examples have embarked on a new lease of life with the enormous increase and interest in water sports of all varieties and types. Equally, tourism has ensured that the more attractive of England's little fishing villages and ports, have become known in new, exciting and profitable ways.

With its geographic position and the richness of its seas, England has long depended on fish as one of the staples of its diet. The fishing industry, though currently going through a very difficult time, still plays an important part in the economy. Among the principal fishing ports are Hull, Grimsby, Fleetwood, Lowestoft, Plymouth, Brixham and Falmouth, though there are a number of others with sizeable fleets. In all, there are only 8,000 people employed full-time in the industry, the number having decreased dramatically in recent years. In some areas the drop has been by as much as fifty per cent in a decade, although this does not, of course, include the many thousands who are employed on a part-time basis or the increasing number who run one-man operations or fish the seas for pleasure. While fishing is therefore a considerable employer in some areas, it is an industry that has become more and more capital intensive and at the mercy of a wide variety of international pressures. It is for this reason that successive British governments have paid much attention to negotiating international agreements, particularly in respect of conservation of existing fish stocks, and ensuring the protection of England's traditional fishing grounds both in British and international waters.

Despite these efforts, England's deep-sea fleet continues to diminish. At the end of 1978 it numbered only about eighty vessels, operating out of

Sweeping beach at Salcombe, the most southerly resort in Devon.

ABOVE *Charming view of Lyme Regis, Dorset. 'Regis' was added when Edward I used the harbour during his wars with the French. Jane Austen visited Lyme Regis in 1804 and described a holiday, no doubt similar to her own, in* Persuasion.

OPPOSITE *Lyme Regis has been a seaside resort from the eighteenth century, and a port from medieval times. Locals and visitors still find pleasure and profit in the sea.*

Hull and Grimsby, and since then, many more boats have ceased operation. These deep-sea boats are of two basic types: the traditional 'side trawlers' that preserve their catch on ice, and the more modern freezer/factory stern trawlers. Their main fishing grounds used to be the eastern Arctic, but unilateral claims to these areas and quota agreements have reduced their operations, and many have now turned to North Sea and coastal waters that were previously fished only by the inshore fleet.

Traditional catches have been cod, haddock, herring and mackerel, but in recent times the attention of the industry has been forced to turn more and more to fish farming in order to survive. Equally, fish by-products, for example, fish meal for animal feed, are important new markets which are being researched and developed by the White Fish Authority and the Herring Industry Board – the two organisations charged with controlling and improving the lot of the industry generally. They keep marketing under constant review, given the fact that Britain is a considerable importer of fish as well. On average, each person in England eats thirteen-and-a-half pounds of fish per year.

Government legislation and international agreement, particularly with the EEC countries, has been a fundamentally important factor in the recent history of the industry. The fishery limits claimed by many countries have, since 1977, been extended on average to 200 miles. The UK has made no such claim, so members of the EEC have negotiated rights in being able to fish up to the twelve-mile limit from our shores and in certain instances up to the six-mile limit. No foreign vessels are allowed to fish at all inside the six-mile limit. These and other Community agreements, for example on the size of catches, have led to many problems and disagreements within the industry. One of the main problems is the conservation of fish stocks, particularly herring; this need must be balanced against the aspirations and economics of the fishing industry generally. A satisfactory solution to these problems has been a goal of successive governments, but at the time of writing, few in the industry are optimistic about the eventual outcome.

The great English sport of yachting has a distinguished history and from earliest times it undoubtedly was very much a 'sport of kings'. Indeed the yacht was originally thought of as a king's vessel, but from the seventeenth century on it has been the general term for more or less any pleasure craft.

From the first, yachts with full-time crews were raced for wagers. One such race was recorded by the famous diarist John Evelyn in the year 1661. It was held on the Thames between the yachts *Katherine*

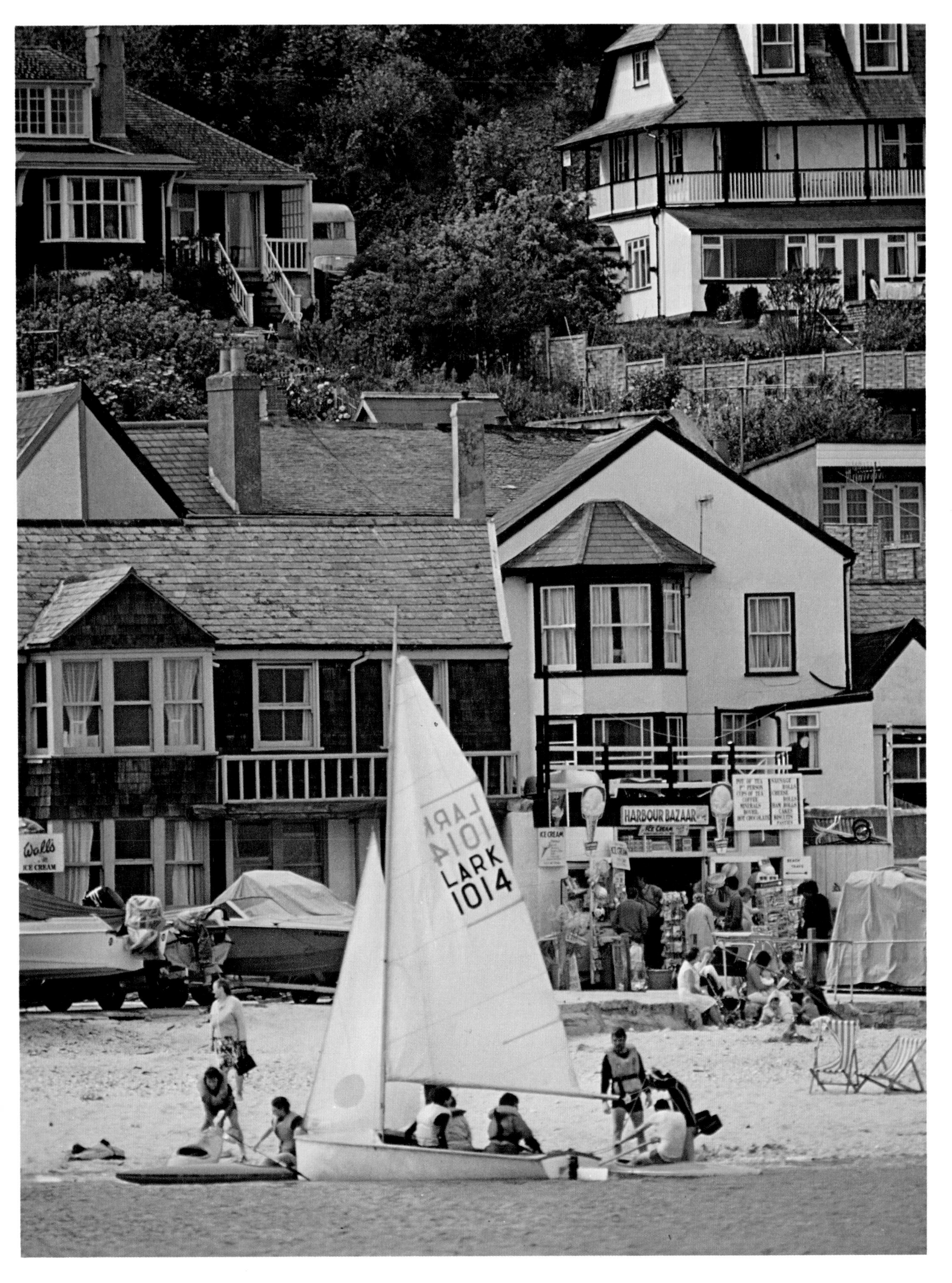
Wall's
ICE CREAM
LARK
1014
HARBOUR BAZAAR
ICE CREAM

and *Anne*, the one belonging to King Charles II, the other to the Duke of York. Consistent reports of yachts and yacht racing occur only in the late eighteenth century. A favourite centre has always been the Thames where the Royal Thames Yacht Club was founded as early as 1775. That other great home of English racing, Cowes, was becoming popular around that time as well, though it was forty years later before the first of its distinguished yacht clubs was founded.

The racing yachts in these early days and indeed up to the 1900s, were all large, professionally crewed, vessels. Since there were high stakes to be won and no attempt to introduce any handicapping system based on size, the tendency of the necessarily rich owners was to go for ever larger vessels, some of which reached a massive 300 to 500 tons. During the first half of the nineteenth century, yacht design tended to be based on the styles of the fast revenue or customs cutters, which were a mixture of fore and aft and square-sail in rig. It was however gradually realised that the yachts themselves, carrying no cargo, did not need to be quite so bulky, and a gradual tendency developed to make them ever more streamlined. But it is a sport in which traditions tend to die hard, and various experiments at smaller cutters and schooners were not always greeted with any enthusiasm or blessed with much success.

One of the great dates in yachting history came in the year 1851 when the US yacht *America*, a schooner of 170 tons, came to Cowes and won a race round the Island to win what was to become the

ABOVE *Trawler fishing at Leigh-on-Sea, which predates the better-known and nearby Southend, with regard to fishing and smuggling.*

foremost cup in yachting, the 'America's Cup' presented to it by the Royal Yacht Squadron. Apart from ushering in this most famous series of all yacht races, the success of the *America* tempted some English builders and owners towards a much smoother streamlined hull, and sails of a lighter and more sheer cut. Despite this, most English yacht-builders retained their cutter styles for many years thereafter.

By the end of the nineteenth century, yacht racing and cruising for pleasure were well established; there were now many yacht clubs in existence all round the English coast. New designs were constantly being tried, and Royal blessing continued to be given to the sport, particularly with the construction by Edward VII of the yacht *Britannia* in 1893, when he was still Prince of Wales. England's builders also kept a wary eye on the increasing success of the Clydeside yards as much as on the American designs over this period.

In the first decade of the twentieth century, internationally accepted rules were first introduced by which yachts of all different sizes and shapes could be classified, and, consequently, handicapped.

After the First World War, the major development was towards a more common use of the so-called Bermuda Rig – the triangular fore and aft sails which are now more or less standard on yachts of all classes, with the spinmaker for the racing classes. At the same time, both national and international competitions were arranged in increasing numbers, though the sport inevitably continued to be one for the rich.

In the post-Second World War period, with the exception of the top class ocean-going yachts, the tendency has been towards smaller and more economical vessels of identical design, to suit the pockets of an ever-increasing number of enthusiasts. Glass fibre as well as other plastics have also revolutionised design, performance and maintenance. Dinghy racing has, particularly in the last two decades, developed very rapidly indeed, with a myriad of classes to choose from. Multi-hulled vessels such as catamarans and trimarans, have also become popular because of the high speeds that can be achieved even in light winds.

Sailing regattas are held at many of England's smaller seaside towns and few of these do not boast their own yacht or dinghy clubs to cater for the enormous range of craft now in popular use. The Royal Yachting Association has over 1,400 affiliated

OPPOSITE *Stern freezer trawler. After about eight weeks at sea the trawler returns to port with up to 650 tons of gutted and frozen fish on board.*

clubs throughout Britain. But it still tends to be the big international races that attract public attention: Cowes Week (each day's racing organised by a different club), the Fastnet Race, the Admiral's Cup (the latter two being organised by the Royal Ocean Racing Club), and (most dramatically) the sponsored Trans-Atlantic, Round Britain and the single-handed round-the-world, races – the most hazardous of all.

* * *

Since the days of Charles II there have been many Royal Yachts which, until the present reign, were mainly used for pleasure purposes. In 1951 however, it was decided to build a new Royal Yacht, *Britannia,* to replace its fifty-year-old, totally unseaworthy, predecessor, the *Victoria and Albert*. *Britannia* was built with a dual purpose role – Royal Yacht in peacetime and hospital ship in times of war, with the Royal Apartments designed for easy adaptation to medical wards. *Britannia* was launched in 1953 and

A Great Yarmouth lugger unloading its catch of herring; from a publication of 1829.

Fish Farming

The rivers of England and the sea around have been harvested for their fish from ancient times. The fish were driven into a bay or inlet where they were then trapped when the outlet was blocked with mud, wicker or stone, the fish being kept alive for a time until they were needed. Later, netting was used and most recently experiments have been carried out with air-bubble screens or electric fences. However, keeping fish in enclosed water may lead to lack of oxygen, variable water temperature, disease and death.

In medieval times almost every village, castle and monastery had its own fish ponds; thousands of archaeological earthworks of these ponds remain all over England. The first documentation of fish farming in the sixteenth century indicates that the skills involved were well established in the medieval period. Highly organised, fish farming included breeding fish and transporting them, sometimes over long distances, to restock the ponds of others. Religious foundations often had complex water-works which fulfilled several needs. At Norton Priory Museum, Runcorn, Cheshire there is evidence that the monks used a huge moat, then in existence, as their fish pond and to run a watermill. A variety of examples exist.

Modern fish farming, less than twenty-five years old in England, is usually carried out in ponds, and includes the supervision and regulation of reproduction, feeding, quantitative growth and control of the size of the fish as well as the stocking and maintenance of the ponds.

Britain led the world in developing techniques for culturing shellfish and marine flatfish, but remains one of the smallest producers. In rivers and ponds current production is mainly trout for the table and for restocking, as occurs at the Bibury Fish Farm in the Cotswolds. Atlantic salmon, mussel, oyster, eel and experimental batches of turbot and Dover sole are also included in the output, which has increased twenty-fold in ten years. At present commercial risks are high, but so too is the scope for growth.

As international competition for the harvest from the sea intensifies, fish farming increases in importance. The problem of ensuring stable fish supplies is aggravated by a heavy depletion of some natural stocks and by the difficulty in achieving a common fisheries policy in the European Community.

Good husbandry is the basis for successful fish farming, but great contributions can be made by scientific breakthroughs. These hopefully will include improved low-cost systems of water-recirculation. At present there is a tremendous diversity of experience and method of operation, which extends to marketing and profitability.

The layout of one hatchery.

A criticism of fish farming in 'intensive' systems (where additional food is given), is that it wastefully converts protein (mainly from fish) of one form into another of a higher quality. Fish meal, however, is mainly produced from low-grade 'industrial' species which do not seem to be acceptable in the human diet; the dietary preference for fish in England tends to be for carnivores.

In the Test and Itchen valleys of Hampshire, where the quality of the water is exceptional, fish farms abound, causing concern to riparian owners and angling interests who feel that the wild fish may be harmed by pollution and overwhelmed by escapees. Evidence of this actually happening is scant. The wild fish in some areas have been encouraged by deliberate policy for 50 years.

The Fish Farming Committee of the National Farmers' Union has applied to the Ministry of Agriculture Fisheries and Food for the adoption of a system of regulation, including licencing. Such licencing will eliminate many problems, so that all groups harvesting the rivers can be accommodated. PP

ABOVE *The Morgan Cup Race, Cowes, organised by the RTYC and the Royal Ocean Racing Club. The cup has been raced for almost every year since 1929, over various courses in the Channel.*

Royal Thames Yacht Club

The origins of the Royal Thames Yacht Club are somewhat obscure. The first records date from 1775, although it is most likely that the club was in existence before then, possibly dating from 1749 when a sailing match was held on the Thames. The race was from Greenwich to the Nore with a plate being presented by the Prince of Wales. There was organised pleasure sailing and racing on the Thames from the mid-1770s.

On 23 June 1775 what was probably the first regatta to be held in England was organised by the club, known then as the Cumberland Sailing Society or the Cumberland Fleet after the Duke of Cumberland, brother of George III and their first patron. According to the *Public Advertiser* the organisers, 'several very respectable gentlemen, proprietors of sailing vessels and pleasure boats on the river', drew up their craft opposite Ranelagh Gardens (a popular pleasure and entertainment centre then on the river in Chelsea), so as to stay out of the way of competing boats. There is no mention of the boats that took part or who won but some entertaining details do remain:

> . . . The whole procession moved in a picturesque irregularity towards Ranelagh. The Thames was now a floating town. All the cutters, sailing boats, in short, everything from a dung barge to a wherry was in motion . . .

The first meetings of the club were held in Smith's tea gardens in Vauxhall, and between 1775 and 1815 the Cumberland Sailing Society was the only one in the world regularly promoting sailing.

In 1823 it became the Thames Yacht Club and in 1830, with William IV as patron, the Royal Thames. The club has been involved in many famous races which have now become legendary, including the 1851 Round the Island Race, the early America's Cup challenges and the Golden Jubilee Round Britain race.

Today the club's main interest is ocean racing, specifically level rating racing, which is racing level without a handicap. The Half Ton World Championship is one such event, held in Poole Bay in 1981. National championships are also held. Longer races usually follow a triangular course: Poole, Cherbourg, Le Havre, Poole. The Royal Thames Yacht Club also organises some of the racing during Cowes Week – a great yachting occasion. PP

commissioned into the Royal Navy in the following year. Not a yacht in the accepted sense, its principal use has not been for pleasure, but to provide a valuable means for The Queen and other members of the Royal Family to make State, Commonwealth and Official visits abroad in a safe, convenient and suitably prestigious manner.

For many people however it is cruising, rather than racing, that has most appeal. Alongside the development of the modern racing yacht has been an equally enthusiastic growth in the number of boats in an enormous range of sizes, in which people with families and friends can explore, in relative comfort, the coasts and waterways of England. This, as much as competitive racing, has led many harbour towns to build and develop special facilities for yachts. Yacht basins and marinas have helped ease the congestion which the growth of the sport has caused, particularly near densely populated areas.

LEFT *The Royal Yacht,* Victoria and Albert *(black ship, centre), at the Review of the Fleet, Spithead, 1887.*

BELOW Britannia, *launched in 1953, enables The Queen to make overseas visits in a safe, convenient and prestigious manner.*

ABOVE *The last crewman on* Camargue *about to be lifted in a Wessex IV helicopter.*

Fastnet Race – 1979

The Fastnet is a supreme challenge to ocean-racing yachtsmen in British waters. In 1979 a violent Atlantic storm struck the 306 yachts as they crossed the Irish Sea, resulting in the tragic loss of eighteen lives. From the first Fastnet in 1925 there had been only one other loss of life.

That 1925 race led to the formation of the Ocean Racing Club, soon to become the Royal Ocean Racing Club (R.O.R.C.) and the governing authority for offshore racing in Britain. The Royal Western Yacht Club of England and the Royal Yacht Squadron are co-organisers of the Fastnet. It is biennial, alternating with the Long Island–Bermuda ocean race. The course of about 605 miles starts at Cowes; the yachts pass the Bishop Rock on the landward side, cross the Irish Sea, go around the Fastnet Rock, and return passing Bishop Rock on the seaward side, ending at Plymouth Breakwater.

In the 1979 race only 85 yachts finished, and twenty-three were lost or abandoned. The disaster was of such proportions that a full-scale inquiry was immediately instituted. Competitors filled out a comprehensive questionnaire, the results of which were analysed by computer.

The storm was caused by a large depression over the Atlantic which deepened rapidly, undoubtedly severe for the time of year, but not record-breaking. There were small areas of extremely strong wind, at times force eleven, with waves of 50 to 60 feet. Although the wind strength was not unusual, conditions were the most serious many knowledgeable competitors had ever experienced – possibly because of the rapid wind veer which resulted in the waves and wind coming from opposite directions.

Many questions arose regarding safety and the official inquiry made a number of recommendations to the R.O.R.C. Some referred to the design and construction of yachts and their watertight integrity, the most serious defect here being the design and construction of the main companionways. Various points were made about safety harnesses, for six lives are believed to have been lost through the failure of safety harnesses or their attachment points. There was 'evidence of shortcoming in the design, standards of, and weather protection afforded by the life rafts.' In short, there are many, many lessons to be learned from this tragedy, which is itself a caution to all who go to sea for pleasure that the sea can soon become a deadly enemy.

In the search and rescue operation more than 100 yachtsmen were rescued by lifeboats, ships and Royal Navy helicopters; the latter – in conjunction with Nimrod aircraft were invaluable, for many rescues took place 60 to 80 miles from land with the yachts spread over a 140-mile area. From the official *Report*: 'The Search and Rescue organisations worked in a fashion which can only excite the admiration of all who can understand the difficulties of the task which they were called upon to fulfil.' PP

OPPOSITE *Pleasure boats in the safety of the harbour at Whitehaven, Cumbria; it is also very much a working port.*

At the same time there has been a rapid growth in motor cruising boats of a wide variety of types. These have developed from the classic and elegant steam yachts of the early days of this century. While there has long been a tradition of condescension in the attitudes of 'real' yachtsmen towards the use of motor power, this branch of the pleasure-boat industry has many devotees. In any event, few yachts of any size set sail without power of some sort or other tucked away for emergency, comfort or convenience. Speedboat racing is also an established and highly dramatic sport, from rubber dinghies

WA39
ANITRA

OPPOSITE, TOP *Sea canoeing: a challenging and exciting sport.*

OPPOSITE, BOTTOM *Shark are the quarry on this Cornish fishing boat.*

RIGHT *Skin diving is increasing in popularity every year. The British Sub-Aqua Club, basically a training organisation, is the largest of its kind in the world.*

BELOW *Motor cruisers at Sandwich, one of the Cinque Ports. The port is now on the River Stour and the retreating sea two miles away.*

fitted with outboards, up to the most powerful and specially designed powerboats built to race long distances and to challenge existing water speed records.

As to other watersports, swimming is undoubtedly the most popular, swimming the Channel being one of the great goals in terms of personal endeavour. Underwater swimming for pleasure (and occasionally for profit, as with treasure seekers) has many devotees and boasts an increasing number of centres throughout England, many of which organise residential courses of instruction as well as holidays for both would-be and experienced divers. It is very much an all-the-year-round sport since, surprisingly, the temperature of the sea does not change dramatically from winter to summer.

Other sports include the most modern one of wind-surfing, and, while canoeing is mainly a calm water sport, there are many places where sea canoeing is practised. The Royal Canoe Club was formed as long ago as 1886 and the sport has developed since then into a highly competitive one with world championships for most classes of canoe. Then there is water-skiing, a sport for the hardy in these northern climes, but still very popular; calm waters are needed which England's rivers and estuaries provide. Sand yachting is practised in a number of places where the beaches are wide and flat, such as Weston-super-Mare: some sand yachts achieve speeds up to eighty miles an hour even in reasonably

The Royal Military Canal at Hythe in Kent. Dug in 1804 to 1805 from Winchelsea to Hythe as part of the defences against Napoleon's expected invasion, it is now an idyllic backdrop for fishing, boating and an annual water pageant.

light winds. Sea fishing, lastly, has one advantage over freshwater fishing: no licences or permits are required. There is even shark fishing – at Padstow and Looe in Cornwall.

As a footnote, that most gentle and relaxing seaside hobby, the delightful pursuit of beachcombing is worth a mention. Who has not indulged in a curious wander among rocks or on deserted sandy shores, discovering and picking up shells, pebbles, sea-shaped pieces of wood and other items of what, more precisely, are known as '*Ejectamenta Maris*'? These are the natural and man-made flotsam (floating wreckage) and jetsam (deliberately discarded items) of the sea. In the old days such items were legally the property of the Lord High Admiral; nowadays, finders, generally speaking, are keepers.

Fishing, sailing and other watersports and a diminishing but still significant coastal trade – these, with tourism, are the main economic activities of the smaller harbours. It seems inevitable that the first will, sadly, continue to decline. But given the fact that people have more and more leisure time available to them, it is, consequently, pleasure-boating in all forms and styles that will allow the little harbours of England to survive and to prosper.

10 Shipbuilding and the Merchant Fleet

Shipbuilding is among the most vital industries for any island communtiy, English shipbuilding being no exception. It is necessary to stress throughout how difficult it is to write about English rather than British shipbuilding, because of the fundamentally important part played by Scottish shipyards. Here we consider the recent past, the present and the future of England's shipbuilding and her merchant fleet.

We have seen how, mainly in southern England, shipbuilding was developed and encouraged after organisations such as the Worshipful Company of Shipwrights received their charter in 1612. Thereafter, many other bodies, including the Institution of Naval Architects, came into being to make their contribution to improving the standards of shipbuilding generally.

It was from the middle of the nineteenth century on, with the coming of the end of the age of sail, and the gradual introduction of steam-driven vessels, that great advances in the technology of the industry were required. To take one obvious example, the pressures and vibration set up by ships' engines meant that wood, lacking the strength to cope, had to give way to iron and then to steel for the safe construction of hulls and superstructure. That the supply of wood for shipbuilding could less and less be met from home resources, coupled with the development, from the time of the Industrial Revolution, of a major English iron-and-steel industry, meant that this transition was a natural and not too difficult one. The use of iron plates also meant that much larger ships with greater cargo-carrying capacity could be built, while steel in its turn was in universal use by the turn of the century. This led to lighter weight and greater strength of hull construction; other light metals for interior and superstructures gave a reduction in topweight and added stability.

This change to iron and steel and the consequent need for convenient supplies of coal had an effect, not only on the design of ships, but also on where they were built. There was a gradual but inevitable move north to the neighbourhood of the iron ore and the coal mines. Today, the main English shipyards are in the north-east, at Barrow-in-Furness and on Merseyside, although there are also yards on the south coast and North Devon.

Some of the milestones in the change from sail to steam and the progression to diesel and on to other forms of power include the first recorded commercial steam-propelled ship in Britain, the *Charlotte Dundas*, which was built in 1801 to travel the Forth and Clyde Canal; there were many other experimental vessels in the years that followed. The change from paddles to propellers as the means of propulsion came rapidly between 1840 and 1850, but even at this stage steam was considered an auxiliary in the aid of sail. It is interesting to note that sail finally disappeared in the British Navy only in the 1880s. The first recorded trans-Atlantic crossing, entirely by steam, was made by the British and American Steam Navigation Company's ship, *Sirius*, in 1838. The journey took eighteen days and, by repute, much of the ship's furniture and one of her masts were burnt to keep up a sufficient head of steam. Iron-built ships of the day included Brunel's *Great Britain* (1845) which was of over 3,000 tons, and a powerful advance in ocean-going design. From then on the increase in size, particularly of passenger liners, was rapid, as builders and owners competed for thriving new markets.

The change from steam to the internal combustion engine took place gradually around the turn of the century, while the diesel engine was first introduced in the years just prior to the First World War.

The most recent and potentially very exciting development in engine design has been the introduction of gas turbines and nuclear power, but these, so far, have been largely confined to naval use.

One of the fundamental problems as far as nineteenth-century shipbuilders were concerned was how to launch ships as they grew and grew in size. Most launches now take place stern first, but some ships were floated out side on from the yards. Brunel's huge *Great Eastern* refused all

Liverpool — the Docks and Shipbuilding

In 1207 King John granted a charter for a new town, which was located on the narrowest part of the Mersey estuary, where there was a short and wide-mouthed tidal creek. The name – Liverpool – probably came from a hamlet which lay on the other side of the 'pool' created in the creek at high tide.

In the seventeenth century the Mersey was a broad, fast-flowing and dangerous river. Only a few buildings fringed the shore and the receding tide left behind a wide expanse of 300 yards of sandy foreshore. On these sloping and protected shores running down to the banks of the pool there were excellent places for constructing ships and launching them. Sometimes even the streets of the town were obstructed by boat-building and there are several references to this activity in the town records of the sixteenth century. An order of 1586 stated that 'no cockboat should be built in the streets in prejudice of the King's highway'.

The supervision and enforcement of the regulations relating to shipbuilding and shipping generally was the business of the water bailiff. With his silver oar as a badge of office and in his livery coat, he (in 1690) collected a shilling for every stranger's ship drawing ten feet of water and sixpence for those drawing less, with half such fees for the ships of the town.

Liverpool first rose to prosperity with the increase in Irish and coastal trade in the late sixteenth and early seventeenth centuries; the Dee began to silt up – a long, slow process – and so this trade shifted from Chester to Liverpool. In the latter part of the seventeenth century and the early years of the eighteenth Liverpool was running equal second with Bristol as the most important port after London. Another substantial contribution to this trade was the infamous 'Liverpool Triangle', in which manufactured goods from the growing Lancashire textile towns, such as Manchester and the salt districts of Cheshire, were exchanged for slaves from West Africa, who in turn were traded for sugar, molasses and spices in the West Indies. This undoubted economic boost stimulated manufacturers and in turn led to the industrialisation of the area.

The first Liverpool dock was begun in 1710, the pool being filled in as part of this project, and the first enclosed public commercial wet dock in Britain, possibly in the world, was also made in Liverpool. Four more docks were built by the end of the century, enclosing thirty acres of water and forming two miles of quays. Liverpool now outranked London in dock space. An economical transport system, tremendously important to a burgeoning trading community, was created with ferries, canals, and railways.

In the last two centuries, with the introduction of ships with a deeper draught, the tidal basin of the Mersey and the depth of water became a true asset. By the 1720s the shipbuilding industry was well-established and thriving. 'View of Liverpool' of 1728 by V. and N. Buck, lithographers, shows eight vessels being built on the foreshore. A few orders were received from the Admiralty and the East India Company. Wooden shipbuilding reached its zenith in 1799 with thirty-one master shipbuilders in the port. These days are recalled in *The History of Toxteth Park* by Robert Griffiths, Liverpool, 1907:

> All along the river frontage of the South end, from Stanhope street to where the Herculaneum Dock now is, (the yards) stretched over a mile in extent. Most of the frigates . . . were built here. It was a general holiday at the south end of Liverpool on the occasion of these launches, and the busy yards of Messrs. Baker, Sutton, Fisher, Barton, Fearon, Wilson and Rogers and Smallshaw, were aglow with bunting as the 'wooden walls of old England' left the stocks . . . At a later period, we have Roydens', Potter's, Miller's, Catto's, Jones & Quiggin and other well-known names . . . A launch was a big day in Toxteth . . . No one thought of working and everyone gave themselves up to rejoicing and festivities. What an army of ship carpenters there was in those days! At the dinner hour, when waiting for a vessel to pass through the old bridge across the Union Dock, they appeared like a regiment of soldiers, and everyone gave way for them to pass first. Ship carpenters received good money in those days; and it used to be a common saying in Toxteth that no ship carpenter's wife would select butter unless she had a sovereign to taste it with.

The docks system along the estuary continued to expand to the detriment of shipbuilding. Liverpool experienced consistently high levels of immigration in the 1800s and by 1901 there were over one million people in Merseyside as a whole. The dock authority required the yard sites which they owned, and the shipbuilders, on short-term leases, were forced to quit – one of the many factors that led to the tremendous decline in

Cammell Laird shipyard today.

shipbuilding in Liverpool. Another important factor was the enormous number of cheap wooden ships launched in North America; by 1854 over half of the ships owned in Liverpool were from the other side of the Atlantic. Liverpool had become the centre of seven miles of docks and was now the premier exporting port in Britain, handling one quarter of Britain's foreign trade. Now almost nothing remains to show that these shipbuilding yards ever existed.

The salvation of shipbuilding in Liverpool was the widespread use of iron and steam engines in ships. In the early 1820s William Laird's boiler works became a shipbuilding operation; the first three ships were built in 1828. This was the first local yard to specialise in steamers and iron construction. Now Cammell Laird, the main shipbuilders on the Mersey today, the firm has a long, colourful, sometimes exotic history, including such famous warships as the Confederate commerce raider, the *Alabama*. Such was the quality of Cammell Laird's building that several of their Victorian vessels survive today in South America. Among these is the iron vessel, *Yapura*, built in 1871 for service on Lake Titicaca in Peru. Renamed *Puno* in 1975, it is still being used as a hospital ship for villages around the lake.

During the First World War a variety of ships were built for the Royal Navy ranging from large battleships to destroyers and submarines. The first all-welded vessel was built, propelled with the firm's own new design of diesel engine. The third *Ark Royal*, the first aircraft carrier, was also built here, as was the fourth ship of that name.

Cammell Laird Shipbuilders Limited is now part of British Shipbuilders. In 1975 the first of the company's standard tankers was launched, and in 1976 the first of a type of guided missile destroyer. In 1978 the new covered construction hall, designed to facilitate production of ships in a factory-type environment, came into use.

A great variety of small craft were also built on the Mersey (and the Weaver) in considerable numbers over the years. The construction of these sailing yachts, tugs, barges, steam and motor launches, life-boats and many other types was carried out in scattered shipyards and workshops, mainly around Birkenhead, Runcorn and Northwich. PP

attempts at such a broadside launch and remained *in situ* for several months before eventually being floated. Problems such as this were gradually removed as the skills of marine architects improved, particularly through the use of models of the ship being used in pre-building trials. Nowadays, increasingly elaborate model-building and testing in simulated conditions in water tanks, goes on side by side with the architects' work on the drawing board.

The years before and after the First World War were those in which the world's great passenger liners and the shipping companies that owned them came into their own. Looking briefly at one of the most famous names, the history of the Cunard Line gives a good indication of the style of the age. The company was founded in 1840 to operate regular passenger services across the Atlantic; it prospered largely because of gaining the contract for the carriage of the Royal Mail. The Line's first ships were wooden paddle steamers, but Cunard kept at the forefront of current developments and thus maintained its position as the pre-eminent passenger line. Famous among its ships were the ill-fated *Lusitania*, the *Mauretania* and then the two great Clyde-built Queens – *Queen Mary*, built in 1936 and *Queen Elizabeth*, built in 1938, both, in their turn, considered to be the greatest of all liners constructed before or since. Since the Second World War, Cunard, faced like so many others by the collapse of the passenger market in the face of airline competition, has been reduced to operating only cruise ships, such as the *Queen Elizabeth 2*.

Launched by the Prince Consort in 1843, Brunel's Great Britain *saw nearly forty years service before she was damaged in a storm. She was then used as a storage hulk in the Falkland Islands until the 1930s, by which time she had further deteriorated and had to be beached. There she remained until 1970 when she was towed home to her original dock in Bristol. Now a museum, her restoration is underway.*

Isambard Kingdom Brunel

Brunel (1806–1859), a civil and mechanical engineer of exceptional ability, is particularly noted for having designed the first transatlantic steamer.

His famous father, Sir Marc Isambard Brunel, was an engineer who solved the problem of underwater tunnelling, and it was on one of his projects – the Thames Tunnel – that the younger Brunel began his own career as resident engineer. But he was injured when one of the shields collapsed and there was a sudden flood of water, an incident which resulted in work being stopped for seven years. While Brunel was recuperating he prepared designs for a suspension bridge over the Avon Gorge, one of which was ultimately adopted – today's memorable Clifton Suspension Bridge.

His numerous engineering feats included designing several docks, and a number of railways in England, Ireland, Australia, Italy and India. In 1853, when chief engineer of the Great Western Railway, he introduced broad-gauge railway tracks, amid much controversy, which allowed trains to attain high speeds. He also built a tunnel and several other important bridges. When building Maidenhead Bridge, which has the flattest arch in the world, he used compressed air caissons to sink the pier foundations.

His contributions to maritime projects were outstanding. He designed three ships, the *Great Western* (1837), the *Great Britain* (1843) and the *Great Eastern* (1858), each of which was the largest ship in the world at the time of launching.

The *Great Western* was a wooden paddle vessel, the first steamship to provide regular transatlantic service. The *Great Britain*, an iron-hull steamship, was the first large iron ship and the first big ship to be driven by a screw propellor. She was one-third longer than any battleship in the Navy. There were sixty-four staterooms, a music room and boudoirs. Queen Victoria visited the ship, and Brunel explained the workings of the ship to her on a specially constructed model. The *Great Eastern* was propelled by both paddles and screw and was the first ship to utilise a cellular double bottom over its entire length. She was large enough to carry in her hold all the coal necessary for a voyage to Australia – a dream of Brunel's. This ship remained the largest in the world for forty years and was equally famous for laying the first transatlantic cable. Only days before she left on her first voyage, Brunel suffered a severe stroke and died shortly after.

Brunel also worked on the improvement of ·rge guns and designed a floating armoured arge which was used for the naval attack on :ronstadt during the Crimean War. 'remendously versatile, he also designed a ompletely prefabricated hospital which was ›ipped in parts to the Crimea.

Many elements of his design, for example, a ›rm of construction later to be developed into ıe modern double bottom, remain standard ractice to this day.

Today the *S.S. Great Britain* is being restored ı her original dock in Bristol. The aim is › restore the exterior of the ship to her riginal appearance of 1843 and to restore nough of the interior to enable visitors to isualise life on board this famous Victorian ner. In time, there will be demonstrations of arious technical features, such as the massive eplica engine, which is now being built. Special ttention has been given to the bow, where the ›rty-two-foot bowsprit stands above the gurehead and trailboards. Beneath the stern allery, a replica of the ship's propeller has been ıstalled.

Visitors can inspect the progress of restoration, ıe historic dock in which the ship was built and a ockside museum – featuring Brunel, the *Great Vestern*, the *Great Eastern* and, of course, the *Great Britain* with her replacement main mast and ınnel towering above all. PP

ABOVE *Isambard Kingdom Brunel and the anchor chain of the* Great Eastern.

LEFT *Brunel's Clifton Suspension Bridge, built in 1864 to span the Avon Gorge.*

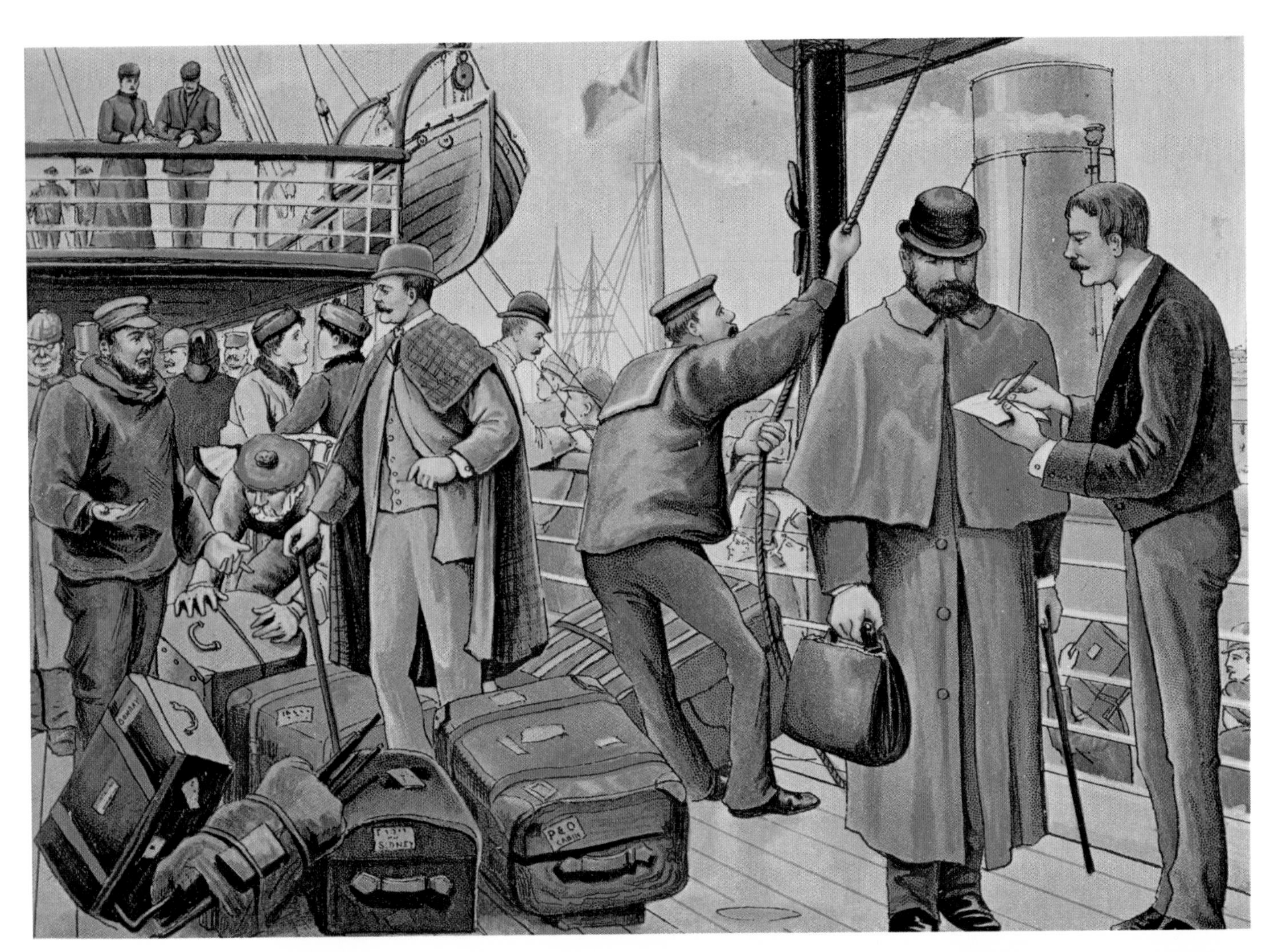

ABOVE *P & O passengers leaving London in the 1880s; from W. Lloyd's* P & O Pencillings.

RIGHT *The Lounge on the* Mauretania, *launched in 1907.*

The Cunard Company's Queen Mary. *Launched in 1934, this trans-Atlantic liner was the ultimate in luxury and speed. Converted to a troopship in the Second World War, she was able to carry over 15,000 troops.*

There are many other famous lines whose history reflects that of the industry, such as the Union Castle and the P and O Lines, which are still among the largest shipping and liner groups in the world. They too were hard hit by the collapse of passenger traffic, but adapted successfully by moving rapidly with the times and changing over to ferry services and tanker and bulk-cargo fleets in order to survive.

Looking at the most recent developments in English shipbuilding, the years between the wars and the post-1945 era were periods when the yards were first badly affected by the depression and then, later, savagely exposed to international competition. This, after a time of complex and apparently insoluble problems, led to the gradual involvement, then a final take-over by the Government.

The 1966 *Geddes Report* in particular proposed that the industry should be rationalised into four major groups, and though, eventually, the reform was much less sweeping, the Government was from then on much concerned in providing both direction and the finance necessary to restructure the industry. Eventually a nationalisation bill was published in 1975, though it did not finally become law by Act of Parliament until March 1977.

At the present time, British Shipbuilders, the body which was formed under the Act to operate both English and Scottish yards, incorporates nearly seventy different trading companies, with more than twenty active yards capable of building a wide variety of different types of naval and merchant ships. The Corporation also operates a number of ship repair establishments which account for around fifty per cent of the value of such work carried out in Britain, as well as companies concerned with the construction of marine diesel engines, offshore equipment and general engineering products. In all, British Shipbuilders make a large contribution to the national economy, in 1979 (with Scottish yards) earning £137,000,000 in overseas sales.

Because of the range of yards under their control, British Shipbuilders have a wide mix of skills and can consequently produce everything from small fishing vessels to the largest tankers and the most sophisticated warships. As far as the latter are concerned, it currently has the greatest capacity for naval construction anywhere in Europe. In order to cope with new developments and markets, they have undertaken an extensive programme of redevelopment, enabling them to produce modern vessels in the most efficient way, taking advantage of the latest shipbuilding techniques.

ABOVE *This sub-sea drilling template, designed to accommodate ten oil-well slots, was completed by Blackwall's in 1980. The huge structure, measuring 50 by 120 ft and weighing 200 tons, was designed by Sedco Hamilton for Occidental Petroleum (Caledonia) Limited. The template is now in use at the Claymore Field in the North Sea.*

OPPOSITE, TOP *The* Queen Elizabeth 2 *dry-docked at Vosper Thorneycroft (UK) Limited for a refit.*

OPPOSITE, BOTTOM *The hovercraft was invented in Britain. This one is at Dover.*

One reason for the current high priority placed on modernisation, is the considerable over-capacity in world shipbuilding resulting from the simple fact that there are too many ships. As a result, international competition for the orders that do come up is intense. Despite this, British yards, through diversification, manage to maintain a hold on a considerable share of world markets, in building both merchant and naval vessels for foreign owners and governments.

Among the range of vessels currently being built for the navies of the world in British yards are fast patrol boats, landing craft, frigates, through-deck cruisers, destroyers and submarines. For merchant navies, they have on their stocks, at the time of writing, standard cargo ships, bulk carriers, refrigerated vessels and have built container ships, passenger ferries, and a range of special purpose ships – lightships, floating cranes, fire ships, dredgers – and a variety of fishing boats and modern trawlers. Very few ships are now built entirely for passenger traffic with the exception of conventional ferries and that particular British development, the hovercraft. This was invented in Britain and has been in regular passenger service here since the mid-1960s.

Hovercraft, which currently operate on cross-Channel services and elsewhere, take about a third of the time of normal passenger ferries, the largest accommodating over 400 passengers and sixty cars.

Finally, to cope with the new offshore oil technology, British (mainly Scottish) yards are currently engaged in building drilling rigs, oil platforms, supply vessels and a host of other types of equipment essential to the safe extraction of the oil necessary for western industrial requirements.

It would be impossible and meaningless to try to break down shipping figures specifically for England, but the British merchant fleet (1978 figures) totals around thirty million gross tons and comes fourth in the world maritime stakes after Liberia (a flag-of-convenience State), Japan and Greece. Her oil-tanker fleet comes in third place, but perhaps most important of all, in terms of age of vessels, we have the most modern fleet in the world. Britain imposes regulations which ensure a greater rapidity of obsolescence than all other maritime nations, particularly because of the high safety factors and other conditions imposed by British owners and the Department of Trade alike. Nearly all the British merchant fleet is privately owned, the shipowners themselves having, as an umbrella organisation, the General Council of British Shipping. Over half the tanker fleet belongs to the major oil companies. The constant pressure of world competition has led many shipping companies, including some of the largest, to work together to ensure best possible use of vessels at most profitable rates. That London is still very much the maritime capital of the world is shown in many ways, including the fact that the major volume of the chartering of cargo ships is still done at the Baltic Exchange in the City.

It is a telling statistic that, despite worries of a recession in shipping and the growth in air cargo handling, eighty per cent by value and ninety-five by bulk of Britain's total overseas trade is still carried by sea; about forty per cent of this is still carried in British registered ships.

As to the future, it is difficult to speculate with any degree of confidence. One thing is perhaps fairly certain: most bulk cargoes will continue to be carried by sea; to that extent, the future of English (British) shipbuilding is also assured, provided that yards remain commercially viable and exchange-rate problems can be overcome. The cost and efficiency of the alternative, air transportation, is unlikely to prove a serious competitor for most purposes in the foreseeable future, provided that speed of delivery is not an increasing prerequisite. But ships will undoubtedly be built with the realisation that they will have much shorter lives, as costs continue to be cut to retain competitiveness and, as a constantly accelerating process, new designs for new

Memorial windows at the Baltic Exchange commemorate the dead of two World Wars – an unexpected reflective corner amidst the frenetic activity of the exchange.

functions are demanded by perceptive shipowners.

Britain's shipyards, building high-quality vessels, will be at risk, not because of inefficiency, but because countries such as Japan will, on present evidence, continue to build at lower overall costs, particularly in labour terms. But given our national maritime needs, our yards should survive on new ideas and initiatives in which fuel-saving must play an ever larger part. As a result, England's shipyards will, hopefully, be able to respond quickly and efficiently to the cargo and military demands of the future.

11 The Royal Navy Today

The end of the Napoleonic Wars left the British Navy with undisputed mastery of the oceans, and it was natural that the task of policing the seas in both hemispheres should devolve upon it. In the Mediterranean, the Corsairs along the North African coast were routed by Lord Exmouth and his Fleet, and the Turkish and Egyptian Fleets were destroyed soon afterwards.

It is, however, a fact that British warships up to the nineteenth century had changed little in design and capability over some 300 years. When the Crimean War ended it was evident that the British Fleet would have to be transformed to take account of the introduction of steam propulsion, the substitution of iron and steel for wood, the change in armaments to enable the new explosive shells to be used by ships' guns and to give those guns the manoeuvrability necessary to make them fully effective.

This transformation took some fifty years, but despite the progress of modernisation, there was such a variety of ships that it was difficult to operate them as a cohesive fleet. Practically every ship differed in armament or speed and even manoeuvres at sea produced great difficulties. Essentially, most ships could only operate effectively in an independent, rather than a fleet, role.

Consequently, in 1889 the *Naval Defence Act* was passed, which provided for the building of ten battleships, nine first-class cruisers, twenty-nine second-class cruisers, four third-class cruisers and

H.M.S. Dreadnought, *1906. She was the first big gun battleship in the world; painting by Frank Wood.*

RIGHT *Sea Harrier jump jet. Harriers now have full operational capability. There are two frontline squadrons – No. 800 squadron is attached to H.M.S.* Invincible *and No. 801 to H.M.S.* Hermes *– and a back-up squadron.*

BELOW *Over forty historic naval aircraft are on display at the Fleet Air Arm Museum, Yeovilton, Somerset.*

eighteen torpedo gun boats. This gave the designers and builders the opportunity to concentrate on standard designs and by the end of the century vast improvements had occurred.

More improvements followed in the opening years of the twentieth century with the increasing threat posed by the other maritime powers, in particular, by the German Naval Rearmament programme. Admiral of the Fleet Lord Fisher, who was then the First Sea Lord, introduced for the first time the big gun ship, H.M.S. *Dreadnought*, which mounted ten twelve-inch guns and was driven by steam turbines – a revolutionary innovation. Between 1906 and 1912, twenty-four battleships of this type were built and once again the Royal Navy was predominant in strength and capability.

Many other classes of surface ship were developed before and during the two world wars of the twentieth century. But it was the terrifying and silent submarine, with its highly effective Whitehead torpedoes, that posed the most serious and deadly threat to ships of all types and classes. During the 1920s another highly significant advance was the birth of the aircraft carrier. This enormously increased the reconnaissance and the offensive capabilities of fleets, and the carrier was for some thirty years the greatest card in the naval pack. Sadly, and despite the tremendous advances in maritime aviation and the skills which it demanded, in historical terms the carrier has had a very brief life due to its enormous expense and its vulnerability in conditions of total war.

The latest and most significant developments which have occurred since the Second World War have been the nuclear-powered submarine and ship, with their unparalleled endurance; armed with long-range ballistic missiles, they have added a totally new dimension to warfare. The ballistic-missile submarines are now the most formidable of the weapons at the disposal of all the modern Navies of the United States, the USSR and the United Kingdom.

In statistical terms, by September 1945, the wartime strength of the Royal Navy comprised fifteen battleships, fifty-two aircraft carriers, one hundred and thirty-seven submarines, sixty-three destroyers, as well as thousands of smaller vessels. The Fleet Air Arm alone was equipped with 1,400 aircraft.

Dartmouth Royal Naval College, beautifully situated above the River Dart. Naval cadets have been trained here since 1905.

This compares bleakly and is in striking contrast to the figures for 1980. Now there are fewer than 200 warships of all types in the Fleet, in addition to some 400 aircraft, crewed and maintained by under a tenth of the immediate post-war manpower. However, in terms of capabilities, one single nuclear submarine, armed with its standard issue of intercontinental ballistic missiles, has more destructive capability than the whole of the British Fleet had in 1945. Equally, modern destroyers and frigates, packed with sophisticated weapons and navigation systems, have introduced a new dimension into maritime operations that makes the numbers game, without regard to capabilities, an increasing irrelevance.

The number of shore bases has also shrunk dramatically in the last three and a half decades. The traditional naval bases were, as we have seen, centred on Chatham, Portsmouth and Plymouth. Abroad, the Fleet sailed out of Malta, Gibraltar, Alexandria, Singapore, Bermuda, Simonstown and Hong Kong. Now, only two small overseas naval bases remain, at Gibraltar and Hong Kong, and the three major Royal Naval Fleets, that did exist, have been contracted into one Command.

But the changes have not all been in one direction. Over the last thirty-five years, social developments, along with sweeping scientific and technological advances, have led to vastly improved conditions of service for officers and men to match the totally new techniques in ship design and weaponry that have been introduced. Where social change is concerned,

ABOVE *Royal Naval College, Greenwich. The superb buildings were, for the most part, designed by Sir Christopher Wren.*

the year 1948 saw one major break with tradition. Over the previous centuries, direct entry into the officer grades of the Royal Navy had largely been confined to those with a certain inherited status in society. For example, naval cadets going to Dartmouth were, with the relatively small exception of the public-school entry, expected to enter at the early age of thirteen. In 1948 this was raised to sixteen and subsequently to eighteen; from then on, criteria for entry hinged entirely on academic ability and personal suitability, without regard to antecedents. In much the same way, the age of entry for regular ratings who had been recruited at the age of fifteen as Boy Seamen, was raised to seventeen-and-a-half.

The training of the modern Royal Navy is pursued on a number of levels, one of the most distinguished centres for which is the Royal Naval College at Greenwich. Here, in one of the finest architectural groups of buildings in the country, Royal Naval officers are given the highest professional training, including courses in Nuclear Science and Technology.

In terms of pay and conditions it has never been possible to establish total comparability between the Navy and civil employment in terms of hours worked, mobility, or the inevitable long periods of separation from home and families. All these factors are now acknowledged so that, in the 1980s, the British sailor for the first time in history is comparatively well paid and his conditions of service are based on a sensible understanding of his way of life.

At sea however, even with the advances and changes in technology, the age-old problem of maximising fighting efficiency at the same time as providing a reasonable degree of comfort for ships' companies, remains as much of a problem in the 1980s as it was in the 1780s. Nowadays the approach is different, and living conditions are looked on as a major, rather than a subsidiary, factor. Bunks have replaced hammocks, recreational space has been provided, and, in all but the older ships, design techniques are now producing the optimum degree of comfort and efficiency in what are still inevitably very confined spaces. More importantly, professional and academic demands on the sailor of the 1980s are immeasurably greater than on his predecessors. The emphasis has, consequently, switched from the making of the all-round 'salt', to the technician who has to acquire a mastery of increasingly complex and expensive equipment.

Given that Pax Britannia is a thing of the past, let us turn now to look other ways in which the modern Royal Navy is equipped for its new role. It finds

OPPOSITE, TOP *Men of the R.N. today master increasingly complex equipment. The four men here control all the mechanical machinery on a large ship.*

OPPOSITE, BOTTOM *Life was harsh for Naval men in the eighteenth century, but there were some moments of ease – as shown in this off-duty scene.*

The Royal Navy Submarine Museum and H.M. Submarine Alliance

The first British submarine, H.M. Submarine *No. 1*, was built by Vickers Sons & Maxim at Barrow-in-Furness to a design by John P. Holland and launched in 1901. She was around the length of a cricket pitch, displaced 104 tons and had a crew of only seven. *No. 1* could dive to around 100 feet and stay down for only a few hours at a time. In 1910, while under tow off the Eddystone Lighthouse, she foundered and sank. Her exact position is known and it is hoped that she will be raised and restored for the Royal Navy Submarine Museum in the future.

From the early days all Royal Navy shore bases were known as 'stone frigates', and even today they are privileged to be named as ships. Thus, the shore base at Fort Blockhouse, Gosport, is known as H.M.S. Dolphin. Dolphin, built on the site of one of Henry VIII's forts, dates from 1905 and is the premier shore base for the submarine service today; some of the Tudor fortifications built to guard Portsmouth Harbour can still be seen. The Royal Navy Submarine Museum, located at H.M.S. Dolphin, probably has the largest collection in the world of models

LEFT *Overview of* Alliance, *now a unique museum.*

›f all types of submarines, numerous artefacts, ›hotographs and displays. H.M.S. *Alliance* aunched in 1947, is now part of the museum. 'his A-class submarine rests on cradles above the evel of high tide with gangways leading to doors ut in the sides, forward and aft, for the benefit of 'isitors, who are able to see every compartment. *Illiance*, fully restored to her serving condition, vas designed for service in the Pacific, but the var ended before she was completed. In the eepest diving class, she could dive to 500 feet, and, with her snort mast, had no need to surface fully for several weeks at a time. In the galley, about six feet by four feet, one chef prepared all the meals for a crew of about 64 – and made bread. She was streamlined for faster and quieter service in 1957 and was finally retired in 1973.

Today the Royal Navy has four Polaris missile-firing nuclear submarines, about twelve nuclear Fleet submarines (still made by Vickers) and about sixteen diesel-electric patrol submarines in service. PP

OPPOSITE, TOP *Rare photograph of H.M. Submarine* No. 1 *with her crew.*

OPPOSITE, BOTTOM *Interior of H.M. Submarine* Alliance *at Gosport.*

The launch of H.M.S. Invincible *by Her Majesty the Queen in May 1977.* Invincible *was built by Vickers Limited at Barrow-in-Furness. She is the first of a new class of through-deck cruiser.*

itself in third place in the league table of blue-water navies after the United States and the USSR. While a nation of the size and resources of the United Kingdom cannot match either of the superpowers in numerical terms, this is made up for in the quality and ingenuity of its capabilities. Thus it continues to play a predominant part in the NATO alliance to which virtually all Royal Naval ships are committed. In particular, the Royal Navy's four nuclear missile submarines maintain a round-the-clock deterrent force, which, while committed to NATO, remain firmly under national control. They operate on a patrol cycle of some eight-weeks' duration. That they do so submerged, yet at immediate call, is indicative of the human resources required. They are to be replaced gradually over the next decade by new submarines equipped with Trident missiles.

As regards surface ships, the first of a new class of through-deck cruisers (also called anti-submarine warfare carriers), H.M.S. *Invincible*, is now in service with the Fleet, as are two others, H.M.S. *Ark Royal* (another in the long line of distinguished ships to bear this name) and H.M.S. *Illustrious*. All accommodate Sea Harrier vertical-take-off aircraft and Sea King helicopters and all are armed with Sea Dart missiles. Two helicopter cruisers, fourteen guided missile destroyers, fifty-four frigates, about twelve nuclear-propelled Fleet submarines, four Polaris submarines and about sixteen diesel-electric patrol submarines, are other main elements of today's Fleet. Some thirty mine-sweepers and minehunters, eight manned by naval reservists, and seventeen patrol craft and offshore protection ships are further essential components of an all-purpose Navy.

As additional strength, Royal Marine Forces, as well as providing four Commando units for amphibious and support operations, are deployed in small detachments in most ships of frigate size and above. The Marines, specially trained to contribute to overall Naval warfare capability, were founded in 1664 and originally known as the Admiral's Regiment. From 1755 they have been a permanent part of British maritime power and from the Second World War, their major role has been centred on commando-style operations. Two Commando Carriers and two Assault Ships today provide the important nucleus of their seaborne attack capability.

An important back-up, a modern Hydrographic Service of no less than thirteen ships, continues to provide material for the traditional Admiralty charts, while some twenty-nine support ships and tankers, many with a world-wide capability,

Ark Royal

Five illustrious ships have carried the name *Ark Royal*. The first, originally the *Ark Ralegh*, was renamed *Ark Royal* when bought by Elizabeth I. As the flagship of Lord Howard of Effingham, Lord High Admiral of England, she took part in the attack on the Spanish Armada in 1588.

The second, built in 1914, was an aircraft carrier. She was renamed *Pegasus* in 1934 to make way for the third, launched in 1937, also an aircraft carrier; after many attempts, this ship was finally sunk by the Germans in 1941.

Queen Elizabeth, now The Queen Mother, launched the fourth H.M.S. *Ark Royal* in 1950. At 50,786 tons, this was the largest warship ever built in Britain.

Continuing the association of the name with seaborne aircraft, a new *Ark Royal*, built by Swan Hunter on the Tyne, was launched in 1981. An anti-submarine warfare carrier, she is third in this class, following H.M.S. *Invincible* and H.M.S. *Illustrious*. At 19,500 tons she is a lighter and more manoeuvrable ship than her predecessor and will do 28 knots. She can accommodate both Sea King helicopters and Sea Harrier jump jets for which there is a 'ski jump' to facilitate take off. The new aircraft carrier provides command and control facilities for the Sea Dart missile system. PP

H.M.S. Ark Royal, *launched in 1950. The last Royal Navy carrier of this type, she was retired in 1978. Once the pride of the Fleet, the fourth* Ark Royal *was sold for scrap in 1980, various campaigns to preserve her having failed.*

A general-purpose Tribal Class Frigate, now part of the Stand-by Squadron.

provide the fuels, provisions, stores and ammunition required on a continual basis by ships of the Fleet.

Successive Defence Reviews beginning in the 1960s have had a profound effect on both the size and capability of the Royal Navy, and on the confidence of and in the Service. This situation is continually changing and, although educational and technical standards required for entry into the Navy are higher than they have ever been, recruiting levels remain good. The Royal Navy believe that, in the face of the relentless build up of the Soviet Navy, it must do the best it can with the resources placed at its disposal by the Government of the day – always the aim of the Senior Service.

12 Hazards of the Sea

From the earliest days, men have placed fixed and floating markers to indicate safe channels, dangerous sandbanks and inhospitable reefs. For England has long depended on the sea for her defence and her wealth, and has always been concerned to ensure the maximum degree of safety for ships sailing in her domestic waters and using her harbours – and she has a full share of hazardous coasts. Only in the past few centuries has this been done to any notable extent, and only comparatively recently has charting and marking the coast been carried out in any consistent and standardised manner.

A first maritime safety requirement is a knowledge of navigation, the history of which is a vast subject. Suffice it to say that, in its primitive stages, inshore navigation consisted entirely of land sightings, assisted, closer in, by the use of leadlines or rods for measuring depths of water. Stars by night and prevailing wind directions were guides used by those travellers venturing further afield.

It was not until the fourteenth century that magnetised floating needles, set against the so-called 'Cardinal Points' – North, South, East, West and their subdivisions, set out on a card – were used as the earliest form of compass. The charts of the age amounted to no more than written instructions which allowed mariners to follow certain coasts with minimal hazard and to enable them to reach harbour safely. Major distinguishing features on the shore would be listed and described, as would depths of water and notes on tides and currents. The modern chart is in many ways only an advanced form of this.

The centuries of growth of England's sea power and her trade led to ever better methods of position-finding and the development of instruments of navigation, such as the sextant. Equally importantly, lighthouses were constructed on dangerous reefs or promontories, standardised marker buoys were placed in channels, as were leading lights and other aids to navigation.

Pre-eminent amongst organisations that have developed, and still maintain, our coastal navigation network is Trinity House. This body is charged with responsibility for the provision of lighthouses and other navigation aids for England, Wales and the Channel Islands (and Gibraltar). It is also pilotage authority for many of the larger ports. Trinity House is controlled by a small management board which runs its affairs on a day-to-day basis. Better known, however, is the largely honorary corporation within the organisation of 'Elder and Younger Brethren' – experienced mariners for the most part – who act as an overseeing body to ensure the safety of shipping in all British waters.

The history of Trinity House dates back to its incorporation, by Henry VIII, in the year 1514, as a 'gild' or 'brotherhood' of 'shipmen and mariners'. The basic reason for its foundation was the widespread concern in the maritime community at so many ships being needlessly lost along the English coastline. The headquarters were at Deptford and the first Master was also Controller of the Navy, thereby signalling, from the first, the close links between the Navy and the Brethren.

In Elizabeth I's reign, Trinity House took over from the Admiralty the responsibility for laying buoys and placing other seamarks including the erection of fire beacons – the earliest form of lighthouse. It gradually gained more and more rights over pilotage, James I giving it exclusive control over pilots in the Thames. By the seventeenth century it was involved in many other fields including the testing of Master Mariners and examining the proficiency of ships' navigating officers.

While many of these functions have dropped away, Trinity House remains the major English organisation connected with maritime safety in all its forms, and has sole responsibility for erecting and maintaining all lighthouses, buoys, and markers, both fixed and floating, including the provision of a number of lightships. In all, they maintain about twenty-one light vessels and many hundreds of lightbuoys. In addition, as a constant reminder of the fallibility of any system, they look after the wrecks of ships round the English coastline. Trinity House also has certain residual and charitable functions in regard to the welfare of seamen.

Aside from Trinity House, certain port and river authorities do have local powers within their own limited areas, but even these are subject to control and inspection by the Trinity House authorities.

For centuries, lighthouses in a variety of forms have played a major part in this process of marking sea-routes and dangerous rocks and reefs. The earliest of them were simple fire beacons or braziers on prominent rocks and headlands which could be lit in time of poor weather. On one or two islands along the English coasts, monks maintained a tradition of keeping a light at the top of their church towers to warn sailors of impending danger, as, at a later stage, did certain civic authorities on watch-towers at the mouths of busy ports. The earliest known lighthouse in England is one erected by the Romans at Dover, which matched another they had built on the French coast; these were used to guide their cross-Channel galley fleet.

Private enterprise lights were, during the periods of greatest growth in maritime activity, built in increasing numbers on dangerous rocks out to sea. For example, the history of the Eddystone Light dates back at least four centuries, the earliest structures being built out of wood, only to be destroyed again and again by storms. Oil-burning lights were introduced in the second half of the eighteenth century: one of the first of these was set up by the harbour authorities on the river Mersey in 1763. Over the years such lights had their intensity and visibility increased, first by the use of paraboloid mirrors, and later by special glass lenses or a combination of both.

Full control over lighthouses came relatively late to Trinity House, since, for centuries, the Crown issued patents or authority to private individuals to operate such lights. The individual paid a rent; in return he was allowed to collect dues, as and when he could, from ships which 'used' the particular light concerned. Because standards varied enormously and the upkeep and maintenance of many of these private enterprise lights was constantly found to be faulty, Trinity House were allowed to buy them out and eventually brought them under their unified control in the year 1836.

Nowadays, on almost any stretch of coastal water round England, one is within sight of some light, each recognisable by a system of varied and timed flashes. This network is backed up by a regulated pattern of floating buoys, some lit, or with foghorns or bells, which are anchored to mark rocks, reefs and approaches. The earliest buoys would have been floats of timber; nowadays they are generally of metal and of different shapes and colours, each indicating, on a co-ordinated and internationally accepted basis, certain navigational rules. The first lighted buoy was, incidentally, introduced by Trinity House in 1880.

Trinity House also run a fleet of tenders which are used to service and support this complex navigational system. They also keep pace with modern technological developments by carrying out constant modernisation and experimentation, particularly with regard to bad-weather navigation aids.

As was mentioned above, one of their additional concerns is the lightships which are strategically placed on major sea-routes where the water is too deep for fixed lighthouses and the danger and traffic density too great to be left to buoy-marking alone. Lightships, each with a crew of five, are always painted red to distinguish them from normal vessels. They are equipped, not only with powerful beams, but also with foghorns and the latest technological navigation techniques. Gradually, however, the number of lightships is decreasing. Some have been replaced by fixed structures based on the seabed, such constructions having only recently become possible with the improvement of underwater building techniques. The once famous lightships, the *Royal Sovereign* and the *Inner Dowsing*, have now been replaced by light towers, while several other ships have been superseded by what are known as 'Lanbys' – Large Automatic Navigation Buoys.

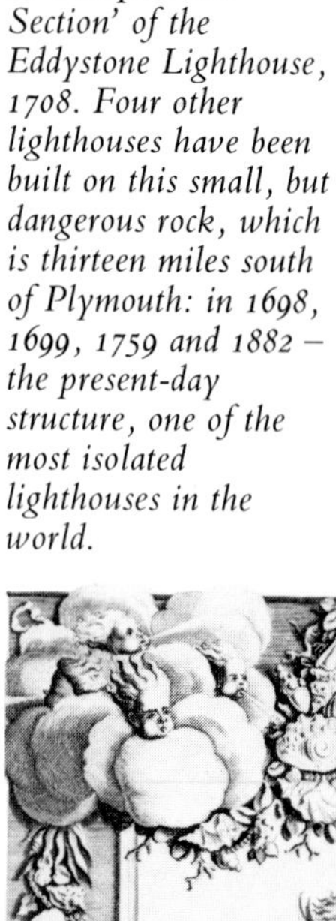
A 'Prospect and Section' of the Eddystone Lighthouse, 1708. Four other lighthouses have been built on this small, but dangerous rock, which is thirteen miles south of Plymouth: in 1698, 1699, 1759 and 1882 – the present-day structure, one of the most isolated lighthouses in the world.

LEFT *Southwold, Suffolk, built on cliffs overlooking the North Sea. The lighthouse is very much part of the town.*

Trinity House is very active in the pursuit of better rules and regulations for sea passage generally, for example, by working with the French authorities and the UN's London-based Inter-Governmental Maritime Consultative Organisation, to ensure a safe traffic separation scheme through the busy English Channel and Dover Straits. Finally, through its scheme for licencing pilots, Trinity House, which is entirely self-financing, ensures the maintenance of the highest possible standards of pilotage for vessels entering English ports and harbours.

Chart-making in England has traditionally been a preserve of the Admiralty. A sea chart is, in essence, a sea map showing coastlines, depths, hazards, buoys and other navigation markers. In their earliest form, they were no more than coastal route guides with information on them on how to follow leads into safe harbour without striking rocks or running aground. The greatest of all the earliest map makers, including Ptolemy and Mercator, gave some guide to early English mariners, but it was not until late in

BELOW *Hartland Point Devon. The cliffs and rocks on this stretch of coast are among the most exciting in the country.*

OPPOSITE *The first light tower to replace a light vessel: the* Royal Sovereign, *seven miles off Eastbourne.*

RIGHT *Very early chart of the Scilly Isles.*

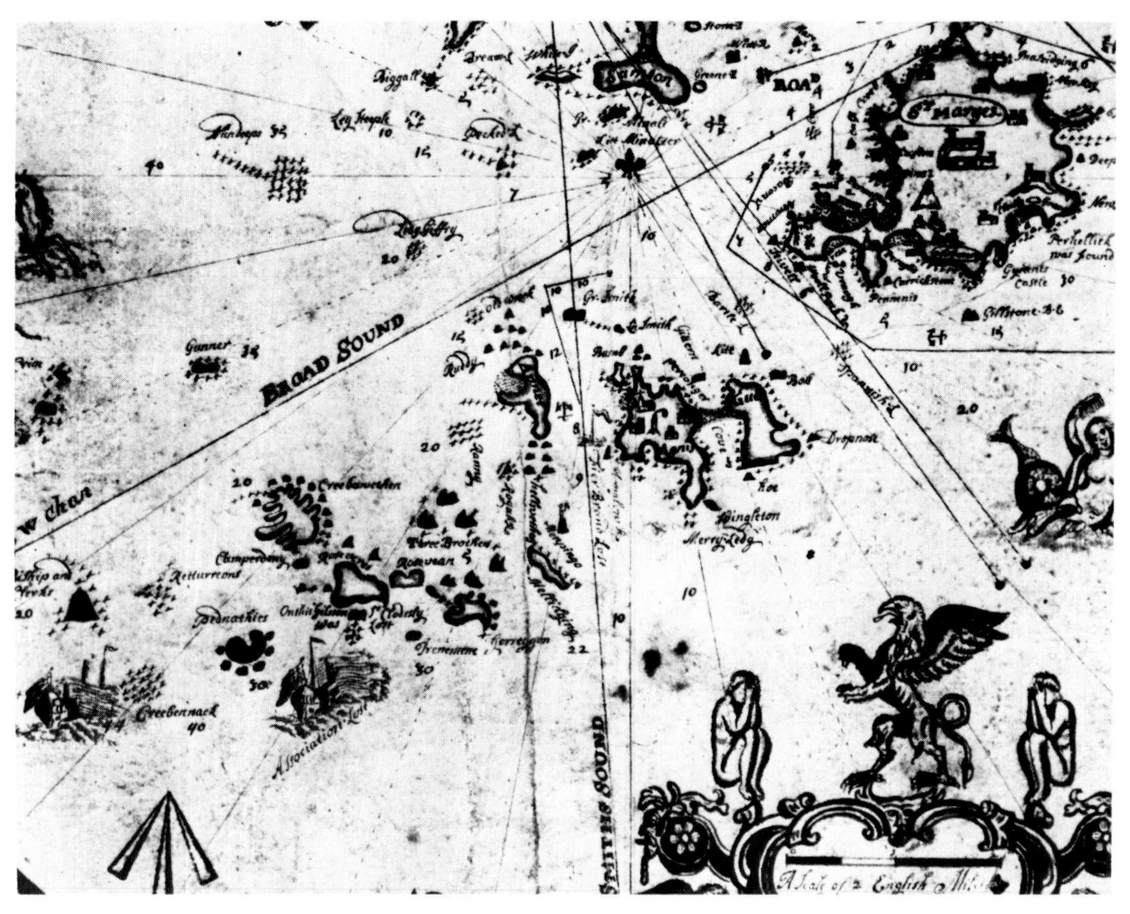

BELOW *Admiralty chart of the Thames Estuary.*

the sixteenth and early seventeenth centuries that any concerted effort was directed at charting the entire coastline.

In 1681, Samuel Pepys, as Secretary to the Admiralty, was among the first to recognise this requirement. He appointed a naval officer, a Captain Collins, to survey all British coasts and harbours. Collins' work *Great Britain's Coasting Pilot* was eventually published in 1693, and for long thereafter was the standard guide to navigation in English waters. In international charting, the name of Captain James Cook is among the greatest in the history of hydrography.

Slowly, through the eighteenth century, new methods of position-finding, such as establishing longitude and latitude, were developed, but it was not until as late as 1880, that international agreement was reached to accept Greenwich (and Greenwich Mean Time) as the prime meridian from which longitude and time at sea should be measured.

The British Admiralty's Hydrographic Service began to produce their own charts in 1801, and since then these have been pre-eminent in terms of overall reliability, and readability. They are the standard to which other nations in the world subscribe. They still provide the most comprehensive available coverage of all the seas and oceans of the world.

Today, the Department of Trade handles overall supervision of the many aspects of safety at sea, in-

Greenwich Observatory on the summit of the Park. Zero meridian of longitude is marked on a brass plaque on the path.

cluding the administration of the numerous Merchant Shipping Acts. Its predecessor, the Board of Trade, acquired powers in the late nineteenth century to inspect ships to ensure their seaworthiness and to regulate, for example, the 'Plimsoll Mark' which merchant ships must have painted on their sides to indicate the levels to which they may be loaded in safety. The Department currently issues many booklets to improve safety at sea, both on ships, fishing vessels and also, increasingly importantly, on pleasure craft. One of the Department's most important subordinate organisations, is H.M. Coastguard Service, which co-ordinates search-and-rescue activities round the coastline. It has a permanent corps of around 600 but many thousands of volunteers back them up by manning their coastguard stations on a part-time basis. Some of these stations are staffed continuously, while others only operate in times of bad weather. They are there to call, as needed, on the air-sea rescue units of the RAF and the Navy as well as on the Boats of the Royal National Lifeboat Institution (RNLI).

The RNLI, which is entirely supported by voluntary contribution, depends largely on voluntary workers and crews for its existence. It was founded

The RNLI and the Ramsgate Life-Boat

The Royal National Life-Boat Institution was founded in 1824, following the publication of *An Appeal to the British Nation* by Sir William Hillary, who lived at Douglas, Isle of Man. Hillary had witnessed many shipwrecks and had himself rescued over 300 people. From the thirty-nine life-boats that were in service in 1824 the number has risen to 258 today, the aim being to reach a casualty up to thirty miles from shore in four hours.

In the history of the RNLI there are innumerable stories of heroic rescue. One of the most famous took place in January 1881, when the Ramsgate life-boat, *Bradford*, rescued eleven men from the *Indian Chief*, a 1,238-ton ship that had left Middlesbrough a few days before bound for Japan. When the ship was about halfway across the Thames estuary and thirty miles from Ramsgate, she struck a sandbank broadside. A great flare was kindled and distress rockets fired, which were answered by both the Sunk and Knock lightships.

When the news finally reached shore, the tug, *Vulcan*, with *Bradford*, the Ramsgate life-boat, in tow, set out. It took almost five hours to reach the casualty, with seas so rough that the *Vulcan* was thrown up like a ball, her starboard paddle clear of the water and with enough room to pass a coach underneath. Coxswain Charles Fish described the wind as the coldest he had ever known, more like a flaying machine than a natural force. By then, night had set in and, unable to see the wreck, they resolved to wait until dawn. With dawn, fourteen hours later, they spotted the wreck – only the foremast remained. In boiling seas, the life-boat went in close and with the seas sweeping over her, took the eleven survivors aboard one by one; the life-boat then rejoined the tug. Both returned to Ramsgate Harbour twenty-six hours after setting out, the waiting crowd stunned by the anguish on the men's faces. Coxswain Fish, a national hero, was awarded the RNLI gold medal, the other men in the life-boat and tug the bronze medal.

While this rescue remains deservedly famous

in the year 1824, by Sir William Hillary who had been much concerned by the great and, in his view, needless, loss of life through shipwrecks. The most famous of early life-boat exploits was that of Grace Darling who, with her lighthouse-keeper father, rescued a number of people from the wreck of the steamer *Forfarshire*, in the Farne Islands, in the year 1838. While lifeboats in one form or another had been in existence since the end of the eighteenth century, Hillary's was the first attempt to co-ordinate their activities.

Round Britain today there are, under the control

The Ramsgate Life-Boat today.

nore than a hundred years later, there are umerous outstanding examples of courage every ear. In February 1979 the Humber life-boat put ut in a force-ten gale, with snow storms and hirty-five-foot waves, to help the Panamanian reighter, *Revi*, which was sinking in the North ea.

The coxswain, Brian Bevan, had to bring his ife-boat alongside the listing freighter thirty-five imes before all of the crew of four were taken ff. On the tenth attempt to rescue the captain, he freighter rose twenty feet above the life-boat nd began to crash down on the life-boat crew vho were lashed to the rails. The coxswain mmediately put his engine hard astern and nanaged to pull clear by a few inches. The aptain disappeared under the waves, but the life-boat went in again, taking him aboard only five minutes before the freighter went down. Bevan was awarded the RNLI gold medal for gallantry, only the second time it had been awarded in a thirteen-year period. The other members of the crew were awarded the bronze. At the same ceremony Bevan also received the silver medal for a rescue in December 1978, when, in appalling conditions, six people were taken off a crippled Dutch freighter.

In 1980 the life-boats put to sea 2,769 times with 1,191 lives being saved. All income is from voluntary contribution. Although the organisation is free from government control, there is close co-operation with H.M. Coastguard and the rescue helicopters of the Royal Navy and the Royal Air Force. PP

of local RNLI committees, around 130 off-shore lifeboats (with a range of some thirty miles) and a further 120 smaller inshore craft. Some of the 200 lifeboat stations are equipped both with inshore and off-shore boats.

It is a telling and heroic statistic that, since the end of the Second World War, while fifty-three lifeboatmen have lost their lives round Britain's coasts, in the process over 25,000 people have been saved by the Service.

The design of lifeboats is constantly under review, particularly with regard to the buoyancy, power and robustness of the boats used. On shore stations one of the most important standard pieces of equipment is the breeches-buoy, which consists of a line-throwing gun by which a light line can be projected to any ship that has run aground. The line is then used to haul a stronger cable from ship to shore along which a harness (breeches-buoy) can be drawn. But increasingly, the most important life-saving vehicle is undoubtedly the helicopter, by which people can be rescued with a speed and reliability that often defeats the most modern lifeboats. The latter will, however, long remain the mainstay of the life-saving services, because, in capacity, endurance and local availability it is still a constant factor independent of Government economics or military requirements.

Ask any seaman for a list of 'safety' aids and the weather forecast will be very high on it; as far as the pleasure- or fishing-boat captain is concerned it will be at the top of the list. Yet meteorology in any modern meaning of the term, is less than a century-and-a-half old. One of the 'fathers' of the scientific study of the weather was Admiral Robert Fitzroy who, after many journeys on the famous survey ship the *Beagle* (on which Charles Darwin also sailed), began to produce weather charts and introduced gale-warning systems – such as the hoisting of warning cones at harbour mouths. Incredible advances in weather forecasting have taken place in very recent years; while the weatherman is still the butt of so many jokes, the use of satellite information weather station reports and internationally accepted standards of measurement, such as windforce (the Beaufort Scale, developed by Sir Francis Beaufort, the nineteenth-century Hydrographer of the Navy), along with a host of other devices, have ensured an increasingly effective maritime service.

But it can all go wrong and, if it does, it is better to be insured. On this basis, the name Lloyd's looms

Grace Darling and her lighthouse-keeper father row out to rescue passengers on the Forfarshire. *Grace became a national heroine, and the story inspired countless writers and artists.*

National Data Buoy

This prototype data buoy was designed and built to enable the U.K. to learn about the problems of collecting meteorological and oceanographic data from a remote station at sea and to successfully transmit this information back to shore. The buoy was built by a consortium of companies: Hawker Siddeley Dynamics Limited, EMI Electronics Limited and Blackwall Engineering (R. and H. Green and Silley Weir in 1975–6). Each was responsible for different aspects of the overall design. The project was funded by the Department of Industry, with technical supervision provided by the Institute of Oceanographic Sciences.

On completion the buoy was placed on station in the southern part of the North Sea, so trials could be carried out. In 1977 it was withdrawn and modified – at Blackwall's – to withstand the more severe conditions of the Atlantic.

In June 1978 it was relocated some 150 miles west of Land's End to provide oceanographic data for the U.K. Offshore Operators Association (U.K.O.O.A.), who are particularly interested in wave amplitude and directional data. It also provides meteorological data for the Meterological Office at Bracknell.

The relevant data is transmitted each hour to Culdrose Naval Air Station at Helston, Cornwall and is then automatically routed by land-line to the Woking Division of EMI Electronics Limited, who are responsible for the present contract. Here the data is automatically checked and made available to the Meteorological Office and U.K.O.O.A.

It is planned to bring the buoy ashore in 1982, after four years of operation. It has had to withstand wind speeds of 90 knots and wave heights of 70 feet. Apart from its routine tasks of helping to provide advance warning of weather arriving from the west, and wave information for the offshore petroleum industry, it gave valuable background data in two severe 1979 storms. One was the storm that devastated the Fastnet Race and the other that which damaged the Chesil Beach defences. PP

The completed National Data Buoy at Blackwall's.

large in English maritime history. Firstly, there is Lloyd's Register of Shipping which was established in the eighteenth century by a group of underwriters as a system of classification of the standards of construction and equipping of merchant ships in order to protect the interests of the insurers both of the ships themselves and of their cargoes.

Secondly, there is Lloyd's of London, the association of these underwriters, which, since the year 1601, has been heavily involved in marine insurance. It also acts as an information centre for the latest reports on ship movements which are published daily in *Lloyd's List*. One of the most famous traditions of Lloyd's is that a bell, known as the Lutine Bell, is rung when there is news to impart of importance to its underwriting members. This occurs, most notably, when confirmation is received that a ship insured with Lloyd's has been wrecked or otherwise irretrievably lost. The Lutine Bell itself came from the French frigate *La Lutine*, captured by the Navy in 1793, and put into British service. It was lost on passage from England to Holland in the Friesian Islands in 1799, when carrying a cargo of one and a quarter million pounds in coin and bullion,

At Lloyd's of London the prominently situated Lutine Bell – from a captured French frigate – is rung when a ship is lost.

and there was only one survivor. Only a small amount of the money was recovered, but the bell itself was salvaged.

Despite the continuous improvement in maritime safety techniques and skills, the hazards of the sea are many. Even the best-equipped ship is at risk as is exemplified by the fact that, at the time of writing, news has just come through that the Lutine Bell has been struck as the result of the disappearance and presumed total loss, with all hands, of a modern well-equipped and tested British cargo ship, somewhere in the South China Seas.

13 'Beside the Seaside'

The seaside is healthy, the seaside is fun.
So off to the briny, to plunge in each one.

In most societies man swims for pleasure. But it was in Victorian times that the great English public was first urged to make an annual pilgrimage to the healthful, bracing sea with its 'briny' and 'ozone', its bathing huts, its piers and its promenades.

Today the typical seaside resort, while usually fully up-to-date on modern attractions and entertainments retains much of what can be considered Victorian folk culture. For the buildings, guesthouses, landladies, whelk stalls, ice-creams, fairs, fortune-tellers and trips round the bay, have been standard items for well over a hundred years. Brash, boisterous and good value for money have been the cries from the Blackpools, the Bridlingtons, the Brightons – well perhaps Brighton is a little different. In all, seaside resorts, backed by a few inland spa towns, are still the holiday goal for the vast majority of the English public. And in case one is tempted to think that nowadays 'most people' go abroad, it's worth remembering that Blackpool alone still attracts around four million holiday makers a year.

In the seventeenth and eighteenth centuries there were already a number of fashionable, and less fashionable, coastal watering places in existence.

By and large, it was in the period of the Industrial Revolution, with the arrival of mass transportation in the form of the steamer and then the train, that gave millions their first easy access to England's beaches. Scarborough was one of the earliest seaside villages as far back as the 1660s; inspired by a certain Dr Wittie, people went for pleasure and relaxation and to take the waters of a local spring for medicinal purposes.

Such taking of the waters both internally and externally had a very much longer history – as the existence of Roman towns such as Bath itself proves. Quite apart from the proven or unproven medicinal benefits of drinking mineral waters – some of which are pretty foul-tasting – there were and are many places whose waters have long had a mystical or religious significance or other presumed healing powers. England has many such 'holy' wells and fountains. Spa treatments, while frequently considered dubious by modern authorities, were probably no better nor worse than other medical practices of past ages. As far as the creation and use of artificial pools for swimming and bathing is concerned, many many centuries elapsed after the collapse of the Roman Empire before the very high Roman standards of internal and external

Sandcastles and dreams.

cleanliness were again aspired to in England.

There is no doubt, therefore, that England's doctors were largely responsible for creating the English seaside. Apart from Scarborough's Dr Wittie, a Dr Richard Russell writing, ninety-odd years later, his 'Dissertation on the use of Seawater in Diseases of the Glands' is credited with having 'invented' not only the seaside but also Brighton, which had, until then, been a little fishing village known as Brighthelmstone. Dr Russell advocated drinking seawater by the half-pint, mixed with port for taste, as a cure for everything from gout to syphilis. And what the good doctor had created was, at the end of the century, given royal patronage by the Prince of Wales who built his seaside holiday home there in the shape of the strangely fascinating Royal Pavilion. Students of building style see the Pavilion's characteristics of oriental design as being the model for much of the whimsical civic architecture soon to appear in other resorts and towns the length and breadth of England. George III gave his blessing to Weymouth and Queen Victoria herself is recorded as having gone sea-bathing in July 1847.

Up until then, Brighton and the other resorts with bathhouses and pseudo-medical establishments by the score, were still watering places for the upper classes. But all that was to change and change quickly. In the mid-Victorian age, the building of resorts accelerated rapidly, a movement driven by the need to cope with the new influx of the middle and working, rather than the leisured classes, the latter until then being the only segment of society able to afford the delights of the seaside.

These new leisure-seekers came from the great cities by steamer; later, when cheap railway transport arrived, the resorts reached their zenith as places of mass entertainment and relaxation. This development was boosted even further by the passing of the *Bank Holidays Act of 1871* which gave people their first real opportunity for carefree, inexpensive outings – Sunday was still very much a day of rest and Saturday a workday. Hotels, ever more grand, civic buildings, long and ornate piers, wrought-iron bandstands, promenades, bathing machines and a blossoming souvenir industry – all were introduced by rival resorts in increasingly imaginative bids to attract custom. To these resorts came entertainers, Punch-and-Judy men, street musicians, Pierrots, minstrel shows and bands, and fairgrounds were built . All of this was backed up by an infant tourist promotion industry that turned out posters, leaflets and guidebooks enticing everyone with the promise of sunny skies, golden sands and the bracing air of Skegness and other towns.

During the first years of this century the idea soon took root that one somehow behaved differently when on a seaside holiday. There was, for instance,

*Some essential features of a popular seaside resort: (*BELOW*) rock at Skegness; (*OPPOSITE, BOTTOM*) merry-go-round at the amusement park, Whitley Bay; (*OPPOSITE, TOP*) cockles-and-whelks stall at Folkestone.*

an almost absolute ban on mixed bathing until the outbreak of the First World War, but beach clothing subsequently became scantier, suntan became fashionable and entertainments like vaudeville, saucy postcards and beauty competitions flourished. The idea of being able to behave unselfconsciously in a way that might seem somewhat inappropriate, perhaps improper, in one's own community still accounts for much of the attraction of sun, sand and sea. Seaside resorts are masters at creating an ambience that gives a raciness and glamour to life, a brief suspension of some of the more tedious realities that prevail in a workaday setting. At the same time sports began to play a bigger role in holiday activity; this was the age in which golf courses, tennis courts and boating for pleasure started being offered as additional attractions to the holiday-makers.

England's seaside resorts experienced a tremendous growth period during the late nineteenth and early twentieth centuries. Today this undoubtedly presents the resorts with many problems: what was built in the past is now suffering – as all buildings do – the ravages of time and taste. Newer resorts on the Continent have been able to start from scratch and very often represent serious competition. On the whole the English seaside has been able to compete, to sustain a healthy level of tourist business while undertaking the important modernisations that the

Brighton Pavilion, the exotic and fantastic creation of the Prince Regent, later George IV. This eighteenth-century extravaganza influenced seaside architecture up and down the country.

RIGHT *The Banqueting Room.*

tourist of the future is going to demand. Often this means treading a delicate balance between what older customers expect and younger customers seek: between alienating the traditional market and meeting the expectations of a new generation. Responding to this challenge, resorts are integrating new tastes into a traditional structure with considerable skill and delicacy. As innovators with a hundred-year-old tradition theirs is not an easy task, but they stand to gain from a large home market that wants easy-going, easy-to-arrange fun at the seaside without the problems of passports, airports, foreign languages and customs of overseas holidays.

With greater mobility there has been a trend towards the farther-away places, the little seaside towns and villages where things are more personal and life less raucous. Counties like Devon and Cornwall, with all their charm, have long been favourites. But there are so many more refuges that are off the beaten track for those who do not demand the company of crowds and amusement arcades. Mass car ownership means that people know more of England's coastline. They travel more; they go on day trips more than ever before; they experiment; they find new beaches and new beauty spots. The style of vacationing and tourism is changing all the time. The resorts must keep pace with changing life styles without losing their charm and architectural inheritance in order to continue to attract – indeed to survive. The growth of interest in sailing and a wide variety of other water sports is one encouraging development for the future. There are many others.

Brighton, for example, has invested wisely in a major new conference centre and a marina, rather than make expensive attempts to revivify past amenities; the piers, previously the main attraction, have problems of maintenance and falling public interest, so new interests have been sought.

All the major resorts, and many of the smaller ones, run tourist information centres according to a standard pattern evolved by the English Tourist Board. People nowadays tend to regard resorts as bases from which to explore the surrounding coast and countryside; the information centres have an important role to play in helping with this, as well as providing data on local events and attractions.

Another trend has been towards shorter and more frequent holidays. Families that used to go to a resort for a fortnight now, more often than not, opt for a week or ten days. Holiday periods are spread throughout more months of the year and the same people may take several different types of holiday – a summer family holiday at the seaside, shorter breaks for the parents only, and weekends or periods of two or three days taken at no great distance from home. Seaside resorts stand to benefit from this new short-break market.

Among the hotels many of the larger traditional establishments continue to flourish in an almost timeless way and there is still a healthy business at seaside boarding houses run by the much maligned

Lithograph of Southsea Common, c.1865. With its stately hotels, promenade, pier, and bathing machines, it was a well patronised resort. Note the early steamship.

OPPOSITE *In a continuing tradition of imaginative posters enticing people to the seaside.*

RIGHT *Bandstand at Weymouth. Intricate cast-ironwork is a feature of seaside architecture. Some of the town's Victorian houses have fine ironwork balconies.*

BELOW *Eastbourne, elegant and festive – and reputedly the sunniest resort in England.*

landladies of music-hall jokes. Today's landladies put a great deal of hard work into providing simple, homely accommodation for millions of families who might otherwise not be able to afford a holiday. Despite this, the stock of serviced accommodation generally has fallen to be replaced by a range of self-catering establishments: flatlets, apartments, chalets, houses and cottages to rent, static and touring caravan sites and camp sites.

English seaside life has a variety of fascinations that still appeal to many people. One of these is the pleasure steamer. While steamers were a feature of many of the coasts of England, it is mainly with Kent and Sussex that they were especially associated. Day-trippers out of London have long sailed down the River Thames, the earliest recorded trip being in the 1820s, when a vessel left the East End packed with people bound for Margate; the journey from London took about eight hours. Figures for the year 1835 indicate an annual influx to Margate alone, mainly by steamer, of over a hundred thousand people. Because it was so popular, it was well recorded in the songs and writings of the age. Similar developments were happening elsewhere: people from the industrial grimness of Manchester and Liverpool went to Blackpool, Southport and the Welsh resorts. Steamer companies vied, often bitterly, with each other, to provide entertainment, refreshment and speed at the lowest possible cost. And when the trippers arrived, they were greeted by a host of subsidiary entrepreneurs, offering transport, entertainment, food and accommodation.

The period of relatively large fleets of paddle steamers was a short one, as mass rail transportation came in rapidly to undercut even the most economic operators. Their numbers dropped, but the steamers were far from finished, since many people preferred,

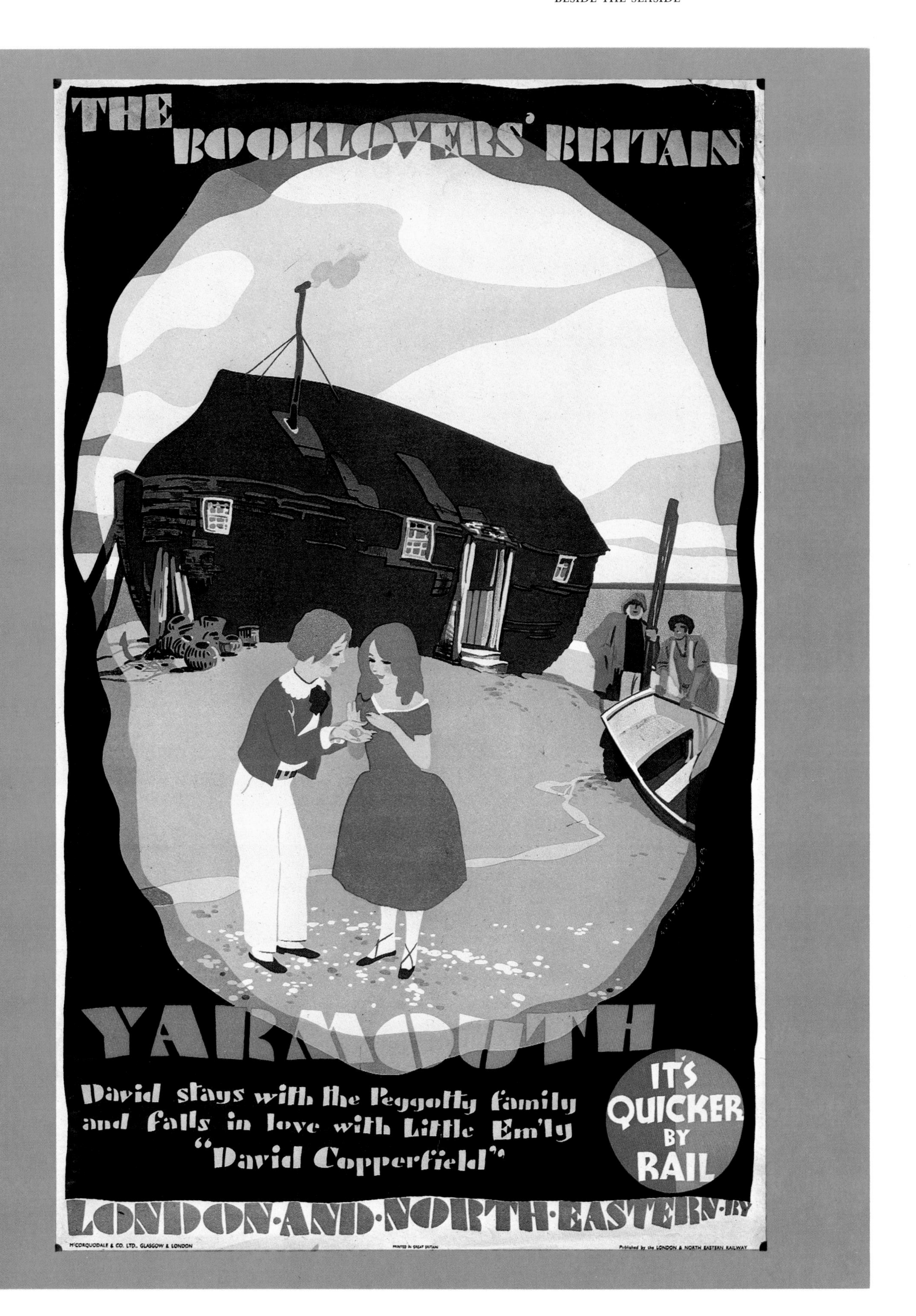
THE
BOOKLOVERS' BRITAIN
YARMOUTH
David stays with the Peggotty family
and falls in love with Little Em'ly
"David Copperfield"
IT'S
QUICKER
BY
RAIL
LONDON·AND·NORTH·EASTERN·RY

and still do, a more leisurely nautical approach to a holiday, quite apart from the delights of the journey for its own sake. Equally, the passenger vessels became more and more luxurious, offering ever more reward and pleasure in return for the fare. New types of steamers were constantly being introduced, but as railway networks and passenger-carrying capacity increased, by the beginning of the First World War only a handful of boats was left.

The most famous of these holiday vessels were undoubtedly the paddle steamers, built on classical lines, highly decorated and easily manoeuvrable in limited space and thus useful for river work and negotiating alongside piers. Some of these vessels had a long and illustrious history right up to the days of the Dunkirk evacuation when a number of these steamers, in J. B. Priestley's words, 'made an excursion to Hell and came back glorious'.

Though tragedy and neglect have taken a heavy toll, no holiday resort was worthy of its name without its pier, its promenade, its formal gardens, bandstands and Winter Garden. Cast iron was the basic building material and the designs were, at the least, highly decorative, at the best, an art form in their own right. Lamps, railings and canopies, were an intricate, often strange, mix of the oriental and the nautical.

Some of the piers themselves were built by famous engineers of the day like Thomas Telford (Herne Bay), and John Rennie (Margate). The piers were built, not only to receive ships and their passengers, but also as giant amusement arcades, the focal point of any resort. They were normally based on wooden piles built out into the sea. Depending on the slope of the shore and tidal conditions, some were both huge and extremely long, length being a considerable prestige symbol. Some were very solid structures; others were suspended between piles like the Chain Pier at Brighton, destroyed in a storm in 1896. There were giants: Brighton's West Pier stretched 1,000 feet into the sea, with Southend the longest at 7,080 feet; others were built sideways on to the shore to hold huge concert and amusement halls capable of seating thousands of people. No one had free entry and the shareholders, the civic authorities or speculators who built them, often got good returns on the takings at the turnstiles.

The recent history of piers tends to make depress-

OPPOSITE, TOP *Looe, Cornwall, a perfect setting for bathing and yachting, and a base for shark-fishing.*

OPPOSITE, BOTTOM *Lympstone, Devon, in the estuary of the River Exe.*

BELOW *St Ives, Cornwall. Artists – the famous and the not so famous – are attracted to the light and the scene, as indeed are the tourists.*

OPPOSITE, TOP *Colourful part of the seaside scene.*

OPPOSITE, BOTTOM *A river trip on the Thames, Easter Monday about 1850.*

RIGHT *Hythe, Kent. The shingle beach of this resort, safe and secure in pleasant weather, is sometimes over-topped by the sea in violent storms.*

BELOW *Margate pier, built by John Rennie and one of the most famous in the country. Beautiful sands and the huge 'Dreamland' amusement park make Margate a most popular resort.*

ing reading. Many of the more original and ornate were sadly lacking in the strength necessary to withstand storms or the usual ravages of time, such as rust, rot and erosion. Many became derelict; others, through neglect, possibly in wartime when people had neither time nor money for the upkeep of souvenirs of a more frivolous past, have had to be dismantled. But there are still around fifty resort piers – 'amusement piers' if one likes to be more precise – around the coasts of England. Some of these remain profitable and popular, their functions having been adapted to modern tastes and demands, like the three that remain the hub of Blackpool life. The future of the rest hangs in the balance between the enormous costs of repair and maintenance and the determination of individuals and organisations to conserve a valuable part of the English maritime inheritance.

It is highly unlikely that new piers will be built for pleasure, so we must necessarily guard those that exist. For a lucky few rescue seems to have arrived. At the time of writing it was announced that, as a result of a concerted campaign by conservationists, Southend Pier was saved a mere twelve days before it was to be finally closed. A private company has taken over and will be spared having to pay rates by the local authorities. Similarly, Clevedon's century-old pier has been saved, provided the trust that runs it can raise the million pounds needed to restore it.

Blackpool

Before the arrival of the Romans the area round about Blackpool was thick with oak and impassable bogs. Much later, records dating from 1416 refer to 'Le pull', a pull or pool, the stream that drained Marton Mere into the sea. The peat lands through which the stream passed discoloured the water, hence Black Poole. By 1602 a collection of cobble and clay huts were spread along the coast near the 'Pool' and by the end of that century a number of the landed gentry had settled in the area.

The first visitors were drawn to Blackpool in the 1720s by the promise of the healthy attributes of the sea. Soon the first cottage was made over to visitors and by 1780 four substantial hotels had been built – all still in existence.

When William Hutton, a publisher and historian from the Midlands, visited Blackpool in 1788 he described what he saw:

> The sea coast at Blackpool forms a strait (*sic*) line for many miles. The bank or cliff, which is clay, rises various heights, from three feet to sixty feet above high water mark. Although about fifty houses grace the sea-bank it does not merit the name of a village because they are scattered to the extent of a mile. . .

Hutton also described the recreations enjoyed by visitors. The rich rode in carriages or on horseback along the sands while poorer visitors 'find equal pleasure in using their feet'. Of the promenade, a two-hundred-yard length of grass, six feet wide, he says, 'A perpetual assemblage of company, when the weather permits, may be seen upon this elegant little walk'. There were bowling greens, facilities for archery and 'a place dignified with the name of The Theatre; if that will bear the name, which, during nine months in the year, is only the threshing floor of a barn'. But the sea, then as now, was the principal attraction. A bell was rung when it was time for the ladies to bathe, and any gentleman found on the shore was fined a bottle of wine.

The 'Father of Blackpool', Henry Banks, and the coming of the railway in 1846, albeit with some difficulties, soon transformed the resort and brought an entirely new Blackpool into being. The town was scarcely prepared for the thousands of visitors from Lancashire and Yorkshire, who could now reach it with comparative ease. There were still only 420 dwellings, gas lighting was a year away and piped water thirteen years away.

The North Pier, designed by Eugenius Birch, was opened in 1863 and soon became a promenade for 'quality' visitors. It is now a listed building. The Central Pier – with its open-air dancing for the 'working classes' – and the Victoria Pier (now the South Pier) were added. Pleasure gardens, an aquarium, Winter Gardens and an Indian Pavilion followed.

In 1879, in the midst of a depression that threatened the newly created borough, the Council decided to hold a grand fête and carnival on the sea to publicise the installation of the world's first electric arc street lighting. This event featured a 'Naval Attack on Blackpool' which was watched by up to 100,000 people on the promenade, piers and ships – the beginning of the Blackpool 'Illuminations'.

The 1890s saw the development of many of the resort's most famous attractions – the Opera House, the 'Eiffel Tower', a permanent circus, a ballroom and the 'Gigantic Wheel' (each carriage held thirty or more passengers).

In this century the transportation system was improved, itself outdated by the 1960s leaving the Promenade trams as the only commercial electric tramway in England. Between 1902 and 1905 twenty-two acres were reclaimed from the sea in the building of the Promenade between the North and South piers. At about the same time the foundations of the Pleasure Beach were laid in the sand dunes beyond South Shore – for many years the home of gypsies and fairground artists. One of the very first rides, Sir Hiram Maxim's Captive Flying Machine (1904), remains today, though in a somewhat different guise. Innumerable attractions have been added to create the present forty-acre fun park.

The Illuminations as such were erected in 1897, 1912 and in the following years, with a few interruptions, until the present day (now from September to November).

The principal role of Blackpool in the 1980s is that of a holiday resort with the tourist industry employing thousands of people. There is also a variety of light and engineering industries, mainly vehicles, biscuits and confectionery. Blackpool's new shopping centre gives it the largest shopping area in Lancashire and one of the finest in the north of England. Many special events are held in Blackpool throughout the year, from the Magicians' Convention and the Junior Dance Festival to the Lions' Carnival.

The 'Seven Golden Miles' of beaches and the bright lights of Blackpool are chosen by around four million people every year for their annual holiday with several millions more enjoying shorter visits. PP

ABOVE *Blackpool Tower and the bright lights.*

LEFT *Blackpool's piers epitomise the seaside.*

That the trust members are optimistic is, hopefully, a pointer to the future.

* * *

Among the best of traditional English cuisine, and, indisputably second to none, are her fish dishes. England's seafood has a considerable range of taste and flavour from the straight-forward, wholesome and universally appreciated fish and chips, through to some of the famous rich and complete dishes, based, for example, on Dover Sole, or the many types of English shell-fish, such as Whitstable Oysters.

Quite apart from the nationally known dishes there is also a range of famous regional delicacies. Underlying this gastronomic phenomenon is the fact that England is blessed, through its fishing industry, with excellent supplies of a wide variety of fish. Because of an efficient marketing system, this fish reaches the kitchens of England in a prime and fresh condition. In London and some of the larger cities and towns there has, as a result, long been a tradition of some of the great restaurants specialising only in fish.

The most common white fish found at table are cod, haddock, whiting, sole, plaice and halibut. There are also worthy and delightful dishes featuring whitebait, skate, turbot, red mullet and mackerel. Freshwater fish include, principally, salmon, eel and trout. Among the shell-fish are crab, lobster, oysters, shrimps, Dublin Bay prawns, scallops, whelks, winkles, mussels and crawfish.

Fish and chips, now so much a part of the English way of life, is of quite recent origin. In the last century there were many street traders who sold hot food, and fried potatoes and fried fish in batter were

ABOVE *Watercolour of Harry Ramsden's Fish-and-Chip Restaurant – reputedly the most famous in the world.*

BELOW *Smoked herrings at Lowestoft.*

OPPOSITE, TOP *Kippers and oysters at Scarborough.*

OPPOSITE, BOTTOM *Sadly, piers continue to disappear. This one at New Brighton, Merseyside, is, even now, a memory.*

popular – although not sold together. One account maintains that fried-fish selling started in Scotland and spread south while chips appeared in south-east England and travelled north. The two met in the industrial belts of Lancashire and Yorkshire and the combination, wrapped in newspaper, proved very popular among hungry mill workers on their way home. The fish-and-chip tradition is still strong in northern England and it is no accident that Harry Ramsden's, probably the world's most famous fish-and-chip restaurant, is at Guiseley in West Yorkshire.

Another speciality is our smoked fish based mainly along the east coast. Herring was the backbone of this industry and our kippers are one of the high-spots of English gastronomy. Few, perhaps, realise that in France they are referred to as the *'le jambon de Boulogne'*. Many coastal towns and villages are strongly associated with one type of seafood. Craster in Northumbria is a village whose succulent, oak-smoked kippers are justly renowned. Great Yarmouth was once the centre of a massive herring industry and gourmets regularly used to travel there to sample the bloaters. In the days before canning and refrigeration much of the catch was salted, the product being either red herrings or the even more pungent black herrings. Salmon was also smoked in great quantities and has become an internationally renowned delicacy. Some of the finest in quality is prepared in London, perhaps a reflection of the fact that until the early nineteenth century the best salmon in England reputedly came from the Thames.

In Cornwall pilchards used to be an important item of food, special towers being built to watch for passing shoals of the fish. It was the pilchard that was used for that strange dish Stargazey Pie, nowadays made in an ordinary pie dish with the fish heads projecting through the crust. Originally the fish were laid side by side on a strip of pastry, another strip was laid over the top and the whole thing was baked. These were then sold like sausage rolls, a section containing a fish (with its head sticking out) being cut off for each customer. Other specialities from around our shores include the Dover sole, red mullet (for which the town of Weymouth was especially renowned), shrimps – particularly from the Morecambe-Bay area – and crabs and lobsters. Eels and oysters seem to be associated with London, one of the reasons being that both will tolerate water of different levels of salinity. This meant they could be carried to inland markets alive – once a very considerable advantage with something as perishable as seafood.

On the whole the cookery of fish in England has remained simple, probably because there has been such a wealth of different kinds readily available. Poaching, grilling or frying is still the usual order of the day with a very few well-known specialities like soused herrings or mackerel, Arnold Bennett

Great Yarmouth and the Herring Fishery

Three silver herrings feature in Great Yarmouth's coat-of-arms, granted by Edward III in recognition of the great number of ships sent when Edward won Calais. From ancient times the town has been a shipbuilding, fishing and exporting centre. Yarmouth began on a sandbank across the mouth of Breydon Water, an expanse formed by the Rivers Yare, Bure and Waveney, the combined waters of which enter the North Sea at the southern end of Yarmouth Harbour. The sandbank was probably used by the early fishermen to pull their boats up on and spread out their nets. The estuary was important from Roman times, and earlier, as it was a main route inland. The location was of great value to this region of medieval England, for it was close to the important trading areas on the Continent.

From the early days herring was the most significant commodity exported, although by the 1300s wool was a strong rival; but it is to the herring fishery that Great Yarmouth owes the foundation of its prosperity. In what is believed to have been the earliest part of the town, excavations have revealed large numbers of fishbones, particularly of cod and herring, and fish-hooks. This is evidence that the community depended on fishing from at least the eleventh century and almost certainly earlier.

According to Damet, a sixteenth-century historian, the vast shoals of herring which congregated off the coast of Great Yarmouth each autumn attracted large numbers of the fishermen of France, Flanders, and

> of Hollande, Zealande, and all the low countryes yerelie, from the feaste of Sainte Michaell the Archangell, untylle the feaste of Sainte Martine, about the takinge, sellinge and buyenge of herringes.

C.H. Lewis, Curator, Great Yarmouth Museums, gives a colourful account of the annual Herring Fair in his booklet, *Great Yarmouth – History, Herrings and Holidays*. Administration of the fair, granted by Edward the Confessor to Hastings and eventually to all the Cinque Ports, led to much bitterness, even when it was agreed that the Fair should be controlled equally. Years later, in 1297, there was still so much hostility that when fleets from the Cinque Ports and from Great Yarmouth were escorting the king to Flanders, the former attacked the latter, burning twenty-nine ships and killing 200 men. After 1663 the Cinque Ports gave up their control.

Scottish women packing herring at Great Yarmouth, about 1902. Fishermen from Scotland gave new impetus to the industry from the mid- to late-1800s.

Great Yarmouth has been one of the largest :rring ports in the world and even in medieval mes was famous for smoked 'red herrings'. hen, in just a few days dozens of foreign vessels ould load up with herring. In the seventeenth ntury Yarmouth was still the most important shing port. The Dutch, particularly adept at ganising their herring fishery, had their own mmunity in Yarmouth. Charles I legislated ainst Dutch activity off the coast, prohibiting eir fishery except under licence and he sent a eet to enforce it. These restrictions, the Dutch /ars and then the French Wars ruined the Dutch shery, which left a vacuum for the British to fill.

Herring boats were improved by introduction of e lug rig and, later in the nineteenth century, the ff rig. The ultimate improvement was the development of steam drifters in the 1890s. The Fishwharf as built in 1869 and distribution improved with e coming of the railways, making the 'Yarmouth oater' available to even larger numbers of people. the mid- to late 1800s fishermen from Scotland ve a new impetus to the Yarmouth fisheries.

In 1913 all records were broken when about oo vessels fished from Yarmouth, the herring catch being worth a vast sum of money.

With the First World War many drifters were used as mine-sweepers, putting an end to the fishing for the duration. Markets were damaged by the war, and then there was increased foreign competition. The latter, with new methods, began to destroy the fish stocks. Although there were record catches, over-fishing led to very low prices. During the Second World War, drifters were again used by the Admiralty, giving the fish stocks a chance to recover.

The stocks were soon reduced again and the fishing fleet dwindled. Finally, by the mid-1960s, the last Yarmouth vessels were sold and Scottish vessels came for the last time.

Today herring is imported from places as far away as Canada, although some herring curing firms remain on the South Denes.

Herring always was the most important fishery at Great Yarmouth, although there were others. Whales were hunted and cod and ling fished.

Great Yarmouth today is still inextricably tied to the sea as a resort for seaside holidays, and, since the early 1960s, as a base for oil and gas exploration in the North Sea. PP

Stargazey pie – today's version.

omelette, fish pie and kedgeree, the latter derived from the days of the British Raj. More widespread travel has resulted in a broadening of interest in gastronomy generally; fish shops today often offer squid, mussels and unusual fish, necessary to fulfil the promise contained in many an exotic cookery book. With a wider range of ingredients our restaurateurs are becoming much more innovative and it is good to see dishes like curled whiting or trout stuffed with black pudding appearing on menus.

★ ★ ★

In conclusion, one oddity of fishing history is worth brief mention. Under a statute of the year 1324 whales, dolphins and sturgeon were claimed as 'Royal' fish and consequently the property of the monarch to whom they had to be offered. In the days before refrigeration such offers were normally (and understandably) waived by the Crown, and the need to give them by right was renounced as recently as 1971. This has not stopped the tradition continuing, particularly in relation to sturgeon, and one or two are so offered to The Queen in any year.

14 England's Offshore Islands

There are between 120 and 130 offshore islands which can, for our purposes, be classified as part of England's natural geography. It is, of course, dangerous to be too specific about which islands 'belong' to England: few Channel Islanders would think of themselves as other than Jerseymen, Guernseymen and so on, and the same applies to those who hail from the Scillies or, more especially, from the Isle of Man. Aside from these, there are many additional islands, most of them very small, which, like the largest and most comfortable of all – the Isle of Wight – must be thought of as entirely 'English'. Together they make a considerable contribution to the heritage of maritime England.

Many of these islands are well inhabited and known or visited by many thousands of visitors and tourists each year. Others are remote and difficult to reach, accessible to a tiny handful of the population – lighthouse keepers, naturalists and ornithologists. Some of them are privately owned, some belong to the nation. Together, they have a richness, a variety and a fascination that is specially theirs, for who has not felt that special feeling of isolation and of leaving cares behind, as one sails towards them from the mainland?

Some of England's islands have significant climatic and natural differences from the rest of the country. For example, the mainland can be in the depths of a blizzard while Tresco in the Scillies or Herm in the Channel Islands basks in warm sunshine. Peace and calm may reign in north-east England, while gale force winds and high waves batter the most remote of the Farne Islands a few miles off shore – all part of their very attraction.

The history of this pattern of islands is sometimes of considerable importance in itself; there are very few of them which have not had a part to play in past centuries as refuges for both the holy and the ungodly – the monks of Lindisfarne and St Michael's Mount, or the pirates and smugglers of that haunted island of Lundy. Equally, the geography varies from the inhospitality of some of the more remote Scilly Isles to the gentle greenness of the islands of eastern England. Many that were inhabited in the past are no longer, since they lack the conditions to support modern ways of life.

Obviously the lure of islands is different to different people. What to a child in a school classroom is a wistful green dot amid a patch of blue, can be an exciting challenge to an archaeologist digging at some prehistoric or early Christian site. To an ornithologist or naturalist an island can be the ideal place to study some rare seabird or the habits and special characteristics of animals that have developed in a properly isolated setting. Sociologists may be equally fascinated by the reasons why certain islands have been abandoned by man or, conversely, resettled by those who want to escape the noise and frustrations of urban or suburban living. Geologists in their turn find much that is exciting in the rocks and nature of an island itself.

Islands have long been places of refuge or escape from political or religious persecution. They have, equally, offered to England's rulers suitably isolated places to banish or imprison. The Isle of Wight was a prison to Charles I; it fulfills much the same function to the inmates of Parkhurst today.

As the geographic outposts of the English mainland, islands have not always been looked on with favour by sailors and navigators. They have frequently acted as barriers to safe havens and are, consequently, littered with the shipwrecks of all ages. Thus man has spent much time and effort in erecting safety devices on them so that almost none of these islands today lacks a lighthouse of one form or another. Lighthouses are by no means an island monopoly although the most famous of them are: the Longstone, the Needles, and the Farne Light, to name but three.

A clockwise tour of the islands of England must begin with the islands of Northumberland, the most notable of which is Lindisfarne or Holy Island. Six miles to the north of Bamburgh and connected to the mainland by a causeway at low tide, it has strong religious associations which stretch back to the beginnings of Christianity in England. Today the age-old monastery is a ruin, but it, the castle and the land round it, now all owned by the National

Longstone Lighthouse from Brownsman Island.

The Longstone Lighthouse

Longstone is one of the principal islands in the Farnes, a lonely and isolated group lying off the northern coast of Northumberland that has constituted a danger to shipping over the centuries. Longstone and Inner Farne each bear a lighthouse.

A light had been requested for the Longstone Rock several times in the seventeenth and eighteenth centuries, but each time the request was turned down by the Elder Brethren of Trinity House, who as the General Lighthouse Authority for England were, and still are, responsible for lighthouses; but the Brethren were unable to obtain the consent of the affected parties to pay a toll for the maintenance of the lighthouse.

By 1826 a light was found to be absolutely essential. The lighthouse was designed and built by Joseph Nelson. It was a red circular tower of rough stones with iron railings around the lantern gallery. The light came from Argand lamps with twelve burners, parabolic reflectors and an optical apparatus. The lighthouse and dwellings cost approximately £4,771, the lantern alone £1,441.

The island was a bleak situation to endure and the isolation must have been terrible. Often storms were so bad that the family were driven into the upper rooms of the tower to seek refuge, the waves being so enormous that they covered the living quarters.

The Longstone lighthouse is famous because it was here that Grace Darling lived with her father, William, who was the lighthouse keeper, as his father had been before him. She became a national heroine when, in September 1838, she and her father set out in a coble to reach *Forfarshire*, a merchant vessel which was being wrecked on Big Hawker about a mile away. In the tremendous seas they knew they would not be able to return unless survivors helped them. In two trips a woman and eight men were rescued – the sole survivors. The heroic story of this brave young girl who had a delicate constitution caught the public imagination and there were many stories, songs and plays written about her. The Trinity House boat which formerly carried supplies to this station was aptly named *Grace Darling*. Nowadays the relief is carried out every twenty-eight days by helicopter – R.A.F. *Boulmer*. The Grace Darling Museum is located at Bamburgh (on the mainland opposite), the town in which she is also buried, having died when she was only twenty-six. There is a memorial tablet to her in the chapel on Inner Farne and one in her room in the lighthouse.

Longstone lighthouse was bombed with remarkable accuracy in 1941. As a result, major alterations were made in 1952 when the light was converted to electricity with an intensity of 3,200,000 candle power. The light's range is twenty-nine miles and is a white flashing every twenty seconds. The fog signal is a siren sounding every sixty seconds.

The Farnes were bought by national subscription in 1925 and handed over to the National Trust. They now form one of the most important nature reserves in the country. Since 1964 a special Sanctuary Order has offered protection to the birds – gulls, guillemots, puffins, terns and turnstones. During the nesting season of the tern, landings on Longstone are forbidden and a landing permit is required at other times of the year. In the summer the island is also a 'hauling-out' ground for seals. PP

Trust, make a fascinating and worthwhile visit. The Farne Islands nearby, largely barren and treeless, were bought for the Trust in 1925. They are teeming with birdlife and many offer a breeding ground to a large grey seal colony. The most famous of these Farnes is Longstone where the Victorian heroine Grace Darling, lived with her lighthouse-keeper father.

Moving on down the coast to the south, one comes to Coquet Island at Alnmouth, a flat and treeless island that is named after a twelfth-century Danish hermit. By Whitley Bay is St Mary's or Bates Island, also a high-tide island, while, at the mouth of the Humber, lies Read's Island. Scolt Head, off the north Norfolk coast is flat, marshy and shingle-ridged, curved like a bow and home to many different species of bird. So too is Havergate at the mouth of the Ore in Suffolk.

Further south again are the Hamford Water Islands, a maze of low lying patches of land divided by meandering channels. The Mersea Islands and the waters round them provide in turn the setting for yachting and other water sports, as does Osea in the Blackwater Estuary. The Isle of Wight itself, prosperous, attractive and accessible, has long been considered an England in microcosm. Queen Victoria chose it as the site for her summer retreat at Osborne – a place of refuge. The island's thick chalk layer provides the geological base for its attractive scenery, most famous of which are the white teeth of the Needles. Against this picturesque background, tourism and yachting provide much of the island's prosperity. Cowes harbour is the cradle of maritime England's favourite and most varied sport. It is no coincidence that, because of the value placed on Wight's coastline, the National Trust have concentrated much attention on ensuring that it is preserved and defended for posterity.

A casual examination of a map of the south coast of England suggests that the only island of note is Wight. But there are many more. Further along the

Inner Farnes Lighthouse.

RIGHT *Lighthouse on St Mary's Island, Whitley Bay, Northumberland. The first 'light' was a lamp kept burning in the sanctuary of a chapel.*

BELOW *The castle on Lindisfarne, or Holy Island, Northumbria with the tide in.*

coast are the eight or nine islands sheltered in Poole Harbour. The largest and most famous of these is Brownsea, which is best known for being the birthplace of Baden-Powell's Scouting movement. Nowadays it is an attractive recreation area for the region. Among the other islands in the harbour is Long Island, said to have been the base for the activities of the notorious privateer and pirate, Harry Paye.

Seven miles south-east of Plymouth and a quarter of a mile from the Devon shore, is Burgh Island which today is a lively holiday centre. In the past it was the centre for pilchard fishing. Moving west, off Wembury Point, is the conically shaped Great Mew Stone, where in medieval times monks kept an oil lamp burning in bad weather as a primitive form of lighthouse to warn passing ships. In Plymouth Sound, is the historically important Drake's Island, of which Sir Francis is said to have stated: 'He who holds the island, holds the town.' It has, in turn, been both fortress and prison and nowadays is home to a youth centre which offers courses in seamanship and marine biology.

There are a number of islands off the south Cornish coast including St George's, the strangely named Asparagus Islands and Mullion Island off Porth Mellin.

ABOVE *The village on Holy Island.*

LEFT *Pier at Shanklin, Isle of Wight. There is also an esplanade, marine gardens, a natural gorge of great scenic beauty, a sheltered beach – and a Victorian seawater bath.*

St Michael's Mount, Cornwall. This fairy-tale castle has inspired many legends.

Then one comes to St Michael's Mount, that well-known and dramatic pyramid which is linked by a low-tide causeway to the mainland. The castle at the peak of the island imparts a fairy-tale quality to the view and this has given rise to many romantic legends. In maritime terms St Michael's Mount was a major base for the early tin trade, and because of its close monastic connections with Mont Saint Michel in France, it was a trading and migration centre from the earliest days of English Christianity.

The Isles of Scilly were, to ancient mariners, situated at the edge of the known world. There are half a dozen inhabited islands in the group with, depending on how one defines an island, between fifty and a hundred others, some large, some mere rocks and skerries. Together they are a scattered archipelago of contrasts where, despite the fact that they are exposed to the extremes of Atlantic gales, a rich harvest of early spring flowers is produced as their main export. In myth they have been called the mountain peaks of the legendary drowned world of Atlantis, or the romantic land to which King Arthur's dead were borne to their final rest.

The Scillies have also been the burial ground of another kind, for, across the centuries, many a ship has sunk on the treacherous rocks that spread over this part of the sea. Stories of sunken Spanish galleons with the eternal promise of gold bullion in their holds, continue to attract treasure seekers to this day. One of the most famous multiple wrecks of all was that of four ships of the Fleet, under command of Admiral Sir Cloudesley Shovell, which were wrecked around the Gilstone Rock in the year 1707. Recently, the hulk of the Admiral's flagship the *Association* was found, and numerous gold and silver coins and other relics have been brought to the surface. The Scillies were also to spell doom for a number of the storm-struck yachts in the ill-fated 1979 Fastnet Race.

Pirates, Vikings, smugglers – now all that is gone and the Scillies have the prosperity which tourism brings. To the visitor they offer a world of their own, variety yet peace.

Turning back to the north-east and into the Bristol Channel, there are a number of interesting islands, such as the rocky Brisons to the west of Cape Cornwall, and the Godrevy Islands at St Ives Bay. Further up channel is the 120-foot high rock pillar known as Newland, while at Pentire Point, stands the Mouls islet, now owned by the National Trust; it is said that on this rock, Laurence Binyon was inspired to compose his Remembrance Day verse, 'At the going down of the sun and in the morning, we will remember them.'

To many mainlanders it is Lundy, standing eleven miles off Hartland Point in North Devon, that is most like a 'real' island. A 400-foot-high bluff of granite, it is just over three miles long by half a mile wide. Likened to a huge ship moored forever in the centre of the channel, its maritime history is a long and fascinating one, since it served as a refuge for many lawless seafarers of the past. At one time it was a virtual pirate kingdom and smugglers haven which gave it its title of 'Tollgate of the Channel'. Today it is a noted bird reserve and, while it has a resident population of only a dozen or so, its splendours are seen by thousands of tourists annually.

Other islands in the Bristol Channel include Stert, which lies off Burnham in Somerset, and Steepholm (and its sister, Flatholm, which belongs to Wales) on which early Christian remains have been discovered. It too was noted as a Viking base.

For the purpose of this book, the Isle of Man is classified as part of Maritime 'England', though its inhabitants, the self-governing Manxmen, would doubtless protest. Nonetheless, Man has always been part of England's nautical history. As an island it offers a varied diet and range of attractions, from the liveliness of its capital to the peace of some of its remoter beaches. At various times it has belonged to Norway and to Scotland; now it is a sovereign state within the Crown and The Queen is known as Lord

ABOVE *Ruin on the site of a tin mine. St Michael's Mount was a major base for the important Cornish tin trade.*

LEFT *The wreck of the* Association *and three other ships of the Fleet on Gilstone Rock, the Scillies, 1707.*

of Man. Wight is only half its size, yet the latter has twice the population. Unlike Wight, Man has few similarities with the nearest mainland, and its many strong traditions with its own parliament and laws are carefully and jealously guarded today.

There are a number of satellite islands, round Man including the Calf of Man (owned by the National Trust), St Patrick's Isle on which stands the famous Peel Castle, and, on the east coast, the isthmus of St Michael's Island, where, it is said, the predecessor of today's Derby was first run.

Finally, on this brief tour of England's other islands are those that lie off the north-west coast. Among these are the almost uninhabited Hilbre Islands, standing close to the Wirral Peninsula, which are of interest mainly to ornithologists. South of Barrow and joined by a causeway are Roa Island and Foulney, while Piel Island and Walney Island lie close to the mainland by Barrow-in-Furness. Piel is a mainly play-and-picnic area, well known to trippers from Morecambe and elsewhere. Walney does not really deserve island status, linked as it now is by a permanent road-bridge to the mainland.

While all these islands are separate entities, they form an intrinsic part of the whole, to be developed, to be protected and to be enjoyed by all who love the freedom that they offer.

ABOVE *Ramsey, Isle of Man. Deep-sea fishermen fish for whiting, gurney, mackerel and plaice. Ramsey is a good base for exploring the north of the island.*

RIGHT *Castle Peel, Isle of Man. Peel is noted for its Manx kippers, which are smoked on fires of oak woodchips. A Viking Festival is held here each year to commemorate a Viking invasion.*

15 The Natural Heritage

The coasts, shores and beaches are treasured and valuable aspects of our natural heritage, part of the framework of maritime England, though one in seemingly permanent danger from a wide variety of natural and man-made attacks. The richness of the scenery and the wildlife along our shores must be safeguarded, the very variety of seascape being our greatest asset – from the placid and peaceful through to the wild, inhospitable and bleak. The long sandy beaches, rocky foreshores, muddy flats, dramatic cliffs, all blend together to offer a stupendous choice.

In general, the west coasts are more subject to attack by wind and waves; in the east the sea waters are more subtle and the dangers to the land, as round the Blackwater and Crouch estuaries, are usually of gentle erosion, thus the need for man-made sea walls to protect the farms of the hinterland.

In geological terms, most of the shaping of the coastline has been a gradual one, wearing away rocks and cliff faces over thousands of years. But there are many other places where the encroachment is much more dangerous and where the shoreline is receding by several feet each year, unless stopped by beach defences. Noticeable is the fact that the sea often

Durdle Door, near Lulworth Cove, Dorset. This quiet, unspoiled beach is part of the Heritage Coast and has also been designated an area of Outstanding Natural Beauty by the Countryside Commission.

gives back what it has taken away, not always to anyone's advantage. Rivers and estuaries get silted up by sand and mud banks, while spits of shingle can rise out of the sea drying up an inland lagoon.

To some people flat coastlines and tides that meander hundreds of yards out and back are the seaside; to others a precipitous climb down rocks to a tiny stony beach is the annual holiday goal. Both types of beach have their attraction.

Cliffs have a peculiar fascination. Some of the most spectacular are at Countisbury Hill on Exmoor which rises nearly 1,000 feet above sea level, and Golden Cap in Dorset, the highest along the south coast at 619 feet. Perhaps the most famous cliffs in Europe are, however, the white cliffs of Dover. Other striking chalk cliffs stretch from Flamborough Head round to the Needles on the Isle of Wight, and, further west, to the grey outcrops of Devon and Cornwall. The red sandstone of St Bee's Head in Cumbria and Boulby Cliff by Cleveland in North Yorkshire – the highest in England – are also notable.

Caves often occur in conjuction with cliffs; this is brought about by differing strengths and consistencies of rock which have allowed the sea to carve out its own rich patterns of geological form. Flamborough Head is riddled with such caves.

Firths, estuaries, bays, Broads, flats, river mouths – all add their own character to the coastline. Some

ABOVE *The Cuckmere River near Cuckmere Haven on the South Downs. Secluded, the bay was once used by smugglers. To the west are the chalk cliffs at Peacehaven (*OPPOSITE*), and to the east at Beachy Head, the dramatic chalk cliffs known as the Seven Sisters.*

LEFT *Marsden Bay, Durham. The sea has carved caves and arches from the cliffs. Many birds nest on the rocks and ledges.*

were created before or just after the ice age, through glacier action or the melting of the ice pack. Other features have been formed and reformed in comparatively recent times by tides, river flows and erosion.

Beaches are sandy where sandstone or glacial sand deposits occur; clay will produce less appealing mud flats, while in the chalky areas, flint and shingle beaches are more common. Sand dunes are mainly a west-coast phenomenon since they are the result of strong prevailing winds piling up sands from the shore. Examples are most common in Devon and Cornwall, but also around the Duddon Estuary in the north-west.

Spits or bars have formed relatively rapidly in geological terms at a number of places round the English coast. Perhaps the most famous is the sixteen-mile-long Chesil Beach, largely composed of flint pebbles, forming a lagoon on the shore side. There are other major spits at Scolt Head in Norfolk and off the Devon and Cornish coasts. Where such spits run together, areas of sea are claimed by the land, most notably at Romney Marsh in Kent where the old coastline is now well inshore of Dungeness.

England has a rich range of seabird life – herring and black-backed gulls, kittiwake and, more rarely, puffins, cormorants, gannets and a host of other largely

ABOVE *Stodmarsh near Canterbury: lush farmland cradled between the Great Stour and the Little Stour.*

cliff-dwelling species. On the shoreline are terns, and the many species of waders. In bays, estuaries and mud flats, protected partially from the sea, many varieties of duck live with other wildlife that need quiet waters in which to survive and prosper. In the offshore waters, particularly in remoter areas, seals are to be found.

Seaside plants are equally varied, from delicate wild flowers to the ubiquitous marram grass – in many areas more useful than man-made fortifications in binding sands together in the never-ending battle against erosion by wind and water.

But the liveliness and the variety of the natural inheritance along the coastline is constantly under threat. Natural and man-made pollution is an unrelenting problem, but one that is being looked at with increasing concern by both local authorities and central government alike. Pollution of the land adjacent to the shore is, by and large, now legislated against in relatively effective ways. There are still, however, unprotected stretches where strip building, 'caravan blight' and other indiscriminate use of the land is allowed. Nonetheless, this is now a less significant danger than other types of marine and coastal pollution, including pollution of estuaries, resort beaches, ports and harbours. All these areas are at risk from discharges from shipping, dumping, seabed operations, and from rivers and pipelines bringing out waste and effluent from inland areas.

England is fortunate in a number of ways. The seas and oceans around her are strongly tidal and, for centuries, have been able to cope by diluting, dispersing and otherwise neutralising waste materials. This is unlike the circumstances elsewhere in the world, for example, in the largely land-locked Mediterranean with no tide, where heavy pollution has created fundamental biological problems. England's coasts are subject to deep tidal variations and to strong currents both of which add to the natural dispersal process.

Nowadays the sea is polluted, not so much by sewage, a relatively tiny problem (except in enclosed or still water areas), but by oil and chemicals either deliberately dumped (bulk carriers cleaning their tanks) or by accident, through shipwreck or because

OPPOSITE, TOP *Solway Firth, Cumbria. The waters of seven rivers flow into the firth – notorious for its dangerous tides. But the flat sands are a wonderful source of food for a variety of birdlife.*

OPPOSITE, BOTTOM *Fleswick Bay. The beach is an obvious attraction for those who collect semi-precious stones.*

OPPOSITE *Heather-covered hillside at Boscastle, Cornwall. There is a sturdy-walled harbour where the Valency and Jordan rivers meet the tide – sometimes dramatically.*

LEFT *New-born seal pup on Brownsman Island in the Farnes. Pups stay on shore for at least three weeks.*

of the malfunction of some piece of equipment. The latter can be either from ships or from land-based undertakings, where, for example, poisonous chemicals may accidentally be released into a river or open-drainage system through irregular pipe-line switching.

Controls over dumping and pollution are subject to a large number of national and, more importantly, international controls. The latter have been drawn up under the auspices of the Inter-Governmental Maritime Consultative Organisation, a UN organisation whose headquarters is in London. It is now an offence for any ship to discharge oil in British, or indeed in any, territorial waters.

Various Ministries of the British Government are involved in pollution control, but principally the Department of Trade which, working through H.M. Coastguards, the Marine Survey Service and the Royal Navy, oversees the watch-dog arrangements. Oil slicks, for example, once sighted and identified, will, if possible, be dispersed using spraying equipment and chemicals which are stock-piled against such eventualities. Extensive contingency plans, drawn up in consultation between central and local authorities, exist to deal, not only with sea pollution, but also with oil and other forms of pollution washed up on beaches, in harbours and estuaries.

Fishery interests are safeguarded by the Ministry of Agriculture and Fisheries, and wildlife by the Nature Conservancy Council, and there is constant research into the complex methods needed to remove, for example, oil from sand, rock and mud flats, as well as from bird life which is so often particularly badly affected. The urgency of any cleaning operation naturally depends on the extent to which the particular stretch of coast has a high amen-

BELOW *Nesting gannet with chick. Gannets are rarely found inland, preferring to breed on remote islands.*

Chesil Beach looking towards the mainland from the Bill of Portland.

Chesil Beach

Chesil Beach near Weymouth in Dorset is a shingle bank that may be the longest ridge of pebbles in Europe – an unbroken sixteen miles in length extending from the Isle of Portland to West Bay near Bridport. The bank forms a large tidal lagoon, the Fleet, before it rejoins the coast at Abbotsbury for the last six miles. At places it is 50 to 60 feet above sea level and 200 yards in width. The gradient is sometimes 1:80.

Chesil Beach is unique in that the pebbles are graded. The stones are largest (about the size of a man's fist) and roughest at the Portland end, becoming the size of peas at Bridport. In a dense fog local fishermen landing on the beach reputedly can tell their position from the size of the pebbles. The pebbles consist of limestone, chert and flint as well as coloured jaspers and quartz; some seem to be far-travelled. Stones from Chesil Beach have been found at Maiden Castle, a prehistoric earthworks near Dorchester, where they were apparently used in sling-shots.

The beach itself may be rearranged somewhat during storms when the violent breaking of the waves and the rattling of tons of pebbles is an impressive sight and sound.

Massive seas sometimes overtop Chesil Beach. In November 1824 a vessel was washed right over the top and relaunched on the Fleet, while in 1853 a great wave stranded a ship on the heights of the beach itself. Particularly destructive storms occurred in 1930 and on February 13, 1942. The most recent, on February 13, 1979, was described by a local citizen as 'the worst attack by the sea in living memory'. A distant depression radiated particularly long-period, high-amplitude waves up the English Channel. The waves hit Portland, destroying houses and flooding the streets in seconds; Chesil Beach Road subsided, temporarily cutting off the island.

Chesil Beach is of great interest to naturalists. The lagoon contains a unique collection of eel grass as well as characteristic shingle flora. Many waders and wildfowl winter in the lagoon, and in the spring mute swans nest at the Abbotsbury swannery, where a swan herd has lived for hundreds of years.

ity value or has substantial and important widlife. In other less immediate circumstances, for example small spills in a busy dockland area, it may be largely left to nature to break down and disperse oil leakage.

This is not to suggest a lack of concern for traditionally highly polluted areas, for example the river and estuary of the Thames. There has been a constant improvement in water quality in recent years and the level of pollution in the tidal Thames has been reduced to a quarter of the 1950s level with some one hundred types of fish identified as now being able to survive in waters that would have been totally toxic half a generation ago.

The rapid development of the offshore oil industry has increased the dangers of oil pollution in the North-Sea areas; however, extracting companies all have contingency plans to deal with any spills and the incidence of this sort of pollution has so far been very slight. Another form of potential pollution that has been given much attention of late is the deliberate dumping of highly toxic, chemical or nuclear waste in very deep water. The present state of knowledge suggests that, given sufficient precautions with the containers used, the risks are slight; but many people are concerned about the long-run dangers to both life and the natural environment.

Brief mention has already been made about the importance of planning coastal land use to provide recreational facilities and pleasure to both residents and holiday-makers alike. In this, the safeguarding of the natural beauties and attractions of the coastline is pre-eminent. The result of a full and all-embracing study, undertaken by the Countryside Commission, of the coastline of England and Wales over the years 1966 to 1970, was the decision that certain undeveloped stretches of particular beauty and interest should be designated 'heritage coast'. In all, some 800 miles (1,300 kilometres) of coast have been listed in this way.

In addition, in 1965 the National Trust, recognising that one of the greatest and most pressing of all conservation problems was to protect the remaining unspoilt coastline, launched the campaign known as 'Enterprise Neptune' – to raise the necessary money to purchase, for the nation, stretches of coastline with a great natural beauty. The gravity of the problem was demonstrated by the fact that a third of

Robin Hood's Bay, North Yorkshire. Here farmland is threatened by the sea.

the 3,000 miles of coast around England, Wales and Northern Ireland was already, to quote the Trust, 'ruined beyond redemption', another third was of little recreational or scenic importance – but the last third was worthy of permanent preservation. The alternative was to lose out to developers, haphazard building and industrial projects and other forms of unplanned blight such as badly sited caravan parks. Enterprise Neptune, was an immediate success and has remained so. At present, nearly 400 miles of the coastline of England and Wales are now under the protection of the Trust and the figure is constantly growing.

Some of the most important acquisitions have included several hundred acres around the Yealm Estuary in South Devon, large tracts of the Isle of Wight, in particular the spectacular area of downland overlooking the Needles, and East Head at West Wittering at the entrance to Chichester Harbour, which is a one-and-a-half-mile stretch of dunes, saltings and beaches. There are other important properties: Ridge Cliff at Seatown in Dorset as part of the Golden Cap Estate which now has over five miles of coastline; a further two miles at Clymping in West Sussex; other properties in Cumbria (the southern shore of the Solway), North Devon and South Cornwall, Avon, Kent, Merseyside, Norfolk,

ABOVE *The remains of Dunstanburgh Castle, on cliffs 100 ft above the North Sea. Craster, famous for its smoked kippers, is an easy walk from there along the coast.*

LEFT *Alum Bay, Isle of Wight. As many as twelve different shades of sandstone have been found on these famous cliffs. Nearby is a pleasure Park and the Needles with their lighthouse.*

OPPOSITE *Creativity with shells on a home in Polperro, Cornwall. Cornwall does not, however, have a monopoly on shells. There is a Museum of Shell Craft at Buckfastleigh, Devon, and Norfolk has a Shell Museum at Glandford, which features carved and engraved shells.*

St Bees, Cumbria. The coast here is protected by breakwaters.

Northumberland, North Yorkshire and Suffolk.

The other type of protection for the coastline is the physical, constant and expensive battle to improve the land defences against sea erosion. The costs of such defences – seawalls, breakwaters and so on – are met jointly by funds from central government and the local maritime authorities. The continual struggle for the improvement of these maritime barriers is occasionally overshadowed by reports of problems, such as flooding or serious erosion. The real story is, by contrast, one of very considerable success.

16 Preserving the Past: The London Area

England's maritime inheritance is both priceless and unique. It must be preserved and protected with care. We are increasingly fortunate in that, nowadays, a great deal of skill and experience goes into ensuring that marine traditions and treasures are held for posterity. Up and down the country, voluntary organisations, museums, local authorities and individuals are helping to save old ships, along with a rich collection of nautical equipment, that have survived from past centuries. Many of the events, personalities and items from our history are brought alive for people today when they are allowed to, for example, clamber over and explore an old ship, see early items of navigational equipment or visit the homes of famous figures from English naval history. In many instances it was rather late in the day before it was realised what was being lost. Great and famous ships and significant items of their equipment have too often gone to the breakers or scrap yards before the possibilities of retaining them for posterity have been fully explored. The record, even now, is far from perfect.

The National Maritime Museum at Greenwich is the most important single institution concerned with the preservation of the maritime history of Britain. Its wealth of important historic buildings includes those of the Old Royal Greenwich Observatory. The Museum's scope is enormous, covering as it does all aspects of the history of the Royal Navy, the Merchant Navy, the fishing industry, pleasure craft and the history of navigation. It also records and illustrates developments in maritime architecture such as harbours, lighthouses and other navigational aids. The museum has a large collection of naval uniforms, weapons and medals, an impressive art gallery, an exhibition centre, lecture hall, library and archives, which ensures that it stands at the forefront of international maritime research.

Many special and permanent exhibitions are on display relating to aspects of maritime history, famous naval figures (particularly Nelson), the development of the sailing ship, steam-driven vessels through the ages and marine navigation. Intercontinental migration, arctic exploration and many other subjects are illustrated by means of model ships, charts, maps and contemporary prints and paintings. There are a number of actual ships on display, as well as a collection of ships' figureheads.

In the Old Royal Observatory buildings, much of the pioneering work carried out on marine navigation techniques in the late seventeenth and eight-

National Maritime Museum, Greenwich.

eenth centuries was developed. The O° meridian, which determines Greenwich Mean Time, runs through the aptly named Meridian Building. The building itself houses a unique display of astronomical instruments and of other items illustrating the history of the measurement of time.

The Maritime Trust is the pre-eminent organisation devoted to the practical preservation of historic ships. This trust aims to do for our marine history what the National Trust does for our natural inheritance. Established as recently as 1969, it has already made considerable progress in the great task of identifying, rescuing, restoring and displaying vessels of historic or of technical importance. With the assistance of privately raised funds, the Trust has acquired around twenty vessels from the most famous tea clipper of all time, the *Cutty Sark*, right up to Sir Francis Chichester's yacht, *Gipsy Moth IV*. Many of these vessels have already been restored; the rest are currently awaiting restoration or are otherwise in the process of being reconstructed so that they can be studied and enjoyed by future generations.

The most important development in the Trust's programme has been the formation of a special Historic Ship Collection at the attractively redeveloped St Katharine's Dock by Tower Bridge in London. This notable collection has been brought to what is itself an historic site from various scattered parts of the country. A sort of floating museum, these ships help demonstrate the evolution from sail to steam and include the coal-fired steam drifter, the *Lydia Eva*, the former *Nore* lightship, the steam coaster *Robin*, the *Cambria*, which is a traditional Thames

ABOVE *St Katharine's Dock. The Historic Ship Collection demonstrates the evolution from sail to steam.*

RIGHT *H.M.S.* Discovery, *when moored on the Thames embankment. The ship is now in the collection at St Katharine's Dock.*

OPPOSITE *Mariners' Chapel at All Hallows by the Tower. Sailors came here to be blessed before setting out; on return they presented a model of their ship in thanksgiving. There are also memorials to H.M.S.* Hood *and S.T.V.* Royston Grange.

spritsail barge, the tugboat *Challenge*, a West Country topsail schooner the *Kathleen and May* and now, most recently, Captain Scott's research ship *Discovery*. The latter, handed over to the Trust by the Ministry of Defence in 1979, used to be anchored along the Thames Embankment; the Trust, with the National Maritime Museum, will be responsible for its gradual restoration and preservation.

By bringing all these vessels together in one dock the Trust can cut costs while giving these venerable ships a secure and sheltered berth free from the strains and damage that would otherwise be caused by tidal waters.

At Hartlepool, the Trust is engaged in the restoration of the important nineteenth-century iron warship *Warrior*, the hulk of which lay neglected for fifty years at Milford Haven. She was built in 1860 and was in her time a major advance on the traditional wooden three-deckers. Another warship awaiting restoration is H.M.S. *Gannet*, a nineteenth-century auxiliary steam sloop. Finally, the Trust is also involved in the preservation of the *Cutty Sark* and *Gipsy Moth IV* which lie at Greenwich.

The work of the Trust extends even further. It has

ABOVE *Victoria Embankment: H.M.S.* Wellington, *H.M.S.* Chrysanthemum *and H.M.S.* President.

RIGHT *Nelson's Column, Trafalgar Square.*

provided both technical help and money to regional organisations with common aims and interests, including among others, the Exeter Maritime Museum, the Windermere Steamboat Museum and the Mary Rose Committee. They have also given help and advice to those involved in preserving and displaying individual ships all around England, including H.M.S. *Belfast*, presently in the Pool of London, and Brunel's great iron ship, the S.S. *Great Britain*, which in recent years was brought back to England from the Falkland Islands and now lies at Bristol.

Inevitably, the London area does tend to have the lion's share of what has been preserved of our nautical past. The Imperial War Museum in Lambeth, with its exhibits relating to the history of the two world wars, has many maritime-orientated displays, particularly relating to weapons and armaments.

The Science Museum at South Kensington has a wide collection of model ships illustrating the history of navigation. It also has a display of deep-sea diving suits, which tells something of the fascinating story of this most dangerous of professions. Among other notable collections are Lloyd's of London where there is a Nelson Room filled with mementoes of the Admiral, and Madame Tussaud's famous waxwork museum where a tableau recalls what it all must have been like on board Nelson's flagship *Victory* during the Battle of Trafalgar. The Museum of London, in its turn, with its concentration on the history of the Capital, has much of nautical Thames-side interest including the remains of a Roman ship that was unearthed near Blackfriars.

Apart from the Historic Ship Collection and the warship *H.M.S. Belfast*, the Thames Embankment has an interesting variety of other privately owned historic ships moored along its length, including the paddle-steamer *Princess Elizabeth* and *Hispaniola*, now floating restaurants. The *Tattershall Castle* was, for a time, an art gallery.

There are land-based memorials to London's maritime past as well, and of these the most important must be the 185-foot high Nelson's Column in Trafalgar Square. The statue of Nelson at the top is by the sculptur Edward Baily. Close by is Admiralty Arch, the national memorial to Queen Victoria.

A little way down Whitehall, the Old Admiralty is still a part of the Navy Department. There, in the Ripley Building, is the Admiralty Board Room, with its great table that has a round section cut out of it, reputedly to fit the rotund figure of a former Secretary of the Admiralty; this room is still used by the Admiralty Board. It also has the original wind indicator, directly connected to a weather vane on the roof, which kept the Sea Lords informed of the likely course of shipping in the Channel. The building, in addition, houses the Nelson Room, where Nelson's body rested prior to its final interment.

One important religious centre with strong maritime traditions is the Mariners' Chapel at All-Hallows-By-The-Tower, which is hung with many ship models. By tradition, sailors went there to be

The Cutty Sark, *Greenwich.*

ABOVE *The Tower of London.*

blessed before setting sail and then returned, offering models of their ships as thanks for their safe passage.

A wealth of interesting things can be seen around London's dockland; while the famous maritime areas of Deptford, Rotherhithe, Wapping and Stepney have seen better days, they are all strong in ship-building or sea-going traditions. Deptford was famous for its Royal Naval Dockyard and Victualling Yard; of the latter, some eighteenth-century buildings and a quayside walk are all that remain.

There are, understandably, many statues, sites, and houses in London which have close links with a number of famous English seamen. Nelson lived for a time at 96 (now 103) New Bond Street and also at 5 Cavendish Square; he is buried in St Paul's Cathedral. Captain Christopher Jones, the Master of the *Mayflower*, is buried in the churchyard of St Mary's, Rotherhithe. There is a statue of Drake in front of Deptford Town Hall, and, also in Deptford, a statue of Blake. Memorials to Raleigh include one in Whitehall and a window dedicated to him in St Margaret's Westminster. He frequented the Mermaid Tavern, was held prisoner in the Bloody Tower of the Tower of London, and was finally executed in front of the Palace of Westminster in 1618. Captain Scott lived at 56 Oakley Street; his last diary and the records of his polar expedition are held in the British Library. Captain Cook lived at No. 88, Mile End Road. Samuel Plimsoll, 'The Seaman's Friend,' who did so much to improve the safety of ships at sea, is remembered with a statue in the Embankment Gardens, Victoria Embankment.

Less glamorous, but no less important in the nautical life and economy of London, is Billingsgate Fishmarket in Lower Thames Street, which has probably been the site of a fishmarket from very early times. On the second Sunday in October a service, known as the Harvest of the Sea Thanksgiving,

RIGHT *Entrance to the Ripley Block, the Old Admiralty, Whitehall.*

Samuel Plimsoll

Samuel Plimsoll (1824–98) was a merchant and politician who entered the House of Commons in 1868. He used his knowledge of the sea and his position in Parliament to campaign for safety for seamen, a long and bitter struggle. In 1873 he published *Our Seamen*, a forceful attack on what were described as 'coffin ships' – in which the owners risked the seamens' lives by heavily insuring overloaded and unseaworthy vessels. Plimsoll was a true social reformer who literally dedicated his life to this campaign. He instigated a Royal Commission, resulting in the *Merchant Shipping Act of 1876*; this gave strict powers of inspection to the Board of Trade. At the same time the loading line for ships was fixed – the International Load Line, popularly called the Plimsoll Line.

The law had far-reaching effects because it was applied to foreign ships leaving British ports; this led to the acceptance of loading rules by other maritime countries. In 1934 an International Load Line was adopted by fifty-four countries and in 1968 a new mark came into effect. This shows six loading levels: tropical fresh water, fresh water, tropical sea water, summer sea water, winter sea water, and winter North Atlantic for vessels under 330 feet in length; the registration society is also indicated.

Samuel Plimsoll went on to become President of the National Amalgamated Sailors' and Firemens' Union and continued to fight – this time against the horrific conditions existing at that time on cattle ships. PP

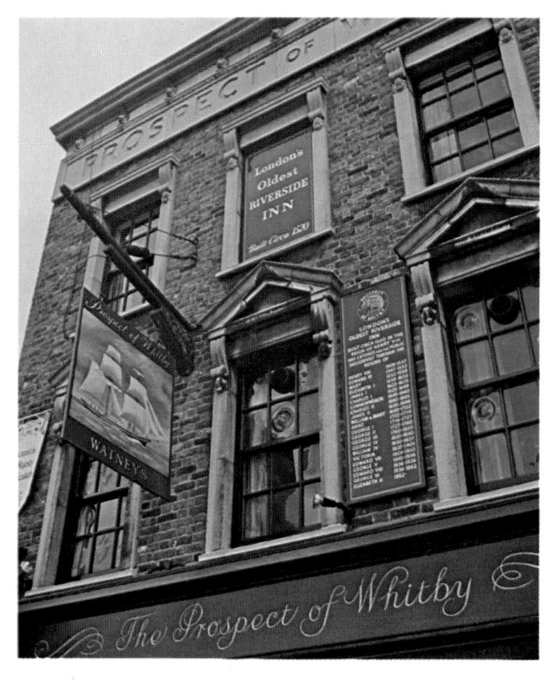

is held at the Church of St Mary-at-Hill, in the City, and the fish-merchants of Billingsgate send up a large selection of fish which is displayed in the church on that occasion.

There are a number of other nautical events in London's annual calendar, the most famous of which is Trafalgar Day, which celebrates Nelson's victory on the twenty-first of October, 1805. On the Sunday nearest that date a ceremony and parade is held on Horse Guards Parade and later at Trafalgar Square. There is also a service at St Paul's Cathedral for seafarers and all those whose lives, in one way or another, are connected with the sea.

LEFT *The Prospect of Whitby, Wapping. One of a number of Thames-side pubs with long and colourful histories.*

Billingsgate comes to life at 5.30 in the morning.

Billingsgate

Billingsgate – the principal fish market in London and the oldest market – is located on a spot that was probably a small harbour in Roman times and a place where royal tolls were later collected. The first documented reference to 'Blynesgate' was in connection with King Ethelred's customs regulations. In 1209, when Old London Bridge was completed, Billingsgate captured much of the trade from Queenhithe, which was west of the bridge. The strong connection with the fish industry dates from the thirteenth century, instigated by the Fishmongers' Company. This trade is mentioned in a Charter of Edward I in 1297 and confirmed by an Act of Parliament.

A Dutch historian in 1773 recorded, 'Billingsgate. . . is the only port for fish in London.' At this time the fish were, of course, brought in by the Thames. For many many years now it has all been brought in by road and by rail.

Until the mid-nineteenth century the fish and seafood was sold straight from stalls and sheds around the dock. A market building was built in 1846 by James Bunning, which soon proved inadequate as a large amount of fish were being brought in by rail. In 1875 the present larger building, designed by Sir Horace Jones, was opened. The building has much charm in a lighthearted Victorian way with its pavilions, mansard roofs, dormers and gilded dolphins. The market halls are robust in character with imposing cast-iron fluted columns and a louvred glass roof supported on lattice girders spanning sixty feet. Massive vaults are under the building; a mezzanine level, put in years ago, is used for chill boxes while the bottom level itself is a cold store.

There are about ninety firms trading at the market, as well as stalls and shops. Between 5.30 and 9.30 a.m., around 190 white-coated porters, with great dexterity and speed wheel about 200 tons of fish into the market on their trolleys. Only one or two of the older porters still wear the famous flat leather hats with deep brims (to catch the drips) on which they can carry up to one hundredweight of fish.

The customers – retail fish outlets, chain stores, restaurants and hotels – can buy every type of fish from a flying fish or a sword fish to the more usual cod, plaice or haddock. The fish may even come from other continents. Live eels are flown in daily from New Zealand and lobsters from Canada.

In 1982, as part of the Docklands Development, the market moves to a new location on the West India Docks, where there is room to expand and less dense traffic. In 1980, Billingsgate Fish Market was listed as being of special architectural and historic interest. 'Save Britain's Heritage' has proposed a scheme to retain the building and restore the river frontage. PP

17 Preserving the Past: The Rest of England

While at first sight London appears to have something of a monopoly of nautical treasures, this is far from being the case. There are many other ports and harbours of historical importance around England, and the range and variety of provincial maritime collections is large and growing. Most big ports and cities have substantial marine sections in their civic museums, including some towns that are neither near the sea nor normally identified with things nautical. Some of these collections are maintained and financed by local authorities; others are run by charitable trusts or owned by private companies or individuals.

Moving clockwise round the coast, we can see what is on offer at museums in some of the more important centres. In Northumberland, birthplace of Nelson's contemporary Admiral Collingwood, the Local Tyne and Wear County Council has done much to classify and display the various maritime collections in its area. At Sunderland Museum there are displays related to the history of the town's Merchant-Navy connections, which include ship models and marine paintings. Similar exhibits exist at South Shields, which also has on display the lifeboat *Tyne*, built in 1833.

Plans are under way to amalgamate several separate collections in one central location at a new Museum of Science and Engineering, which is being developed at Blandford House in Newcastle. This will include the display, as a comprehensive series, of many fine builders' models; these serve to demonstrate the development of steam ships, in which the region specialised during the period 1880 to 1930. The *Turbinia*, the first turbine-driven ship, will also be displayed.

Additionally, there are many fine marine paintings at the Laing Art Gallery in Newcastle, the Shipley Art Gallery in Gateshead and a collection of over fifty ship portraits at the Sunderland Museum.

Hartlepool in its turn has a museum which concentrates on the maritime history of the town, depicting its growth from a small fishing village to its present status as a major port; there are plans to restore the world's first fully ironclad battleship H.M.S. *Warrior* there, before it finds a lasting berth near Nelson's *Victory* at Portsmouth.

H.M.S. Victory *at the Royal Navy Museum, Portsmouth.*

At Marton-in-Cleveland near Middlesbrough, Captain James Cook was born in October 1728. A new museum is devoted to his life, his voyages and his achievements. Other places associated with Cook

Captain James Cook; painting by Nathaniel Dance.

in the area include Marton Parish Church where he was baptised and the Whitby Museum.

The Zetland Museum at Redcar exhibits, as one of its principal attractions, the life-boat *Zetland* and has a number of additional displays relating to life-saving and to the fishing industry in the area.

Moving down to the Humber, Hull is home to the Humber Keel and Sloop Preservation Society, which has renovated and is restoring two locally built vessels, while the Town Docks Museum has displays relating to the local whaling and fishing industries and the merchant ships of the port. At Great Yarmouth the Maritime Museum is housed in a building that functioned as a home for sailors up until 1965. Two years later the museum was opened as a co-operative venture supported by a number of local authorities. Here there are ship models, boat-building tools, early life-saving apparatus and items relating to the history of the local fishing industry.

The whole south-east of England has a strong maritime tradition. This is the land of the Cinque Ports – Hastings, Romney, Hythe, Dover and Sandwich which were confederated in the reign of Edward I with the common duty to protect Crown and country, in return for which they were exempted from certain duties and taxes. Each of them is worth a study on its own. At Dover, its white cliffs the pre-eminent symbol of all England's coastal scenery, one can see what is probably the oldest lighthouse in England – the Roman Pharos. To the north, Deal also has a maritime museum and many other sites of nautical interest.

The Dolphin Yard Sailing Barge Museum Trust is situated on an old barge yard at Sittingbourne in Kent. It exists to restore the yard as a living museum of the sailing barge where visitors can watch the traditional skills of boatbuilding and sailmaking for this form of boat, being carried out by experts.

Among the martime traditions of this part of England is the so-called 'Admiral's Court', held on the Medway in July. The Mayor of Rochester, as 'Admiral', holds his court while afloat on a barge on the river, and makes laws 'regulating the Oyster Fishery and the taking of floating fish'. At Hastings there is the equally ancient annual custom of 'Blessing of the Sea', this ceremony being held in the late spring at Rogationtide.

Moving along the southern coast of England, Portsmouth has a long and distinguished record as the home of the Royal Navy. Today there is much evidence of this, including the old sea defences – the Square and Round Towers and the Batteries – and, of more recent origin, the Palmerston Forts, which were built in the nineteenth century as further protection for the Dockyard. The Naval Dockyard itself, which is only open to the public on Navy Days, contains some of the finest buildings in the City. Round every corner there seems to be some memorial, statue or building reminding the visitor that Portsmouth was and is England's premier naval base. As such, in peace as in war, Portsmouth is also home to the Royal Navy Museum. First opened in 1930, its best-known feature is Nelson's flagship *Victory* which is dry-berthed alongside it. The Museum houses many relics related to Lord Nelson including the state barge of Charles II which was used, in January 1806, to take Nelson's coffin from Greenwich to Whitehall. Here too is the famous panoramic painting of the Battle of Trafalgar by W. L. Wyllie, as are many ships' figureheads and a display of their modern equivalent – the naval ship's badge.

Another ship, the *Mary Rose*, is closely connected with Portsmouth. Built in the years 1509 to 1511 on the orders of Henry VIII, she sank at Spithead in 1545. In the mid-1960s the well-preserved wreck was rediscovered lying under the Solent's seabed silt. Work is actively underway to raise the ship and display it and its priceless Tudor period contents,

Hastings, Sussex. Net shops, some built about 1750, still used by local fishermen; the nets are hung inside to be stored and repaired. These buildings were built upwards instead of sideways to save money on the rent, which was based on beach frontage. They are unique in England. Appropriately, Hastings has a Fishermen's Museum and a Museum of Local History, the latter featuring the history of the Cinque Ports and of maritime life.

POLICE

particularly its armaments, at a special museum to be built at Eastney.

Nearby, at Southsea, the Royal Marine Museum has on show exhibits illustrating the history of the Marines since their formation as the 'Admiral's Regiment' in the year 1664. There are uniforms, colours, medals, arms, paintings and audio-visual displays covering the heroic exploits of the Marines in peace and in war. Additionally, various musical instruments used by the famous Royal Marine Bands throughout the centuries, are the subject of a special display of their own. A further service museum is at Gosport in Hampshire, the home of the Royal Navy Submarine Museum, which records the history of the 'silent service' from its origins at the end of the nineteenth century right up to the present day.

On the Beaulieu River, the Buckler's Hard Maritime Museum stands on a site where ships for the Navy of Nelson's day were constructed. The museum, opened in 1963, is principally concerned with local history, with figureheads, models and other nautical relics, including memorabilia of Sir Francis Chichester who used the Beaulieu River as his sailing base prior to his single-handed circumnavigation of the globe. Nearby, Broadlands in Hampshire was the home of Admiral of the Fleet Earl Mountbatten of Burma, until his tragic death in 1979. It now houses the family archives and exhibits illustrating Lord Mountbatten's career.

OPPOSITE *The 'Admiral's Court', held annually on the Medway at Rochester, Kent. While afloat on a barge, the 'Admiral', the Mayor of Rochester, holds his court, making laws 'regulating the Oyster Fishery and the taking of floating fish.'*

ABOVE *Superb timberwork recalls the Flemish weavers who moved to Sandwich, and elsewhere in Kent, in the sixteenth century.*

LEFT *'View from the saluting platform, Portsmouth.'*

Buckler's Hard on the Beaulieu River, Hampshire. More than fifty naval ships and many merchant vessels were built here, as was Nelson's favourite, the Agamemnon. *Life in the village must have been lively at the time of a launch. In 1804, when* Swiftsure *with 74 guns was launched, 2021 pints of beer were served from the Ship Inn.*

The excellent Southampton Maritime Museum is worth a visit, as is the Poole Maritime Museum.

Across the Solent, at Ventnor on the Isle of Wight, is the Museum of Smuggling History which, with the help of tableaux, tells the nefarious story of smuggling across seven centuries. In describing the exploits of various notorious smugglers, it explains and demonstrates the ingenious methods that have been, and still are, used to hide contraband in order to get it into the country without paying legal duties.

The West Country is fortunate in its maritime inheritance, much of which is on display. For example, the Appledore Maritime Museum has the Bideford collection of shipwrights' tools, Brixham has exhibits relating to the trawling and fishing industry and Dartmouth, with its enormously strong naval traditions, has important items of maritime interest quite apart from the treasures housed at the Britannia Royal Naval College. At Bridgwater in Somerset is the Admiral Blake Museum, housed in the birthplace of this famous seventeenth-century seaman, while the Falmouth Maritime Museum is devoted mainly to the history of the Royal Mail Packetboats.

The Exeter Maritime Museum, situated in the heart of the city, has an outstandingly large collection of working boats. They are housed both in a number of warehouses and on the Exeter Canal. This valuable display includes almost a hundred different vessels: a tug, lifeboat, launch, gig, coracles, a dredger, plus a large and fascinating selection of small boats and craft from all over the world, including the distinguished Ellerman Collection of Portuguese Working Boats. Particularly interesting are a selection of modern open boats including three used in recent attempts to row across the Atlantic.

Plymouth, with its equally long sea-trading and naval traditions is another major centre for maritime study, set as it is on the Sound, one of the best natural harbours in the world. Its record as a naval port goes back as far as the end of the thirteenth century. Here, on the Hoe, famous as the location for Sir Francis Drake's game of bowls, one can visit Smeaton's Tower, a lighthouse that, until 1882, used to stand on the Eddystone Rock. One can also visit the Mayflower Stone at the West Pier of the Barbican, which commemorates the Pilgrim Fathers departure for America in September 1620. From Plymouth too, at a later age, both Captain Cook and Captain Scott set out on their long voyages of exploration. Nine miles out of town, is Buckland Abbey, the house, first of Sir Richard Grenville and then of Drake and his family. It is now a National Trust property housing, among many other relics, Drake's Drum which is supposed to sound at times when the nation is in peril.

There are many other maritime collections and museums in the West Country and on the Isles of Scilly. For example, the Museum of Smuggling at Polperro in Cornwall gives fascinating glimpses of a lawless past with its tableaux of old and modern smuggling techniques, while Charlestown has a Shipwreck Centre, the most important exhibit of which is the entire wreck of a wooden vessel, the *Grand Turk*, among relics of other wrecks from along the Cornish coast and elsewhere.

At Penzance is the Museum of Nautical Art, which houses a substantial collection of items, again mainly from wrecks, including finds from the ships of Sir Cloudesley Shovell's squadron which was

Exeter Maritime Museum, located in the Exeter Canal Basin. A variety of boats are on display, notably a collection of working boats of the world.

Shipwrecks in Cornwall

Shipwrecks and Cornwall have always been inseparable in the public mind – and with good reason. To the majority of people, the sight of a stranded ship is a relative novelty, but not to the people of the West Country. They too flock in droves to watch men battle to save a vessel, or the ocean to tear one to pieces in a single tide, but they watch with an attitude of familiarity and resignation born of experience, for these people know the sea.

The 'foot' of Cornwall, protruding as it does into the Atlantic, experiences the very worst of winter gales; with January come winds that turn the sea into a boiling cauldron. In the days when all ships were wooden and wind-driven, to be caught close inshore or become embayed in such conditions was certain death for ship and men alike; Cornwall proves the point with evidence of more than fifteen shipwrecks for every mile of coastline.

Much has been made of Cornish 'wreckers', who traditionally lured ships ashore with lanterns tied to the tails of wandering cows on clifftops, or displayed on lonely beaches and headlands when 'wrecker's weather' prevailed ('a savage sea and a shattering wind, the cliffs before and a gale behind'). Although there is some evidence that 'wrecking' did occur elsewhere, it seems that there is no firm proof that this happened in the West Country. Nevertheless, while this point may be hotly disputed, there is an eighteenth-century prayer (reputedly from this part of the world), and somehow understandable in this then economically deprived and isolated part of the country, that goes as follows:

> We pray thee, O Lord, not that wrecks should happen, but that if any wreck should happen, Thou will guide them into the Scilly Isles for the benefit of the inhabitants.

In Cornwall the immense catalogue of wrecks is attributable mainly to the elements and the geographical location of Cornwall and the Isles of Scilly. There were other factors as well: charts copied ancient error, placing the Isles ten miles north of their true position; an ocean drift called the Rennell Current was capable of pushing ships off course; and in the days of dead reckoning, a recognisable landfall was essential, but the Bristol and English Channels were sometimes confused. Over the years at least 5,000 vessels, and ten times that number of lives, have been lost. Galleons and men o'war, liners and tramp steamers, sailing ships and tankers, all have come to grief at some time or another on this rocky coastline, many of the wrecks making history.

The most infamous area is the Western Rocks, Isles of Scilly; it was here in October 1707 that Admiral Sir Cloudesley Shovell and some 2,000 officers and men met their deaths in one night – still the greatest single naval disaster of its kind. Near the Gilstone Rock, on which Sir Cloudesley's ship, the *Association*, struck, lie the remains of the German transatlantic liner, *Schiller*, wrecked on the Retarrier Ledges in May 1875 with the loss of 313 lives, and, within less than a mile, the remains of two Dutch East Indiamen, both 'treasure' ships.

On mainland Cornwall, the story continues, with century after century of shipwrecks; the transport vessel *John* on the Manacles, 193 lost; *Mohegan*, a liner, lost in 1898 with 106 deaths – and still there are shipwrecks. In 1977 to 1978 six

BELOW *A four-masted barge of about 1880 – a 'ship-in-a-bottle' at the National Maritime Museum. The model-maker constructs the ship outside the bottle. The masts are hinged, the yards, and so on, laid out and attached to strings. The ship is then slipped into the bottle. When a string is pulled the masts spring erect, the yards square away and the ship is 'afloat'. The strings are then cut away and a cork placed in the bottle.*

ABOVE *Wreck of the schooner* Giles Lang *near Bude, Cornwall on 8 November 1896.*

ships came to grief with the loss of twenty-eight lives, and a further seven vessels were lost during the winter of 1979 to 1980.

A quite remarkable collection of items salvaged or recovered from some of these wrecks can be seen in the Shipwreck Centre and Museum at Charlestown, near St Austell. In the heart of this picturesque Cornish seaport, which has changed little since its inception by Charles Rashleigh in 1790, a building complex houses a fine display of artefacts, pictures, photographs and charts – in fact anything connected with shipwrecks. Outside there is a good collection of ships' guns, anchors and an interesting variety of other nautical items, sad reminders of what lies beneath the sea. PP

wrecked in the Scillies in the year 1707. The museum is also dedicated to illustrating the many forms of art and design found in the construction of England's old ships. Full-size and small-scale models abound along with a number of 'hanging ships' used for church dedication, a 'ship-in-bottles' collection, and an exhibition of small naval cannon.

Bristol, naturally, is particularly wealthy in maritime material. The City Museum has a small, but good, collection of models of ships built in the port, while the *Great Britain*, the most important ship ever built at Bristol, has been berthed there since it was salvaged and brought all the way back from the Falkland Islands in 1970 to be restored. The National Lifeboat Museum is also situated close by.

Moving up to Liverpool, with its Pier Head as the traditional focal point, the whole area has many distinguished buildings recalling the city's maritime heritage. The Royal Liver Building, topped by the legendary Liver Birds, and the Cunard Building are two of many. Nearby, Merseyside's Maritime Museum, which is being created in the heart of Liverpool's dockland, is a project in the making. Against the backdrop of the warehouses of the Albert Dock, restored buildings and quays are the first visible phase of the project. Traditional craft are on display together with Sir Alec Rose's famous yacht *Lively Lady*. Visitors can watch boats being repaired and study sail-making and other practical nautical crafts. There is also a nautical brass-rubbing centre, while the county museums have fine displays of models and paintings.

There is also much to see among England's inland waterways. Near the entrance to the Shropshire Union Canal, is the Boat Museum at Ellesmere Port,

MAGPIE
CAFE
FUN CITY
RIFLES
BINGO
WY12

Cheshire which is being developed to house the largest display of canal craft in Europe. Here are traditional broad and narrow canal boats of a wide variety of styles, this despite the fact that the museum was established only within the last decade. The site itself is based on the terminal docks of the canal which themselves offer an informative picture of the lock and warehouse system of what used to be a busy and profitable port. The project is run entirely by volunteers.

Besides the Grand Union Canal in the village of Stoke Bruerne in Northamptonshire, is the Waterways Museum, housed in what used to be a grain warehouse. Here too one can get a impression of what the life and work of boatmen and their families was like over the decades when canals were such a fundamental part of England's life and prosperity.

There are other centres to show that England's waterborne traditions are not only preserved and protected along the sea coasts. On Lake Windermere, the Steamboat Museum displays steam launches and other vintage craft, the collection including the *Dolly*, built in about 1850, which is reputed to be the oldest mechanically powered boat in the world. Here also is the *Esperance*, built in 1869, and the earliest iron-built steam yacht listed in Lloyd's Register of Yachts. Finally, and even further from the sea at Shugborough in Staffordshire, is the ancestral home of the Ansons among whom was Admiral George Anson whose eighteenth-century exploits included circumnavigating the globe.

These are a few of the many historic maritime attractions that visitors can see and enjoy in England today. There are many others, such as the Marlipins Museum at Shoreham, the Doughty Museum at Grimsby, the Bridewell Museum at Norwich and other collections at Devonport, Whitby, Worthing and Castletown on the Isle of Man – open to the public on a regular basis.

There are also glimpses of that nautical past buried away in corners of general and municipal museums, or, more commonly, allowed to rot and degenerate in forgotten docks and bywaters. But the efforts of conservationists are strong and are growing, and deliberate neglect of our maritime heritage is fortunately becoming less common.

OPPOSITE *Still an active fishing port, Whitby embraces the harbour. Captain Cook lived here when a young man. His ship* Endeavour *was built here, and he sailed from here in 1768.*

BELOW *Fishermen at Whitby, late nineteenth century; photograph by Frank Meadow Sutcliffe (1853–1941).*

Dolly, *the oldest mechanically powered boat in the world, on Lake Windermere in a serene mood.*

The Steam Launch

DOLLY

This Windermere steam launch of about 1850 sank in Ullswater, to which she had been transported, during the great frost of 1895. She lay forgotten in about forty-five feet of water until discovered by members of the Northern Federation of the British Sub-Aqua Club. Even in the cold, dark water her beautiful lines were emphasised by a slender stripe of gold leaf which gleamed from her finely raked clipper bow along her full length. The grace and beauty of this submerged vessel inspired Gerry Jackson and the Furness Sub-Aqua Club during the many thousands of hours of work – often in very difficult conditions and with many setbacks – that were needed to raise her from the brink of an underwater escarpment down which she could easily have slipped. She was raised in 1962.

The launch, forty-five feet in length and seven feet at the beam, was taken to Windermere for restoration. She was duly restored – incredibly there was no rust, scale or pitting on the boiler. Ten years later her true name came to light. She is the *Dolly* and was owned by Alfred Fildes who lived at Sawrey on the west shore of Windermere, where a boat of some sort was a necessity. But this is an elegant steam launch, for such vessels were popular on Windermere during the Victorian period. With the coming of the railway in 1846 tourism was introduced. The lake was a perfect setting for the country homes of wealthy industrialists from Lancashire and Yorkshire, a world of fashion centring on the weekend steamer and tea parties. With the advent of the industrial revolution enterprising engineers from the north-west took advantage of this large freshwater lake for their experiments, as well as for pleasure.

The *Dolly* can be seen at the Windermere Steamboat Museum, located on a former sand wharf site where, for many years, barges unloaded gravel dredged from the lake bed. The Windermere Nautical Trust was set up in 1971 by G. H. Pattinson to ensure that the *Dolly*, the other Windermere steamers, *Branksome*, *Esperance*, *Raven*, *Lady Elizabeth* and a collection of historic craft, could be preserved in working order. In 1976 the Maritime Trust and the English Tourist Board supported the Windermere Nautical Trust in building the museum to enable the public to see and enjoy these beautiful vessels. PP

18 The Nautical Muse

The sea has given great inspiration to English painters, writers, poets and musicians over the centuries. From earliest times the power of the waves and the mystery of the surrounding seas were more potent than any other natural element in the experience of mankind. The sea was considered a manifestation of the supernatural, the all-powerful, as every seafarer knew only too well. Where is that religious awareness more purposefully expressed than in Psalm 107: 23-30?

> They that go down to the sea in ships, that do business in great waters;
> These see the works of the Lord, and his wonders in the deep.
> For he commandeth, and raiseth the stormy wind, which lifteth up the waves thereof,
> They mount up to the heaven, they go down again to the depths: their soul is melted because of trouble.
> They reel to and fro, and stagger like a drunken man, and are at their wit's end.
> Then they cry unto the Lord in their trouble, and he bringeth them out of their distresses.
> He maketh the storm a calm, so that the waves thereof are still.
> Then are they glad because they be quiet; so he bringeth them unto their desired haven.

England's particular relationship with the sea is equally well established in every branch of art, literature and music. Perhaps Shakespeare, who was much taken by things nautical, as *The Tempest* demonstrates full well, developed it most memorably in his play, *Richard II* (II, i, 40):

> This royal throne of kings, this sceptered isle,
> This earth of majesty, this seat of Mars,
> This other Eden, demi-paradise,
> This fortress built by Nature for herself,
> Against infection and the hand of war,
> This happy breed of men, this little world,
> This precious stone set in the silver sea,
> Which serves it in the office of a wall,
> Or as a moat defensive to a house,
> Against the envy of less happier lands.

Many of the great writers and poets have written about the sea. From novels like Daniel Defoe's *Robinson Crusoe*, through to the works of Tobias Smollett, Captain Marryat, 'Taffrail', Kipling and Joseph Conrad, the tradition is constant. These writers managed to convey so much of the sea's majesty and challenge, as exemplified in Conrad's *Youth*:

W. Heath Robinson illustration from A Song of the English, *London.*

John Masefield

John Masefield (1878–1967) could probably be considered the finest English poet of the sea. At the age of thirteen he joined H.M.S. *Conway* in the Mersey knowing almost nothing of this way of life. The *Conway* was an old wooden warship and one of the most famous training ships; and it was here, as a cadet, that he first began to write.

According to the *Conway's* records, he sailed round Cape Horn as an apprentice aboard the *Gilcruix* (White Star Line), a square-rigged ship. He became ill and on arrival was sent to hospital. He never served on a sailing ship again and his indentures were cancelled.

Masefield was rather secretive about his private life but it is known that he journeyed to the United States, by sea, of course, where he spent several years living rather precariously. During this period he worked in a carpet factory, an experience he later described in *In The Mill* (1941). He returned to England and became a journalist on the staff of the *Manchester Guardian*. In about 1897 he moved to, in or near, London, committing himself to writing. Plays, novels, short stories, a naval history and long narrative poems such as *Dauber* (1913) were included in his output. He is best remembered for his sea poems, especially the famous *Salt-Water Ballads* (1902), in which 'Sea Fever' and 'Cargoes' appear. Although his time at sea might be considered short – it ended before he was twenty – the pure essence of the experience stayed with him throughout his life. A romantic, he was able to write about the ships and people of the sea with rare tenderness and passion.

Masefield was made Poet Laureate in 1930, a member of the Order of Merit in 1935 and an honorary member of the Honourable Company of Master Mariners. He once wrote: 'I was beyond all mortals lucky in seeing and knowing something of those decades of the sailing ship, the three in which she touched perfection, as a man-of-war, as bird of passage and as carrier.' PP

John Masefield

> The sea was white like a sheet of foam, like a cauldron of boiling milk; there was not a break in the clouds, no – not the size of a man's hand – no, not for so much as ten seconds. There was for us no sky, there were for us no stars, no sun, no universe – nothing but angry clouds and an infuriated sea.

But not everything is trial and tribulation. Marine pleasures abound in literature, not only relatively modern writing, such as *Three Men in a Boat*, but even in seventeenth-century writings, as with this entry for the first of October, 1661 from Samuel Pepys's Diary:

> I sail'd this morning with his Majesty in one of his yachts (or pleasure boats) vessells not known among us til the Dutch E. India Company presented that curious piece (Mary) to the King, being very excellent sailing vessells. It was on a wager betweene his other new pleasure boats, built frigate like and one of the Duke of York's; the wager £100; the race from Greenwich to Gravesend and back. The King lost it going, the wind being contrary, but sav'd the stakes in returning.

There is literature of the sea which relates largely to the biographies and autobiographies of famous navigators and seamen. Publications by sixteenth- and seventeenth-century writers like Richard Eden and Richard Hakluyt were among the first to open the minds of Englishmen to the study of navigation and exploration. After them came the writings of many famous seamen who recorded for the less adventurous what the seas of the world held in store.

OPPOSITE *Illustrations from an early edition of* Robinson Crusoe.

RIGHT *English and French soldiers dancing on board H.M.S.* Vulture, *1854.*

BELOW *Illustrations from a children's* Pirates of Penzance, Savoy *magazine, 1884.*

Certain areas of the globe were given particular attention. For example, there is much written English material on the attempts to find the North-West Passage to the Orient. In present times one of the best-known books of the sea has a precise and valuable function: *Jane's Fighting Ships* has provided a comprehensive record of the navies of the world since it was first published in 1897.

Among the poetry of the sea, one of the best-known English verses of all time must be Coleridge's *Rime of the Ancient Mariner*, which the poet composed during a West Country walk with his friend Wordsworth:

> Water, water, everywhere,
> And all the boards did shrink;
> Water, water, everywhere,
> Nor any drop to drink.

English poets have been inspired not only by the sea, but also by the ships that sail on her. Probably the greatest of the twentieth-century marine poets, John Masefield, exemplifies this in his poem 'The Ship':

> I march across great waters like a queen,
> I whom so many wisdoms helped to make;
> Over the uncruddled billows of sea green
> I blanch the bubbled highway of my wake.
> By me my wandering tenants clasp the hands
> And know the thoughts of men in other lands.

In 'Cargoes' the inspiration is memorably realistic:

> Dirty British coaster with a salt-caked smoke stack
> Butting through the Channel in the mad March days,

Painting by Willem van de Velde the Younger of English ships and the Barbary pirates, about 1670.

With a cargo of Tyne coal,
Road-rail, pig-lead,
Firewood, iron-ware, and cheap tin trays.

Not all ships arrived safely, of course, and among Shakespeare's 'thousand fearful wrecks; a thousand men that fishes gnawed upon,' was the *Royal George* and crew, a tragedy immortalised in William Cowper's poem:

Toll for the brave!
The brave that are no more!
All sunk beneath the wave,
Fast by their native shore!

To any Briton who, like the author, was brought up on sea lore from a very early age, particularly through the engrossing books of that best-appreciated children's writer, Arthur Ransome, it is as much the music as the words of the sea that is evocative and inspiring. There are many works of English opera (Benjamin Britten's *Peter Grimes*, for example), symphonies, concertos and other music forms that composers have tried to match and dedicate to the moods and conditions of the sea. Not all this is heavy and classical in style: *The Pirates of Penzance* and *H.M.S. Pinafore*, for example, those most famous Gilbert and Sullivan Operettas, incorporate maritime wit and wisdom at its liveliest.

Much of this musical tradition can be linked and traced to the folk music of the sea and of sailors, the sea shanty or chanty. Basically they were work songs to help lighten the load of turning the capstan or pulling on halyards. 'Capstan' shanties tended to be steadier in rhythm, while 'halyard' shanties are strongly stressed, thus giving the sailors a signal as to when to heave together. The standard pattern is to have solo verses that tell a story, and back this up with rip-roaring choruses. Nearly all of these shanties come in many different versions, doubtless improvised or varied over the years to suit the ship, the personalities and the occasion. With the end of the age of sail, the shanties, far from dying out, have retained an eminent position in folk music because of their robustness and the jollity of their tunes. Sadly, the traditional 'sailor's' dance, the hornpipe, is probably only now seen when the theatre, ballet or opera wants to impart a nautical flavour to a production.

Among the best known shanties are 'What Shall We Do With The Drunken Sailor', 'Shenandoah', 'Billy Boy' and 'Blow the Man Down', but many, many more are commonly heard. There is usually a girl left behind or one met, or one to be told of the joys of sailing the world. Some are sad – usually the measured one for working the capstan; others are quite the reverse. And with their tales of women, the promise is always there:

In Amsterdam there lived a maid . . .
And she was mistress of her trade . . .

or

As I was strolling down Paradise Street,
A pretty young maiden I chanced to meet.

Then, after the fun of the tale or the lament, comes the exhortation to work: 'Way-hay-ay, Roll and go', or 'Heave away my bully boys', or again 'Way, hay, an' up she rises'.

But, above all, there is the longed-for reward of the safe return to England, home and family, often

The Battle of Trafalgar as seen from the mizen starboard shrouds of the Victory; *by J.M.W. Turner.*

with words that have a poignancy that belies the vigour of the tune.

> Call all hands to man the capstan, See the cable runs down clear;
> Heave a-way, and with a will boys, For old England we will steer.
> And we'll sing in joyful choral in the watches of the night.
> And we'll sight the shores of England when the grey dawn brings the light.
> Rolling home, rolling home, rolling home across the sea.
> Rolling home to dear old England, Rolling home dear land to thee.

* * *

England has a rich history of marine painting which dates back to the sixteenth century and offers a glimpse of styles and ship design, valuable information that would otherwise be lost to us. Much of the tradition of this period emanates from Holland, where the numbers of both seascapes and ship 'portraits', reflect Dutch maritime power at the time. There is also a strong school of naval battle painters, recording, often with considerable artistic licence, the great maritime exploits from the Armada onwards.

Charles II, presumably recognising the historical value of maritime painting, employed the Dutch painters van de Velde – father and son – at his court, and they were largely responsible for recording the subsequent growth in British naval power. The English school of marine painters owed much to them in the centuries that followed.

A belief held by many art historians is that up till the arrival of Turner on the scene, marine painting was more a technique of record than a proper art form. Be that as it may, it was Turner who, as one of the fathers of impressionism, established the subject in international terms. His studies are less helpful to the historian of marine architecture, and, by definition, lack detail, but this is more than made up for by the luminosity of his style. There are many well-known painters of this, the last age of the sailing ship, people like George Chambers, some of whose paintings hang in the Painted Hall at Greenwich, Sir Oswald Brierly who recorded voyages to Australia and during the Crimean War, and William Wyllie who painted a huge panoramic picture of the Battle of Trafalgar. In this century one of the last great names, before the camera arrived to take over the recording of events, was Sir Muirhead Bone, a Scot, whose brother David, the author of *The Brassbounder*, was equally noted as a maritime writer.

OPPOSITE, TOP *Detail of a pencil sketch made from the bridge of a battleship by Sir Muirhead Bone.*

OPPOSITE, BOTTOM *Painting of the Southsea Life-Boat during a rescue; painting by W.L. Wylie.*

Ordinary sailors have always made their own contribution to nautical art forms in humbler, but no less magnificent ways. In addition to the folklore and the sea shanties described above, sailors have long been noted for their craftsmanship with forms of sculpture that take infinite patience and time to create. Carvings, from ship figureheads through to the intricacies of scrimshaw, model-ship designs, ships-in-bottles and rope 'sculpture', are, equally, part of the sea-inspired heritage of this great maritime nation.

Finally in this chapter, some of the traditions and superstitions of the sea and sailors should be noted, though not part of the nautical muse as such. They are many, strange and varied, for the elemental nature of the seas has always inspired feelings of majesty and awe. Sea monsters have been reported from every ocean and in every age. Mysterious ships, such as the *Mary Celeste* or the *Flying Dutchman,* sail on forever, inspiring theatre, opera and music as they go. Beautiful sirens entice bewildered sailors to their deaths – in marine parlance they end up with Father Neptune in Davy Jones's Locker.

Nor are such superstitions a thing of the past. Who whistles on board ship when the wind is already high? Which new ship or yacht glides down the slipway (and never on a Friday) without a bottle of champagne or wine shattered over its bow? And then the order is 'splice the mainbrace' – a free issue of rum in celebration – the most welcome tradition of them all.

Painting of the 'Flying Dutchman'. Even today, sailors believe that those who see her will perish at sea.

The 'Flying Dutchman'

In a popular and famous legend this ghost ship haunts the waters around the Cape of Good Hope. A sighting of the 'Flying Dutchman' spells impending doom, for sailors believe that anyone who sees her will die by shipwreck. In one story the Dutch Captain Vanderdecken impetuously gambles his salvation by swearing that he will round the Cape in his barque loaded with bullion during a fierce storm, even if he has to fight God and the devil until doomsday. The ship founders as he speaks this oath and he is condemned to round the Cape forever. It was on this version that Richard Wagner based his opera *Der Fliegende Höllander* (1843). In a German version the captain, Herr von Falkenberg, sails forever through the North Sea, in a ship without helm or helmsman, playing dice with the devil for his soul. Samuel Taylor Coleridge used the dice-game motif in the *Rime of the Ancient Mariner* (1798). The 'Flying Dutchman' theme has been used by many other poets, novelists and dramatists.

As a young man, the 'Sailor King', George V, when standing with a group of officers on the deck of a battleship, reputedly saw the 'Flying Dutchman'. PP

19 Past, Present and Future

Today the sea around us offers as much as it has always done: our soundest defence, economic prosperity, and prospects for all levels of leisure and enjoyment. Our naval skills, aptitude for shipbuilding and marine architecture from the humblest coracle through to today's supertanker, have been second to none. While Britannia may no longer rule the waves, that is not to suggest that any other country has replaced her in the same way. For in terms of modern military armaments and strategy, neither the United States nor the Soviet Union has a unique supremacy, and, for its size, the Royal Navy can still hold the candle to anyone in terms of defence technology.

Equally, we have seen that the geography of England has, through exposing the majority of its population to the sea, produced a nation of seafarers as well as nation that enjoys its maritime leisure. The nation is gradually learning to conserve that inheritance, both the natural and the historic, but the pace is at times dangerously slow.

The process is increasingly assisted through education, not only in schools and colleges, but also with the aid of the media. The imaginative 'Operation Drake' was one outstanding example of how young people can be involved in a major maritime adventure. Commemorating Sir Francis Drake's great voyage some 400 years earlier, the 150-ton brigantine, the *Eye of the Wind*, went on a sponsored two-year round-the-world voyage of exploration. Several hundred young people from twenty-seven different countries participated in ten three-month phases, during which archaeological, zoological, biological, botanical, geographical and community-service projects were undertaken. Guided by experienced adults, the young people crewed the *Eye of the Wind* as well as taking part in the projects themselves. They left, as Drake himself had done, from Plymouth and they ended the voyage in London at St Katharine's Dock. And not only did the participants benefit, but so did many others who followed the progress of the expedition at home. In all it was a modern epic voyage which reawakened the Elizabethan spirit of adventure.

What does the future hold? To take one example, at the time of writing, the Royal Institution of Naval Architects is considering a new and important breakthrough in methods of powering ships, the impetus being the constant search for fuel conservation. The revolutionary new concept is wind power. In the western world generally this 'new' development

It is thought that more than a million people enjoy sailing in English waters. Clubs around the country hold training courses at all levels.

Operation Drake

Operation Drake provided superb opportunities for young people from twenty-seven nations in following various stages of Sir Francis Drake's circumnavigation of the world in the *Golden Hind* 400 years before. Lt. Col. John Blashford-Snell and the Scientific Exploration Society conceived the idea of the expedition, which took four years to plan. Blashford-Snell became Director of Operations and led various patrols in Panama, Papua New Guinea and Kenya during the expedition itself, in 1978–80.

Over 60,000 young people (aged 17–24) applied for the voyage in the *Eye of the Wind*, a magnificent brigantine. After stringent and imaginative tests – one was how to weigh and measure an eleven-foot python – to indicate their capability, enthusiasm, fitness and ability to contribute to and benefit from the experience, over 400 were chosen. The Young Explorers, as they were dubbed, over 121 from Britain, each took part in one of the ten phases of the expedition, each phase lasting three months.

The young people were sponsored by charities, individuals and commercial firms, such as Capital Radio. Capital sponsored the largest number of young people, ten in all, and made an invaluable contribution to the project. They sent a producer-presenter on the voyage who broadcast twice-weekly reports. Hundreds of thousands of people were thus involved in the day-to-day life of this marvellous adventure. One Young Explorer who returned to London was trained by Capital and rejoined the voyage as their presenter. The radio station also developed an Operation Drake educational project, which was followed by more than a quarter of a million London school-children.

The Prince of Wales, the Patron, officially launched Operation Drake at Plymouth on 22 October 1978 and the *Eye of the Wind* set sail. During the two-year voyage the brigantine linked a series of land-based expeditions, some lasting several months, in Panama, Papua New Guinea, Indonesia and Kenya. At each of the major sites the Young Explorers were assisted by scientists, archaeologists, doctors, members of the Services and many other specialists in carrying out an immense variety of studies and projects. A host of islands were visited in between each landfall.

A sample of the tasks carried out by the Young Explorers gives some idea of the scope. An active volcano, La Soufrière on St Vincent Island was investigated and subsequently erupted, as was predicted by the Young Explorers who had noted the rising temperature of the water in the crater lake. In Panama there was a 110-mile trek over mountains and through a confusion of rivers and swamps, following the probable route taken by Balboa in 1513; there was a medical research project on the island of Mulatupo, home of 2,000 Cuna Indians. In Costa Rica's Osa Peninsula, a survey was made by dug-out canoe of the shoreline's plant and animal life, sediment deposition and the effects of erosion. On Moala, in the Lau group of islands, teachers' quarters and classrooms that had been destroyed in a hurricane were rebuilt. In Papua New Guinea they searched for and charted aircraft and ships sunk in the Second World War; three aerial walkways were constructed by the Royal Engineers to enable the Young Explorers to make comparative studies of the rain forests' complex ecosystem (part of the first 'round the world' study of upper canopy insects in the rain forest); the Strickland Gorge was navigated in inflatable boats – the most ambitious and potentially dangerous of all projects; there was a surprise encounter with a group of primitive, nomadic people, the Pogaea, who had never before seen white men, nor anyone outside their own valley. In Indonesia observations and reference collections of insects, plants, fish and small mammals were made – the last bat caught on the expedition was of a new species which has yet to be named and published. In the Seychelles they searched for and discovered two of the world's rarest plants. In Kenya they marked the boundary of Sibiloi National Park and went on a 300-mile camel trek, following the footsteps of Count Teleki von Szek who, in 1888, discovered Lake Rudolph (now Turkana); undertook a game count; built cattle dips for the Masai to protect their cattle from tick-borne diseases; uncovered the ruins of one of the earliest and most complete Islamic ports on Pate Island, and much, much more.

By the time Sulawesi (formerly the Celebes) was reached, Young Explorers organised and worked on projects without direct supervision, although all had been given thorough initial jungle training. Later, selected Phase 6 Young Explorers ran similar familiarisation courses for those in Phase 7.

The expedition's scientific work was of exceptional depth and breadth. For example, the collection of bats made in Indonesia, with the material from New Guinea, is believed by the British Museum to be the most valuable sent to them since 1900. The extensive reference collections of beetles, birds and butterflies will be classified, and a representative collection returned to the country of origin. Thus a bank of base-line data has been established.

The *Eye of the Wind*, chartered for the voyage, is a 150-ton brigantine which was built in 1911. This beautiful vessel served as home, transport and laboratory for the Young Explorers. During the long sea voyages they learned radio communication, ship maintenance and studied theoretical and practical seamanship and navigation, including how to furl the sails from ninety feet up the mast in a heavy squall, ride out fierce storms or simply combat sea-sickness. The ship was an important part of many projects. When on long sea voyages marine biology projects were undertaken. In Papua New Guinea the ship was used to support a University of Papua New Guinea study of medicinal plants on various islands.

The problems experienced by the ship itself were resolved, often in true expedition-style fashion. When the twenty-two foot main boom snapped in a violent storm, a tree was purchased and a replacement was made and fitted.

On return from this truly outstanding expedition for young people, one Young Explorer said: '. . .out there, I learnt humility, modesty, I don't know what you call it. I do know it was an experience I will value for ever.' PP

Examining a Giant Tortoise on Frigate Island, the Seychelles. Young Explorers took part in a survey of tortoises, counting and measuring a number of them.

ABOVE *Helicopters are leased by the North Sea oil companies for daily victualling, crew changes and to carry equipment.*

RIGHT *Diving bell (top right) on the* Borgila Dolphin. *The bell, owned by SubSea Offshore Limited, was leased to Chevron Petroleum UK to carry out inspection and maintenance work in the Ninian Field. The divers work in pairs, each locking out for up to four hours. After eight hours the bell returns to the surface, still pressurised, and transfers the divers into the living chambers (in background). A second team, under pressure, replaces them in the bell.*

is looked at very much as a curiosity. By contrast, the Japanese have already launched a sail-assisted tanker. This particular vessel has rigid, fold-away sails built around the ship's masts. Admittedly, even the Japanese will use the sails only to assist other power sources – but that idea too is a mere century-and-a-half old. The developers believe that it will cut fuel bills by around ten per cent, something not to be ignored given current world oil prices.

Other possible developments of the future have been mooted, particularly in relation to the strength of the sea itself. Can not its waves and tides be harnessed to produce cheap and effective power? Developments and experiments are underway in a number of countries on this front, but they are still far removed from being a serious major energy source for future generations.

Again, and increasingly important in the context of the growth in world population, is the potential of the sea in providing food. Fish farming and harvesting is also in its infancy, yet there are those who see it as one of the greatest potential areas of expansion in terms of future food supplies. Small, man-made tanks are one thing; stocking large areas of coastal waters, which can be given artificial 'fences' to contain that stock for harvesting when ready, is an exciting concept with limitless possibilities. Quality and species control, ease of – and carefully planned – harvesting and the consequent speedy delivery to markets, are other self-obvious benefits, though capital costs would undoubtedly be very high.

What, above all, the seabed has offered us in the last decade has been the oil and natural gas that is, with increasing profitability, being extracted from it. While the amount of oil brought ashore from specifically 'English' sectors is small compared to that taken from the 'Scottish' fields, the development of the North Sea oil industry is a spectacular pointer to the future and already having a massive effect on our economy. But it is an asset that will not last forever and while, for example, natural gas from the rich 'English' fields off the Norfolk coast and elsewhere now accounts for virtually all English gas supplies, estimates for the twenty-first century are far from reassuring.

Conservation is essential with regard to both natural gas and oil supplies. It is equally imperative in so many other of the fields discussed and described in this book. Our coastline, our natural environment, wildlife, fish stocks, historic ships, shore-based sites and so much else, are at constant risk. But as people increasingly educate themselves to find their pleasure by and on the sea – sailing, swimming, windsurfing – or be it in pursuit of simpler pleasures – beachcombing, walking, camping, exploring the well-populated or deserted littoral – the dangers recede and the future of maritime England looks ever more secure.

An idyllic day in Hampshire.

SELECTED BIBLIOGRAPHY

Abell, Sir Westcott, *The Shipwrights' Trade* (Cambridge University Press, Cambridge, 1948).
Adamson, Simon H., *Seaside Piers* (Batsford, London, 1977).
British Tourist Authority, *Resorts & Spas in Britain*, Study commissioned 1975 (British Tourist Authority, London, 1976).
Burton, Robert, *The Seashore and Its Wildlife* (Orbis Books, London, 1977).
Callender, Sir Geoffrey, *The Naval Side of British History 1485-1919* (Chatto & Windus, London, rev. ed. 1960).
Clapham, Sir J., *A Concise Economic History of Britain to 1750* (Cambridge University Press, Cambridge, 1949).
Cornwell, E.L. (ed.), *An Illustrated History of Ships* (New English Library, London 1980).
Country Life Books, *The Country Life Book of Nautical Terms Under Sail* (Country Life Books, Feltham, 1978).
Drummond, Maldwin, *Salt Water Palaces* (Debrett, London, 1979).
Gladwin, D. D. *An Illustrated History of British Waterways* (Spurbooks, Bourne End, 1978).
Graham-Campbell, James, and Kydd, Dafydd, *The Vikings* (British Museum Publications, London, 1980).
Howell, Sarah, *The Seaside* (Studio Vista, London, 1974).
Hudson, Kenneth, and Nicholls, Ann, *The Book of Shipwrecks* (Macmillan, London, 1979).
Kemp, Peter, *The British Sailor* (J.M. Dent & Sons Ltd., London, 1971).
Kemp, Peter, *History of Ships* (Orbis Books, London, 1978).
Kemp, Peter, *History of the Royal Navy* (Arthur Barker Ltd., London, 1969).
Kemp, Peter (ed.), *The Oxford Companion to Ships and the Sea* (Oxford University Press, Oxford, 1976).
Lloyd, Christopher, *Atlas of Maritime History* (Country Life Books, Feltham, 1975).
Lobley, Douglas, *Ships Through the Ages* (Octopus Books, London, 1975).
Lubbock, Basil, *The China Clippers* (Brown, Son & Ferguson Ltd., Glasgow, 1st ed. 1929, 1973).
Lucas, Alan (ed.), *The Complete Illustrated Encyclopedia of Boating* (John Murray Publishers Ltd., London, 1979).
May, W.E., *A History of Marine Navigation* (G.T. Foulis & Co., Edinburgh, 1973).
Navy Department, *The Admiralty Manual of Navigation*, 2 vols (H.M.S.O., London, Vol. I new ed. 1971, Vol. II rev. ed. 1974).
Navy Department, *The Admiralty Manual of Seamanship*, 3 vols (H.M.S.O., London, Vol. I new ed. 1973, Vol. II new ed. 1967, Vol. III new ed. 1964).
Rolt, L.T.C., *The Inland Waterways of England* (George Allen & Unwin Publishers Ltd., London new ed. 1979).
Russell, John, *The Shell Book of Seasmanship* (David & Charles Publishers Ltd., Newton Abbot, 1979).
Seymour, John, *Companion Guide to the Coast of North East England* (William Collins Sons & Co. Ltd., London & Glasgow, 1974) and *Companion Guides* to other parts of the coast.
Simper, Robert, *British Sail* (David & Charles Publishers Ltd., Newton Abbot, 1977).
Shrubb, R.E.A., and Sainsbury, A.B., (eds), *The Royal Navy Day by Day* (Centaur Press Ltd., Arundel, 1979).
Smith, Peter C., *Heritage of the Sea* (Balfour Publications, St Ives, 1974).
Stammers, M.K., *Discovering Maritime Museums and Historic Ships* (Shire Publications Ltd., Avesbury, 1978).
Steers, J.A., *The Sea Coast* (William Collins Sons & Co. Ltd., London & Glasgow, 4th ed. 1969).
Trotter, Wilfred, *The Royal Navy in Old Photographs* (J.M. Dent & Sons Ltd., London, 1975).
Wall, Robert, *Ocean Liners* (William Collins Sons & Co. Ltd., London & Glasgow, 1978).
Warner, Oliver, *The British Navy – A Concise History* (Thames & Hudson Ltd., London, 1975).
Warner, Oliver, *Fighting Sail* (Cassell Ltd., London 1979).
Warner, Oliver, *The Lifeboat Service* (Cassell Ltd., London, 1974).
Whipple, A.B.C., *Fighting Sail* (Time-Life International, London, 1979).
White, Colin, *The End of the Sailing Navy* (Kenneth Mason Publications Ltd., Havant, 1981).
Wood, Michael, *Fish Cookery* (Ward Lock, London, 1975).

Additionally, the English Tourist Board publish numerous booklets and pamphlets on touring, historic sites, resorts, water sports, leisure activities and many other subjects with maritime content.

The majority of maritime organisations mentioned in this book, such as British Shipbuilders, the British Transport Docks Board and the British Waterways Board also publish material about their organisations and activities.

INDEX

N.B. Italics refers to illustrations.

ILLUSTRATION ACKNOWLEDGEMENTS

The photograph on page 57 bottom is reproduced by courtesy the Master and Fellows of Magdalene College, Cambridge and that on page 126 bottom is reproduced with the sanction of the Controller, HM Stationery Office and of the Hydrographer of the Navy. The picture on page 191 is from Rudyard Kipling's *Song of the English*, Hodder & Stoughton, London.

Antikvarisk – Topografiska Arkivet, Stockholm 19; Ashmolean Museum, Oxford 21; Stewart Bale, Birkenhead 108 bottom, 109; Baltic Exchange, London 112; Bodleian Library, Oxford 25 top, 45; British Museum, London 13, 14, 23 bottom, 28, 49; British Rail 139; British Shipbuilders, London 35, 110; British Tourist Authority, London 15, 47, 126 top; Cammell Laird Shipbuilders, Birkenhead 105; City Art Gallery, Bristol 73 top; Corporation of Lloyd's, London 132; Corporation of Trinity House, London 127; Crown copyright – Science Museum, London 18, 32; RNAS Culdrose 98; Department of the Environment, London 12; Eastern Counties Newspapers, Norwich 84; England Scene – English Tourist Board, London 2, 8, 9, 16, 25 bottom, 26, 41 top, 42 top, 56, 71, 73 bottom, 75, 76–77, 78, 80 bottom, 85 top, 85 bottom, 87, 89, 91, 92 top, 92 bottom, 96, 99, 100 top, 100 bottom, 101 top, 101 bottom, 102, 107 bottom, 122, 125 top, 125 bottom, 128, 133, 134, 135 top, 135 bottom, 136 top, 138 bottom, 140 top, 142 top, 142 bottom, 143 top, 145 bottom, 146 top, 146 bottom, 147 bottom, 154 top, 155 bottom, 157 top, 159, 160, 161 top, 161 bottom, 162 top, 162 bottom, 164, 167, 169 top, 169 bottom, 170, 171, 179, 181, 183 top, 185, 188, 199, 203; England Scene: Robin Adler 172 bottom, Keith Bernstein 82 bottom, 174 bottom, 176 bottom, Marcus Brown 141, Mike Busselle 55, 83 top, 111 bottom, Tony Craddock 156, John Farnham 88, 174 top, Anne Hills 82 top, 118 bottom, 119, 158 bottom, Tony Holey 163, Neil Holmes 117, 175, 176 top, Ray Palmour 51, 114 bottom, 172 top, 177 bottom, 178, Eric Peacock 202 top, 202 bottom, William Pereira 158 top, Christopher Wormald 140 bottom; Mary Evans Picture Library, London 39, 44, 108 top; HMS Excellent, Portsmouth 97 bottom, 114 top, 115, 121; Fish Farmer, Sutton 95; Walter Fussey, Hessle 93; SS Great Britain Project, Bristol 106; Hamlyn Group Picture Library 36, 46, 48, 50, 52, 66, 86, 94, 97 top, 136 bottom, 150, 157 bottom, 177 top, 196; Hampshire County Museum Service, Winchester 183 bottom; Hudson's Bay Company 72; Institute of Oceanographic Services, Godalming 131; R. Larn Collection, St Austell 187; Library of Congress, Washington 38; Mander & Mitchenson Theatre Collection, London 194 bottom; Mansell Collection, London 24, 192, 193, 198; Mary Rose Trust 31; Merchant Adventurers' Hall, York 69; Ministry of Defence, London 65, 116 top, 120; National Archives, Naval Dept., USA 195; National Army Museum, London 61; National Maritime Museum, Greenwich 34, 41 bottom, 42 bottom, 53, 54, 57 top, 58 top, 58 bottom, 59, 60, 62, 63 left, 63 right, 64, 67, 74 bottom, 83 bottom, 113, 116 bottom, 124, 143 bottom, 180, 186, 194 top; National Motor Museum, Beaulieu 184; National Portrait Gallery, London 29, 74 top, 107 top; Norfolk Museums Service, Great Yarmouth Museums 149; W. Oddy, Berkhamsted 17; Operation Drake – Rupert Ridgeway 201, Operation Drake – Christopher Sainsbury 10–11; Philpot Museum, Lyme Regis – Gerald Silverlock 90; Port of London Authority 79, 80 top, 81; Portsmouth City Museums 137; Harry Ramsdens, Guiseley 147 top; Peter Reeves, Faversham 70; Royal National Lifeboat Institution 129, 130, 197 bottom; Royal Navy Submarine Museum, Gosport 118 top; Staatsarchiv, Hamburg 27; Sutcliffe Gallery, Whitby 189; Homer Sykes, London 182; Tate Gallery, London 197 top; B & S Thomlinson, Carlisle 152, 153, 154 bottom, 155 top, 165 top, 165 bottom; Judy Todd, London 166, 168, 173 top, 173 bottom; Tourism and Attractions Dept., Blackpool 145 top; Universitetets Oldsaksmalung, Oslo 20, 23 top; Urs Graf Verlag, Switzerland 22; Victoria and Albert Museum, London 33, 40; Vosper Thornycroft (UK), Portsmouth 111 top; Windermere Steamboat Museum 190.